AF350452

The Story of
a Korean Policeman
Becoming
an Australian Lawyer

Bruce Yoon

ISBN: 9798223806493

TO MY FAMILY

I DEDICATE THIS BOOK TO MY BELOVED WIFE, SON, AND DAUGHTER WHO HAVE SUPPORTED ME THROUGHOUT EVERY MOMENT OF MY LIFE AND SHOWERED ME WITH ENDLESS LOVE AND ATTENTION. IT IS THANKS TO YOUR UNWAVERING LOVE THAT I WAS ABLE TO ACHIEVE MY DREAM. THANK YOU FOR ALWAYS BEING THERE FOR ME.

The Story of a Korean Police Officer Who Became an Australian Lawyer

CONTENTS

Prologue 1

Chapter 1 Childhood Memories 2

My Childhood 3

Memories of Suni 5

An Accident That Nearly Led to Blindness 8

School Days 10

The Teacher Who Gave Me Confidence 13

Children's Saemaul Movement 16

Puppy Murder 19

Dropout of Middle School 24

Life as a postman at Cheongdeok Post Office 27

Life in Cheongdeok, Hapcheon 30

A pen pal who motivated me to learn English 30

Grandmother's Blessing Prayer 31

Wake up the dawn 32

Eyes moving along the Offering Box 33

Request for Help from Relatives 33

Pay and Get Slapped 36

Sae Ongjima (塞翁之馬) - The Irony Of Fate......................39

Chapter 2: Days of Compulsory Combat Police 44

Nonsan Training Center 45

UDT Member 49

Served at Post in Jeju Island....................................52

Jeju Island Airport Guard...58

The 1st Mobile Unit of the Gyeongnam Provincial Police Department..61

Demonstration of the Airborne Special Forces...........64

Masan Provincial Hospital...66

A Man Called Tarzan..68

Admission to Seoul Police Hospital............................70

Pain is the level of medical technology......................71

The power of 9 boiled eggs......................................73

The little ladies I met at the hospital 74

Chapter 3 During My Tenure at the Police Station........77

First-time Police Officer..78

Two Perspectives On Prostitution 82

Sacrifice of the Homeless..86

Smuggler Crackdown Anecdote.................................89

The Sneaky Detective's Double Play 92

Gochugaru Myungdo 95

Falsely Accused of Bribery 98

The End of a Fellow Police Criticizing Jesus 101

A Thug Out Of Prison 103

An Old Woman Selling Udon on the Street 105

Meet Jejus 109

Why Is a Medical Report So Expensive? 112

Is GoStop a crime of gambling? 115

Foreign Friends 118

U.S. Soldier "George" 118

Musical Band "Mild Coffee" 119

Taekwondo international student - Anthony 120

Napoleon – The Relative of Marcos in Philippine 122

Special Friend Eddie 123

Airport Room No. 100 126

My Friend Detective Kim 131

Bar Exam Preparation Proposal 134

Chapter 4 Poor Life of Overseas Student 138

Preparation for Overseas Study 139

Corruption at the Australian Embassy 143

Most Expensive Banana 145

First Impression of Australia 148

Shocking First News in Australia 148

My Wife's First Impression of Australia 150

Aussie Landlord 151

Memories of the Korean Uniting Church 153

International Student Pastor J 155

Car Accident and Dream 159

Baby Delivery in Australia and Korea 164

My Thoughts On Children 169

Chapter 5 The Trials of My Life 172

Violation of the Reserve Forces Act 173

100 million won in Compensation 176

Neighborhood in the Apartment 183

Tragedy of Partnership 185

Seed of Unhappiness 186

My Own Business 188

Copyright Litigation 1 192

    Re-investigation 192

    Commencement of the Ordeal 194

    Extreme Abuse of Power 196

    My Counterattack 197

David, My Australian Friend 199

Copyright Litigation 2 203

    Failure of Counterattack 204

    Last Defense 208

    Unlawful Confinement 210

Korea's First PC Cafe 212

First Guarantee in My Life 215

Story of Prosecutor's Dismissal 217

Chapter 6 Migration & Life of Faith 223

Migration to Australia 224

Discord with an Aussie friend 226

Prison Visit 229

Theology and Pastoral Candidate 231

The Apostles' Creed 234

Reader's Letter 240

My Reply to the Letter 244

The Reason I Left the Church 248

Pastors who know the secret 249

Pastors, My father's Friend 250

Heaven and Hell 253

My Talents 256

Chapter 7 Troubled Society 258

Reverse Immigration to Korea 259

Reasons for Reverse Immigration 259

First Stock Investment 260

Invisible Force 262

The Purpose of Traffic Enforcement 266

Dotted and Solid Line 266

Crackdown like theft 268

Parking on verge 270

Honesty = loss? 272

Australian and Korean Doctors 276

African Doctor 276

Authoritative Korean Doctor 278

Experience at the Emergency Room 279

A Kind of Social Distrust 283

Difficulties in Transferring a Car 287

Chapter 8 From Entrepreneur to Law Student 291

Founding Director of Avnet Korea Co., Ltd. 292

Origin of the Double Ledger 295

Real Estate Bubble 299

Claim Against Guarantor 307

Venture Registration and Startup 309

Issue of VAT Refund 314

Hospital Abuse 318

The Unfairness of Banking System 324

Bank's Discretion 327

Refusal of Investment and Termination of Merger Agreements 331

Memories With Staff 336

Eccentric Programmer 336

Welfare to the Employees 337

Lead Woo 340

Reunion with Staff..341

Addition of New Business Type..343

Iran like North Korea..347

Betrayal of Samsung Card..354

Last Resort..357

Chapter 9 Life as Australian Lawyer..360

Too Strict Conflict of Interest..361

K Group Litigation and Investigation..368

Negotiations with the Metropolitan Investigation Unit..........................371

A Place Like Swamp..374

A Memorable Flight Turbulence..377

Asiana Airlines Flight..377

Korean Air Flight..379

Unusual Client..382

Difference Between Rich and Poor..390

The Skills of Wealthy People..390

Emperor's Morality..391

Death of My Parents..394

Resentment of My Father..394

The Surgical Decision Dilemma 395

Tyranny of Nursing Hospital 397

Chapter 10 Happiness and Sadness 402

Memories of Tongyeong 403

Reversed Relationship 405

The Daughter of My Father's Friend 408

Little Happiness 412

Taiwanese friend Max Ma 413

Thai Friend Nahtaw 416

Friend's Daughter 419

Passing Fate 423

Good Neighbor 423

Relationship in Chuncheon 425

Precious Relationships 428

Epilogue 433

INDEX 438

Testimonial

Soo Yong (Bruce) has been a great friend since we met him while a student in Australia in 1988. He showed a real enterprising spirit and a strong desire to learn and understand the culture and language of his adopted home. I remember he decided he could improve his grasp of culture if he understood the humour and so he read books of English language humour and so he always had us laughing.

A wonderful and generous host, he and his wife showed us around Korea in 1991, an unforgettable experience, introducing us to many aspects of Korean culture and the changes that continue to sweep that country. Once while travelling we spied a KFC outlet. On first visiting Korea in 1984 my wife and I were a little culture shocked and upon seeing 'the Colonel' in the street we just had to have lunch there because it felt like home. When we passed the KFC with Soo Yong he chuckled and told us how, when he first came to Australia, he went to KFC because it made him feel like home! This illustrates the experience of a unique person who has bridged the cultures of Korea and Australia in a quite unique way.

Intelligent and insightful, Soo Yong's story is an interesting reflection on culture and life. We are privileged to count Soo Yong among our friends, commend his story to you, and look forward to the next Chapter.

Rev David & Debbie O'Brien, Retired Baptist minister and wife (davidnobrien1@gmail.com) in Melbourne Australia

Testimonial

I have known my uncle Bruce for many years and have always recognized his unique character. However, reading his inspiring story of overcoming adversities and pursuing a new career as a lawyer at an older age has significantly elevated my admiration for him.

Through his experiences, he has taught me to acknowledge life's challenges and appreciate all that the world has to offer. As a family, we have faced our own hardships, and his stories deeply resonate with us, bringing us closer together.

I am grateful for his willingness to share his experiences through his book. I am cheering him on as he continues to persevere and inspire us with his stories.

Mac Ma, (comomac@gmail.com)

DevOps / Bankwest

Recommendation

In 2012, a stranger Australian lawyer with a piercing gaze requested legal advice regarding a domestic company-related case and met lawyer Yoon for the first time. As a Korean lawyer, it was a strange occurrence that the Australian lawyer oversaw a case related to a domestic company, but Yoon's meticulousness, firmness, and boldness in handling the case impressed and surprised the writer.

Yoon has had various experiences, including working as a police officer, software engineer, theology student, and entrepreneur. Through these experiences, Yoon developed a resilient mentality that is not afraid of failure, and even the writer, who did not know Yoon well, could not help but respect him.

Yoon has published a book titled "The Story of a Korean Policeman Becoming an Australian Lawyer," in which he candidly recounts his life. Personally, the writer recommends Yoon's book and hopes that it will be a great help to everyone in making decisions or reflecting on their lives.

CHOI Dong Kyu, (magma20000@gmail.com)

Law Office of Choi Dong Kyu in Seoul, Korea

Recommendation

It is intriguing to contemplate the trajectory of an individual's life, who has successfully emerged from a humble upbringing to stand tall in the twilight of middle age, having immigrated from Korea to Australia, transitioned from a police officer to an Australian lawyer, and experienced a gamut of life experiences. However, Bruce Yoon's autobiographical essay is not simply a book that satiates one's curiosity about an individual. Rather, through this book, the life that I observed appears to represent a successful life of someone who faced the world with well-managed time and an almost overwhelming internal pressure. At the very least, that is my impression from this candidly written book.

There is no definitive answer as to how an individual ought to live their life, when to pursue what, or how to do so. However, in the life that Soo Yong YOON has challenged himself with and chosen, we observe a rigor that constantly tightens the loose screws of his life at every moment without causing discomfort to others. It is certainly not an easy life. Rather than following the wind and trends, Soo Yong YOON has clearly walked against the wind to come this far. He seems to have fully savored the 'freedom of choice' granted by God more than anyone else, and if there exists a 'good and faithful servant' praised by the master in the biblical 'Parable of the Talents,' Soo Yong YOON may be one such individual.

It has been over two decades since I first met him, and he is someone I make a point to meet whenever I visit Australia. He possesses an amiable disposition, and his presence is invariably pleasurable. His narratives are always captivating, with his witty remarks never failing to impress. Such dexterity likely stems from his profound experience and composure when encountering life's poignant moments. Those familiar with him are perpetually intrigued by his future endeavors.

In the preface, Soo Yong YOON dedicated this book to his wife and beloved son and daughter, who have given him endless love and attention. It is possible that he endured many years just to write this one sentence, and it is also possible that he wrote this book with their help. His wife, who has stood by him through difficult times, should take pride in being the wife of Soo Yong YOON, who has taken responsibility for her husband's honor. Similarly, his son and daughter, who were raised through prayer and provided with the opportunity for a good education, should also be proud to have Soo Yong YOON as their husband and father.

He is likely currently standing facing the winds blowing in Perth, Australia, as he sets new goals for himself in pursuit of a new challenge. Encouraging himself with the maxim, 'There is nothing to be gained without a challenge,' he is generating internal pressure to motivate his efforts.

Seo Jeong-min, (jmseo@21sma.com)

CEO of Alipex Co., Ltd.

Prologue

Around 2008, before I lost my memory, I wrote an autobiographical essay titled "Korea and Australia I Experienced," which summarized my life experiences. However, my son's and daughter's friends, as well as Australian friends who knew me, expressed interest in reading my autobiography in English.

After careful consideration, I have decided that it would be worthwhile to translate my autobiography into English and have it published. Although my life has nothing to boast about, I believe it could serve as a valuable record for my children or future generations.

Upon reviewing the manuscript and working on its translation during my spare time, I discovered a number of missing stories. Consequently, a complete rewrite of my life story was necessary, rather than a mere translation. Furthermore, previous autobiographical essays have not been pure autobiographies, as they included my theological ideas and experiences in addition to my life story.

This book contains my life story and philosophy, a human life story. I do not try to show the world what success or failure is, but rather wants to express my genuine life in this book. I believe that recording one's life, whether successful or not, can be a valuable resource for future generations.

While writing the book, I was able to evoke old memories and feel nostalgic. How happy would I be if the people I miss from my memories could appear in front of me one day in reality...

Chapter 1 Childhood Memories

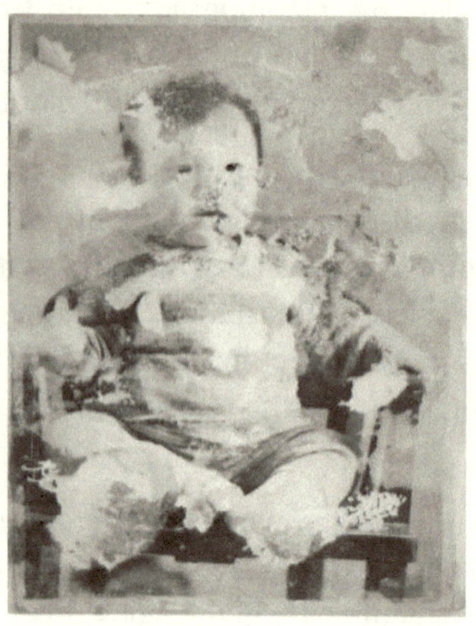

First birthday photo - A fire in the apartment destroyed many memories, but this photo luckily survived.

My Childhood

As attested by my parents, during my early years, I was a mischievous child. One of my standout abilities was my aptitude for mimicking animals. Among my repertoire, I was renowned among many adults for my uncanny impression of a cat that would crawl under tables and let out a charming "meow." Consequently, I would often find my pockets filled with treats and snacks.

As a five-year-old child, my family dynamics changed when my younger sibling was born. Gradually, my mother's attention shifted towards them. Soon after, my third sibling was born, and I found myself constantly criticized with comments like

"You're all grown up now, you shouldn't behave like that."

In retrospect, it felt as if I was expected to be a mature adult from the age of five, and as a result, I often received scoldings from my parents due to my younger siblings. While my younger siblings were praised for their achievements, any mistakes they made were blamed on me for setting a bad example.

As a young child, my toys were frequently taken and played with by my younger siblings, and whenever I attempted to stop them, my parents would reprimand me, saying,

"You're all grown up, yet you play like a child."

It caused me indescribable feelings of resentment as a child.

Due to the presence of my younger siblings, my parents' attention was constantly diverted away from me, leaving me increasingly isolated and alone. The constant scoldings I received from my parents caused me to become withdrawn and insecure, making it difficult for me to speak up for myself and assert my needs even when I was being mistreated by others around me. Despite this, my aunts and uncles admired my quiet and reserved nature, often comparing me to a skilled general.

As I reflected on my past, I came to believe that my parents' parenting methods, which unknowingly favored my younger siblings, were the reason why I, once a playful child, gradually became passive and introverted. Growing up with three brothers and one sister in difficult economic conditions, my parents struggled to give each child the same attention. However, as an adult, I spent time analyzing the reasons behind my parents' treatment of me. Despite their favoritism, I came to realize that they were my roots and decided not to hold onto resentment towards them anymore. While I could have easily blamed my parents for their parenting methods, I rarely discussed my self-taught life, fearing it would seem like I was blaming them for their incompetence. For me, the grace of being born into this world was enough to respect them as parents.

If there is any mention of my personal achievements in this book, I humbly ask that readers recognize that it was not solely due to my own greatness, but also due to my parents' unwavering devotion and fervent prayers for their children. Through their wise approach to education, I believe that all of my siblings have developed a remarkable level of resilience and self-reliance. It is my parents' tireless efforts that have instilled within us an unyielding spirit that persists even after digging countless wells.

Memories of Suni

When I was six years old, I had a severe case of the flu. I was bedridden and unconscious for a week. Due to financial difficulties, my parents were unable to take me to the hospital, so they had no choice but to let me recover at home.

After being bedridden with the flu for a week, I regained consciousness. Though my head ached when my mother instructed me to sit up and stand, I managed to rise.

After a while, I felt well enough to venture outside. Since I wasn't old enough to start school, I joined a group of neighborhood kids my age. I recall watching boys and girls playing with each other's sand.

At that particular moment, a young girl approached our group, showing interest in joining us. When we turned to see who it was, we noticed that she had a noticeable limp, presumably due to polio. Children who were near to her at the time began to make cruel remarks such as

"Don't go near the polio girl,"

while pointing at her as if she was a social outcast.

After being teased, the girl turned away crying and left alone to watch us play from a distance. Seeing this, I felt very sorry for the polio girl. So I approached and befriended her to play with her.

The kids who saw me playing with the girl with polio started laughing at me, calling me names like "retard" and making fun of me for playing with her. I was bigger than the other kids my age, so I used my strength to chase them away and became a reliable support for the girl with polio.

I remember her name was "Suni." That's why my favorite songs to sing are Choi Heon's "Suna" and Na Hoon-a's "Our Suni." It's because I remembered Suni, who needed my help when I was young.

As I matured, I considered marrying a woman who had difficulty walking due to a disability. However, my intention was met with criticism from someone who said,

"That's not true love, it's just pity,"

and advised me that a marriage cannot be sustained by mere sympathy.

Thinking that what he said was reasonable, the sympathy to find a woman with polio and make her my spouse disappeared. As a result, I married a healthy female police detective who did not limp at all, and I am living well with a son and a daughter.

I cannot recall who provided me with the advice at that moment, but through this book, I express my gratitude to that person for giving me sound and rational guidance.

It seems that my quirky personality manifested itself in my childhood. Before I met Suni, there was a pretty girl in the neighborhood who was always dressed neatly and had a delicate look on her face. None of the kids my age had the courage to play with her, so she played alone on the ground. I, on the other hand, wanted to befriend her and decided to run over to her and kick her in the belly, thinking it would be a good icebreaker. Unfortunately, this resulted in her crying out loud and calling for her mother while pointing her finger at me.I quickly returned home, holding my pounding heart, and stayed in my room as if I were dead. My mother asked,

"Why are you suddenly like this?"

but I didn't say anything.

Shortly thereafter, the girl's mother knocked on our door.   Then she spoke to my mother.

"My daughter says your son kicked her belly, I need to know why."

"Yes?　Soo Yong is not such a child"

"What are you talking about?　My child is crying right now holding her belly!"

"Soo Yong!　Come out! Is it true that you kicked her stomach?"

I replied

"yes"

in a dying voice.

Then my mother said:

"Oh, I'm sorry.　My child is not that kind of kid, but he is too introverted, so I think he did it by expressing that he liked her."

"Oh my God! He would be going to kill her if he likes my daughter again"

Even now, in hindsight, I don't recall exactly why I kicked this little girl. Maybe because I wanted to go out with her or because she seemed overly arrogant and I wanted to teach her a lesson.

An Accident That Nearly Led to Blindness

When I was about 5 years old, I remember playing alone in the front yard often while my mother was home. There was a small pond in the front yard, and flower beds were placed along it.   Around the flowerbed, stones with pointed ends were erected for decoration or as a hedge of the flowerbed.   I think this was a place of misfortune for me and my brother.

My newborn brother, who had just started crawling, followed me outside one day. While my mother was busy knitting or doing something else, she probably thought that he was playing with me outside.

My brother fell into a small pond with a splash, his legs flapping in the air and unable to scream.

Thankfully, my mother heard a loud splashing sound and immediately rushed outside to see what had happened. She saw my younger sibling's legs flailing in the air, and quickly went to rescue him.

Another day, I was playing alone in the yard when I saw the neighborhood kids having fun playing tag with their eyes covered. So, I pretended to be "it" and tried to catch them on my own. While walking with my eyes closed, I suddenly tripped and fell on a sharp rock that was placed to protect the flower bed.

My mother, who had come out from the inside hearing my cries, saw me and knew that my eyes were bloodshot. She thought that I had become blind.

My mother quickly took me to the nearest hospital. The doctor cleaned the blood around my eyes with alcohol, and fortunately the sharp stones missed both eyeballs and hit the glabella[1] accurately. Although about 6 stitches were required to sew up the glabella, I was fortunate to avoid blindness. However, this left a scar on the center of my face that looks like a knife mark.

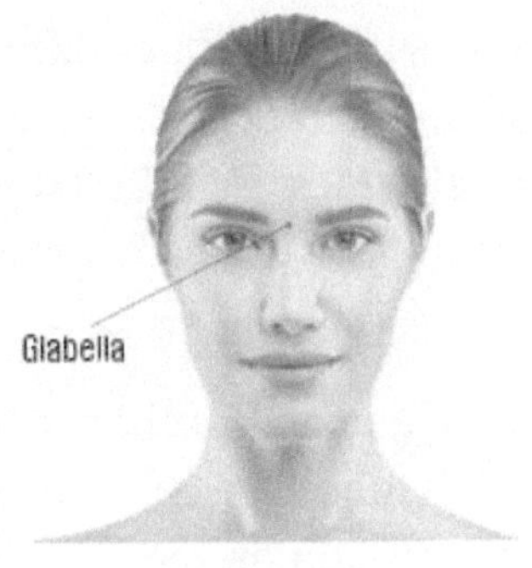

A fortuneteller once told me that my scar may not be considered an advantageous physiognomy and could be causing difficulties in my work. In reflection, I must admit that the fortune teller's prediction may be accurate as my life has been full of challenges and obstacles.

Despite receiving advice from those around me to remove my scars, I did not believe that they were the cause of my difficulties. Since I was not originally a handsome man, I lived my life with resignation as it was.

---

[1] Tthe flat area of bone between the eyebrows, used as a craniometric point.

School Days

Did I have any school days? I changed schools about 5 times until the 6th grade of elementary school (then "Kukmin Hakgyo" meaning "Citizen's School") and dropped out in the 1st semester of the 1st year of middle school, so there are few memories of my so-called school days.

However, even though the memory is from elementary school, there are particular teachers whom I remember vividly. One of them is a female teacher who has left an indelible impression on me. I believe her story can serve as a valuable lesson to many in the field of education. This recollection dates back to when I was in the fourth grade, and she was a slim-faced woman in her early forties. Although many years have passed, she remains a significant figure in my memory. It's worth noting that our class leader at the time was the child of a police officer. I mention this because, having worked as a police officer myself, I am well aware of how prevalent corruption

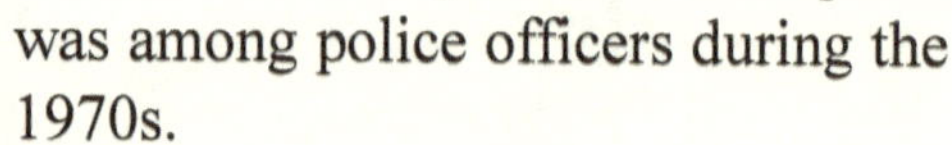

was among police officers during the 1970s.

One day, the class leader gave a writing presentation, and I remember that the classmates laughed out loud because there was probably a content that satirized the teacher in a rather ridiculous way. At this time, the teacher stood up the class leader and shed tears saying,

"I thought of you as more than my own son, how could you do that?"

Then the class leader also wept bitterly at the sight and showed off their friendship.

This teacher had such a soft heart and seemed to take good care of her students like her own children, but in reality, she did not treat all students that way, which made my heart hurt. Everyone could see that the strength of the cane hitting[2] some students, including the class leader, was different from that of other students when they were punished for doing something wrong.

Even when distinguishing children who were in the wrong line during assembly time on the playground, among the children who played together, the teacher punished all students but excluded only the children in her favoritism in a gerrymandering manner. The teacher's discriminatory act hurt a lot of students like me who couldn't even pay the Nurturing Membership Fee [3] properly. She often called the students and sent them home to bring money for payment of the Nurturing Membership Fee.

During class, the teacher asked if any of the students had a ruler that she could borrow. Despite rulers being rare at the time, I happened to have a good-quality 30cm ruler, so I saw it as an opportunity to get the attention of the very unkind teacher. Without hesitation, I lent my ruler to her, saying "Me!". Although I don't know how I was able to acquire the ruler given our difficult family circumstances, the teacher seemed happy when she borrowed and used it. However, even after using the ruler, she did not think of returning it. Day after day passed, and the teacher carried and used the ruler as if it were her own, but she did not return the ruler even after seeing me. Although she was kind to some students from rich families, she was a tiger-like teacher to poor students like me. I couldn't bring myself to ask for the ruler back, and eventually gave up on getting it back as the class changed

---

[2] In the 1970s in Korean schools, it was commonplace for teachers to physically discipline their students.

[3] Since 1970, Nurturing Membership Fee has been prepared in the form of voluntary sponsorship of parents for the education of their children.

during the second semester.

I don't know if that teacher forgot the fact that she borrowed the ruler from me, or if she cheated because she knew I wouldn't be able to ask for the ruler back.   It is beyond my understanding what her intentions were, but I wonder if her home life has improved recently, given her favoritism towards wealthy students in the past.

The Teacher Who Gave Me Confidence

In the second semester of the 4th grade, students were newly assigned to a class as the class changed. I didn't know it at the time, but now I understand it. The teachers were sorting out the so-called children from good families, and they unknowingly sent children like me who had no economic power to the newly transferred teacher's class.

In fact, this played a positive role for me. When a new teacher transferred in, they evaluated students solely based on their behavior and abilities, without taking into account the economic status of each student's household. One day, a poem that I wrote was selected for poetry writing. The newly transferred teacher seemed to be paying attention to me, even though I spoke less. He introduced the poem I had written to the whole class, which made me feel proud. As a result, I gradually gained confidence in my class. However, my time in that class was cut short as I was transferred to another school.

It was Busan Bansong Elementary School, which was located on the outskirts of the city, and since I was a transfer student from the city, I received a lot of attention from my new classmates.   Having gained some confidence in school before, I happened to be chosen as the class leader at my new school.   At the time, the parents of the class leader had a culture of donating to the school, but my parents never visited the school even though I became the class leader because of the difficult family situation.   No, strictly speaking, they couldn't dare to visit because of our family's circumstances. The teacher, who immediately grasped the economic power of our family, didn't like me very much.

The fact that he didn't like me was felt through several incidents, but one thing I couldn't forget was at a drawing contest.   I remember that my homeroom teacher in the first semester of the 4th grade at my previous school praised the robot picture drawn by the class leader at the time, so I drew a robot picture that the class leader drew wonderfully. And when each of them displayed their own picture in front of the class, I also put my picture out.   Then, the classmates exclaimed. However, our homeroom teacher completely poured cold water on us, saying,

"This cartoon-like robot picture has no value as a picture."

I didn't understand the reason why the 4th grade teacher highly praised the picture and the 5th grade teacher dismissed it as nothing. What was the difference? I didn't know which teacher's evaluation was correct at the time, but as I grew older, I could understand.   I'm not sure if it was due to the influence at the time, but I still don't have much interest in painting.   I am a person with poor drawing skills.

An Australian couple, who had adopted a Korean child, informed me of their adopted child's experience at a Japanese school during their time as expatriates in Japan. It reminded me of my own childhood. During drawing class, apples were put on the table and everyone was asked to look at the apples and draw them. Everyone drew an apple-like picture, but this kid drew a picture that was not like an apple at all.   Upon seeing the apple, the child remembered the story of Snow White and the Witch.   She drew an abstract picture of the apple as it came to her mind.   The Japanese teacher scolded the child for not drawing properly according to the teacher's words, despite not understanding the child's unapologetically abstract drawing. After being scolded by the teacher for her drawing, this child came home and cried profusely for a while.   Knowing this, the Australian adoptive parents patted the child and comforted her for a long time. They told her not to cry and to have confidence because the schoolteacher was never right.

Later, as a father of two children, while educating two children in an Australian school, and understanding the Australian education method, I was able to compare the education methods of Korea and Japan in my own way. Teachers in Australia never accuse a child of doing something wrong. No matter how wrong the child is, the teacher always emphasizes only the good side so that the child gains confidence. For example, even if a child has a very bad score in math, the teacher says,

"This child is very good at addition and is working hard to be good at multiplication."

Even if the child is not good at English grammar, the teacher says,

"This child speaks English better than anyone else, but if you put a little effort into grammar, English will be no problem"

and so on. . . Teachers always say nice things to hear.   There seems to be a real difference from Korean and Japanese teaching methods, which always emphasize shortcomings no matter how good a child is.

Children's Saemaul Movement

During the summer vacation of my 6th grade in elementary school, while the Saemaul Movement[4] was in full swing, I proposed to my peers that we should engage in a community service project. I suggested that female students in the neighborhood should also be involved in this effort, which was readily accepted by my peers.

It was during summer vacation when I was in 6th grade in elementary school. At the time, the Saemaul Movement was in full swing, so I thought that we should do something good in the community, so I suggested to my peers that we should do the Saemaul Movement, and they all readily agreed. Upon the suggestion that female students would be needed to do good things together, I proposed that female students in the neighborhood should also join our group.

So we dispatched a sociable boy from our group. He knocked on the window of the neighbor's house where the female students were studying together. A female student peered out the window and asked.

"What's up?"

"We have something to talk about, so come out"

Then, all 4-5 female students who were studying together came out. They also seemed curious when a male student asked them to come out.

---

[4] The Saemaul Movement, also known as the New Community Movement, or New Village Movement, was a political initiative launched on April 22, 1970 by South Korean president Park Chung-hee to modernize the rural South Korean economy.

When I suggested,

"We want to do the Saemaul Undong, let's do it together,"

the female students readily agreed.

So we introduced to each other and from then on we met together every day to discuss what needed to be done to improve the neighborhood.

We initiated the restoration of the village roads by clearing them of debris and other waste materials, thereby improving their appearance and functionality. In addition, we undertook the restoration of a collapsed sewer that was previously obstructed by stones. We carefully removed the stones and reconstructed the sewer, ensuring it was level and functional. As a result of our efforts, the village elders recognized and commended the exceptional work of the children involved.

At that time, it was considered taboo for male and female students to socialize, as they were often scolded by adults for doing so. However, we were able to legally socialize with female students and even received compliments from adults.   It was like killing two birds with one stone. During our participation in the Saemaul Undong, I played the guitar and sang songs with my fellow students, and sometimes the elderly around me who were very excited also attended and played together.

We were the object of envy even among children from the neighboring village, until we experienced a major accident.

In order to restore the collapsed sewer more beautifully, it was agreed that the garbage in the sewer should be collected and the sewer should be dug deeper. To do this, a student brought a pickaxe from his home and started digging deep into the sewer.

In the meantime, we encountered an obstacle that felt hard like a stone. In our efforts to remove it, we accidentally caused a water pipe to burst, resulting in a fountain-like flow of water from the ground. Not knowing how to handle the situation, we promptly reported it to the village chief, who summoned the village elders to take charge of the matter and stop the water flow.

We overheard adults talking to each other.

"The kids made a mistake while trying to do well"

No one yelled at us, demanding that we be held accountable, but we got discouraged and gave up the Saemaul Undong.

Puppy Murder

During my sixth-grade year at elementary school, I participated in the Saemaul Undong and met Moon Kyung-soon, the second daughter of the Moon family who lived next door with their three daughters and one son. Despite my fondness for Moon Kyung-soon, I refrained from expressing my feelings and kept them to myself.

Moon Kyung-soon's mother owned and managed a modest restaurant located in the Dongrae district of Busan, where she displayed a tireless devotion to raising her three daughters with utmost care and dedication. However, her husband, who was unemployed at the time, often succumbed to alcohol and mistreated his children, including Moon Kyung-soon. As a consequence, her eldest son felt compelled to depart from home prematurely and volunteer for military service.

Mr Moon was the proud owner of two dogs, affectionately named 'Zach' and 'Drone'. Upon producing a whistle sound by placing his fingers in his mouth and emitting a sharp blow, the two canines would promptly scurry towards their owner's feet, wagging their tails with fervor. The sight filled me with envy and admiration.

Similar to Zach and Drone

During that period, I nurtured a desire to become a dog owner, but the financial constraints precluded me from purchasing one, and my attempts to secure a free dog from my neighbors were futile. Despite the assurance from the Moon family to gift me one of their pups upon delivery, regrettably, that promise went unfulfilled.

One winter day, while walking down the street in the evening, a puppy was moaning in a trash bin. It appeared that someone had dumped the puppy in the trash as there was no chance of resuscitation. I quickly hugged the puppy and thought that maybe I could save it. So I brought it home and fed it, but the puppy wouldn't eat it.

I forced warm water into the puppy's mouth, but he couldn't swallow it properly. Desperately wanting the puppy to wake up, I tilted the broken earthen pipe beside the briquette fire in the kitchen and laid the puppy there.

I watched the puppy all night in the hope that it would wake up, and I fell asleep, but I heard the puppy whimper and woke up. The dog was whimpering with his eyes wide open.

"Ah! I warmed the puppy and it seems to come to life!"

As soon as I offered water to the parched pup, it eagerly lapped it up, and my heart swelled with delight. Watching it drink to its heart's content, I couldn't help but feel grateful for this moment of simple joy.

The thought of taking this pretty puppy for a walk down the street crossed my mind, and I couldn't resist smiling at the idea.

I moved the puppy closer to the briquette fire, hoping it would help speed up its recovery. The little dog burrowed its head again, as if checking for comfort, before drifting off to sleep. I too dozed off next to it, with the hope that it would wake up healthy and lively in the morning.

Upon awakening in the morning, my attention was drawn to the puppy, which appeared to still be in slumber. In an attempt to assess its condition, I promptly retrieved and lifted it, only to observe a notable laxity in its physical state. Alarmed, I concluded that it had likely succumbed to respiratory failure at an earlier time.

During that moment, I was consumed with a deep sense of emotional distress. The night before, when the puppy briefly stirred, I had the chance to interact with and care for it. Nonetheless, my exhaustion overwhelmed my judgement, leading me to speculate that the puppy had passed away. My mind was riddled with a myriad of thoughts, including the possibility that my actions of placing the puppy in close proximity to the briquette fire had potentially caused its demise. The gravity of these ruminations left me with an intense sensation of sorrow and regret.

When I wanted a dog so much, one day my mother brought me a puppy. I think it was probably bought with some money. It was because my mother said that she would raise the puppy well and sell it. During that time in Korea, it was not uncommon for some households to feed their dogs leftover rice and sell them to restaurants that served boshintang, a controversial dish made from dog meat. The dogs were often priced based on their weight.

I extended my hand and commanded the puppy to "shake" in an attempt to properly train it, but it failed to comprehend my words. In response, I resorted to utilizing a stick, previously employed by my mother to hit me on occasion, as a means of puppy training. It appears that there is a tendency for individuals who have experienced punishment to replicate similar behavior towards their own children, and it seems that I was no exception. If the puppy refused to obey me, I struck it with the stick, despite the emotional pain it caused me, in frustration that the puppy failed to comprehend my commands even when I yelled "shake." Additionally, the puppy's ears were not perked up, making it an unpleasant sight to behold.

From the puppy's perspective, it may have seemed like I was just constantly torturing it under the guise of training. Looking back, my actions at the time, driven by my lack of understanding of animals, are something I deeply regret.

While I was training the puppy, it suddenly started whimpering and losing weight. As its weight dropped, my mother worried that we wouldn't get as much money from the dog meat dealer if we sold it with less weight. She decided that we needed to sell the puppy as soon as possible, even if it meant selling it for less than we had hoped. When a dog meat dealer happened to pass by, she bargained with him over how much he would pay for the puppy.

The dog meat dealer said that since our dog was in a weakened and emaciated state, and he couldn't give us a high price.   Nevertheless, my mother decided to sell the puppy and get some money before it died.

According to the dog meat seller, weak and frail dogs sometimes attack him when he tries to put them in the bag. Therefore, he requested that my mother hold the dog and put it in the bag. My mother then asked me to hold the dog and put it in the bag.

When I tried to hold the dog, it recognized me and weakly wagged its tail. We put our dog into the dog meat seller's bag this way. Looking back now, my mother and her son, who sold the dog before it lost any more weight, seem very cruel. I want to apologize to the puppy whose name I don't even remember, even now.

I learned a lesson that I should never use corporal punishment while training, as the puppy died from an illness allegedly caused by me hitting it with the stick that my mother used. For this reason, I have never punished our children physically while raising them.

Dropout of Middle School

My regular school education in Korea is the drop-out of the first semester of the first year of middle school. At the time, preparing for school at Bugok Middle School in Busan was a significant financial burden for our family. The cost of the school uniform and materials was formidable, and my parents struggled to afford them. Although I was able to manage the initial preparations, my family found it impossible to provide the necessary educational materials for each subject throughout the semester.

I faced various challenges attending school due to financial constraints, including being punished for not having the required materials for classes. For instance, during art class, I was excluded from the class for not bringing a set of crayons, and during drafting class, I was unable to participate due to not having the necessary drafting tools. These incidents made me feel as if school was not a place to learn, but rather a place to be punished. As a result, my enthusiasm for school diminished since I knew that my family could not afford the required educational materials.

When I told my mother that I didn't want to go to school, she promised to provide me with the necessary materials even if it meant going into debt.   However, I knew that this was not a sustainable solution. In addition, because I had already been stigmatized as a child who was punished at school, I hated going to school more than anything. As a result, I dropped out of Bugok Middle School during the first semester of my first year.

Since I did not go to school, the adults around me introduced me to a car painting factory, saying that I should at least learn some skills. When I went to work on the first day, older brothers in their 20s and 30s treated me well.   But the way they treated me well was to talk dirty all day long.   I, who was pure in my faith at the time, could not bear harsh words in my ears.   I came home that evening and told my mother that I could no longer go to the painting factory.   At this time, my maternal grandmother, who stopped by the house for a while, scolded me very much, saying,

"Young lads must endure at one place"

Still, I couldn't go to the factory any longer.   At that time, hearing obscenities was more detestable than death, and hearing such words in itself seemed like committing a great sin.

Eventually, I quit the factory and got a job selling newspapers at a bus stop. I remember earning between 2,000 and 3,000 won (equivalent to $3-4AUD) a day, and later on, my mother informed me that the money was greatly beneficial for our family since, at the time, my father was serving as a pastor on the island and receiving goods in kind, such as rice.

As a former class leader, seeing a boy selling newspapers at the bus stop made me feel shabby. This set me apart from my friends who were attending a regular school, and since there was no class in the church for out-of-school children like me, I couldn't participate in student classes either. As a result, I started hanging out with other kids of my age who came from disadvantaged backgrounds. Although they were young, they smoked out of curiosity and even offered me a cigarette. However, as a child of God and the eldest son of Mr Yoon's family, I knew that giving in to their temptations was not an option for me. Consequently, I couldn't bring myself to get close to them, and I ended up becoming a loner.

I'm not sure if it's the reason, but I still perceive myself as a lynx[5] - a

---

[5] The nickname of a fighter active from the Japanese colonial era to the First Republic. It is said that in the era of romantic fists in the past, no

human who constantly struggles against both the world and himself, rather than finding strength and a sense of existence through the companionship of friends and siblings. I believe that my perspective has been shaped in part by the biblical teachings as well.

---

one was better at fighting than this man, and he acted alone without organization, but was respected and feared by everyone.

Life as a postman at Cheongdeok Post Office

When I was around 14 years old, my father became the pastor of the Cheongdeok Church in Hapcheon. We moved from our neighborhood and stopped selling newspapers to live in the pastor's residence at the church.

One day, my parents heard that the nearby post office needed a mail carrier and suggested I try it instead of lounging around at home. It was my first experience as a mail carrier.

At that time, each household had a telephone connected to the exchange office at the post office. To make a call, we had to first call the operator and ask to be connected to the desired location. At the Hapcheon Cheongdeok post office, a pretty young lady worked as both the operator and the post office clerk.

After finishing my mail deliveries, I sometimes helped the young lady with her duties at the exchange. At that time, there was a system called "Jeonbo," or telegram which meant that if a call was made to a distant post office, the operator would read the message out loud, and I would then deliver it to the appropriate household.

However, sometimes due to poor call quality, I misunderstood the message and caused misunderstandings. The jeonbo system charged by the number of characters, so it was necessary to shorten the message while conveying its meaning. Therefore, I had to have some knowledge of Chinese characters, which I was studying on my own along with English at the time. Creating jeonbo messages by abbreviating words was easy for me.

For example, the four-letter phrase "Please send money quickly" can be shortened to the two-letter phrase "Remittance Urgent". So when adults came to the post office and asked me to send a message for them, I often shortened the words like this for them.

Sometimes mistakes were caused by postal workers who wrote down the wrong message when too many characters were abbreviated, and there were cases where the meaning was not understood by the recipient because too many characters had been shortened.

As an example, there was someone who sent a congratulatory message at a wedding that read,

"Congratulations on your marriage. John 4:18."

However, the post office worker mistakenly wrote down "Gospel of John" instead of "First John" (1 John). The content of 1 John 4:18 was as follows:

"There is no fear in love. But perfect love drives out fear, because fear has to do with punishment. The one who fears is not made perfect in love."

It is part of a letter written by the apostle John, believed to be written to a group of Christians as a message of encouragement and instruction.

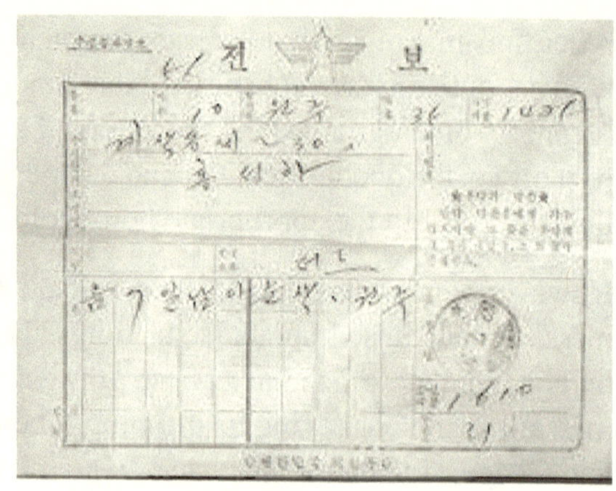

A sample of 'Jeonbo' at that time

However, as the MC read the congratulatory messages, he mistakenly recited John 4:18, which says,

" For you have had five husbands, and the one you now have is not your husband. . . ."

There was a rumor that the wedding reception went topsy turvy.

To deliver mail in Cheongdeok, I had to cross mountains and rivers. Sometimes, in order to reach the next village, I had to take a boat. When a sudden shower caused the river to overflow, it was impossible for me to enter some villages.   In those isolated villages, one of the most welcome people was the postal worker who delivered the mail.

The days of a postman at Cheongdeok Post

So during the holiday season, many people gave me gifts with their mail or packages to send. Oblivious to this, I only had a sense of duty to deliver the mail quickly and would throw the mail into the front yard and quickly ride my bicycle to deliver the mail to next villages.

One day, a plump lady was panting and following me. It turned out that she had to send her letter, and because I ran away quickly after throwing the mail, she had to follow me all the way from the previous village. I felt very sorry but this lady was a kind girl who later gave me a holiday gift.

Life in Cheongdeok, Hapcheon

A pen pal who motivated me to learn English

My life in Cheongdeok, Hapcheon revolved around my occupation as a postal delivery person. During my free time, I enjoyed studying Chinese characters and English. Corresponding with pen pals from overseas was the most enjoyable of all my hobbies. It was through exchanging letters with foreign pen pals that I developed a deep interest in the English language.

Jessica, my first pen pal

The first pen pal I ever had was a girl named Jessica who lived in Washington DC, USA. Her letters were especially exciting because they included high-quality photos, which was not common at the time. I felt like I had my first girlfriend and couldn't help but study English more seriously because of her.

I had always hoped to meet Jessica someday if I ever went to Washington, but when I did visit later on, I didn't even think about her. Although I enthusiastically corresponded with pen pals at a young age out of a sense of curiosity about the world, the process of sending and receiving letters took 2-3 months, so eventually we stopped replying to each other and I forgot about her.

Later, a fire broke out in my apartment and my address book, which contained Jessica's contact information, was destroyed. At that time, there was no internet, so it might be difficult for younger generations to understand this kind of situation.

Grandmother's Blessing Prayer

I remember a few episodes related to my grandmother on my mother's side in Cheongdeok, Hapcheon. She was very sympathetic to her daughter's poor church ministry life and used to visit Cheongdeok church from Busan once in a while to stay with us for several months. During her stay, she helped our family by cultivating the garden around the church and doing other things. She held a position in the church as a senior deaconess, and although she didn't have much education, she worked hard and diligently all her life. She had earned a decent fortune during her younger years as a businesswoman, but she gave it all to her eldest son, who didn't treat her very well in return. Later in her life, she came to live with my father, who was a pastor at the time, and she found peace in her heart.   She spent a lot of time with my mother, who was her youngest daughter.

My grandmother used to lead prayers at church gatherings because of her position as a senior deaconess. However, there was a particular prayer content that bothered me as a child. Perhaps my grandmother wanted to express her desire for the people who received the prayers or their families to receive abundant blessings in a more sophisticated manner.

Her prayer often went as follows:-

"Lord, please bring Gonyok to this household no matter what."

Curious about the meaning of the word "Gonyok", I looked up the word in a Korean dictionary one day because I didn't know what it meant. The definition was

"an intense insult or a difficult experience that causes a sense of humiliation or disgrace."

So, what the grandmother was actually praying for was not a blessing, but rather for "severe humiliation or difficult situations to occur in that household," according to the definition of "Gonyok" that she didn't know before.   However, there was no one who shared the same thoughts as defined in the dictionary, whether it was the person who prayed or the person who received the prayer. It was the first time I had seen someone pray so earnestly for misfortune to occur, but the people who received such prayers even expressed gratitude and treated the grandmother to a meal, which was quite remarkable.

Later on, when I explained to my grandmother what "Gonyok" meant, she exclaimed,

"Oh dear, I made a big mistake because of my ignorance!"

From then on, she never prayed for "Gonyok" again.

Wake up the dawn

During the time my grandmother stayed with us, she was in charge of ringing the bell of our church tower in the early morning. Since she never slept in the morning and always attended the early morning prayer, ringing the tower bell at 4AM was a piece of cake for her.

When the church tower bell rang, it was an important event for the entire Cheongdeok village. Everyone woke up and started their day, going out to work in the fields or beginning their daily routines. However, one day the church tower bell rang at 1AM, waking up the entire village.   My mother, who heard the bell and checked the time, quickly rushed to stop the grandmother from exercising her arm. My grandmother thought her watch had stopped at 1 AM because she forgot to wind it. She quickly wound her watch, made sure it was running properly, and went back to sleep.

Later, at 2AM, the church bell rang again. As it turned out, my grandmother's watch was broken, and the hands moved randomly. When her watch struck 4AM, she rang the church tower bell accordingly.

The villagers came to visit us that day and laughed, complaining that they couldn't sleep that day because of my grandmother's mistake.

Eyes moving along the Offering Box

During the worship service at church with my grandmother, there was a part that was particularly difficult for my parents. From the grandmother's perspective, she was simply concerned for her daughter and son-in-law, but it made my parents very uncomfortable.

Basically, at the end of the service when the offering box was passed around, my grandmother's gaze would follow it and she would scrutinize who was giving how much. Even though the people in the rural area didn't contribute much money, and the amount was far from enough for our family's living expenses and church upkeep, my grandmother hoped that the congregation would make more contribution in the offering.

"Mother, please don't do that. The amount of the offering should depend on each individual's faith. And we should have faith that God will take care of us,"

my mother said to my grandmother.

Request for Help from Relatives

As I corresponded with foreign pen pals, I strongly felt the need to study and develop my abilities beyond my current environment. It became apparent that I would require external assistance, as my family's financial means would not suffice for me to pursue my goals.

Initially, I reached out to my paternal uncles and aunts, who had always praised me as a bright and valuable individual since I was young, seeking their help to financially support my studies and overcome my current situation. Although they responded with encouraging letters, their practical aid was limited. Nevertheless, I was grateful for their encouragement.

As no one among my paternal relatives could offer me economic support, I attempted to reach out to my maternal relatives. I wrote a letter to my youngest maternal uncle living in Seoul, who was reputed to live comfortably. In response, he shared an anecdote of a cleaner who, through hard work and dedication, was eventually recognized and employed by their company, achieving success. He expressed his willingness to help me find employment, even if it meant starting as a cleaner. While I appreciated his kind offer, I respectfully declined, expressing my gratitude in a letter of thanks.

After careful consideration, I decided to go to my big uncle's house in Busan, stay there, find a job during the day, and study at night. I told my parents that I wanted to visit my grandmother in Busan and left home.

At my big uncle's house, there were a cousin brother who was 1-2 years younger than me and a cousin sister who was a couple of years older than me. When I visited without notice, my cousin welcomed me warmly like a friend, and I remember my cousin sister being kind to me as well. However, the problem arose when my aunt-in-law returned from work that night and started worrying that I might end up staying at their house indefinitely, which caused her to confront me.

"What brought you to Busan alone?"

"I came to find a job."

"How long are you planning to stay in Busan?"

"I'm not sure yet."

"Where are you planning to stay from now on?"

". . . ."

During my visits to the big uncle's home, my aunt-in-law always greeted me with a smile and said,

"Welcome, Soo Yong!"

However, the day when I visited, she completely changed her demeanor and didn't say anything like that. I couldn't help but start crying with sadness.   It felt like I had been humiliated.

My cousins, who were younger than me by 1-2 years and older than me by a couple of years, tried to comfort me by patting my back and justified their mother's attitude saying,

"It's okay. My mom was just worried since you came alone."

However, my tears didn't stop for a while. The next day, I left the house without telling anyone and haven't met the uncle's family since. I thought that she didn't have any reason to take an interest in me since I came from a poor family.

My big uncle had inherited all of his wealth from my grandmother, who had saved up a lot of money in her younger days, and they were able to live a prosperous life.   However, my mother was the youngest and a minor at the time, so she didn't receive any benefits from my grandmother and had to grow up without any support.

My disliked aunt-in-law has already passed away, and I haven't been able to contact my cousins either.   Sometimes, I feel like I miss them, but I don't have their contact information.

Pay and Get Slapped

I am a person chosen by God and I take pride in being a descendant of the Yoon's head family. This thought gave me great strength in life, and I was not ashamed to sell newspapers on the streets of Busan. However, I always had the belief that I needed to study hard in my heart.

I tried to study on my own by buying English and math books, but I couldn't understand the content or remember it. Feeling like I was wasting my time not even knowing how to study, I enrolled in an evening institute for English basics. I was deeply moved by the fact that I could learn from a teacher by paying money to study.

I prepared a lot of questions to ask the teacher, hoping to get my money's worth, and concentrated all my energy on listening to the lecture. However, this teacher was a bit strange. Although I had paid a lot of money and sacrificed valuable time to attend his lecture, he spent almost half of the lecture time telling jokes. I was angry. At first, I thought it might happen once or twice, but he continued to waste time with jokes every time, so I finally raised my hand and asked him to give a serious lecture.

Despite being popular among his female students who had praised him, the teacher appeared uneasy when I approached him with such a request and responded to me in a rude manner.

"It's not that there's a problem with my lecture, but it's because of your questions that it's disrupting the class for other students,"

I couldn't agree with this statement because I believed that my questions were helping other students learn as well. So, I stood up and asked the other students around me,

"Am I disrupting the class with my questions? If so, then I won't ask any more questions from now on."

At this, many other students who had been silent during the unsatisfactory lectures spoke up in unison and said,

"It's okay. Please ask more questions."

However, the teacher at the institute was so furious at this sound that he came to me and slapped my cheek, calling me a bad person. Even though I had come to study in a difficult environment and had paid money to learn something, I couldn't bear the injustice of being hit in the face by an institute teacher, and despite at a young age, I felt like I couldn't endure it.

I didn't know what to do under the circumstance, so I went to a nearby police branch in Seomyeon and reported that the teacher had slapped me for no reason. Later, when I became a police officer, I learned that the police branch had already formed a good relationship with the institute, which was a company within their jurisdiction, so they were unable to properly handle the report of a young and powerless person like me.

The chief of the police branch summoned and gave me a lengthy lecture.

"In the old days, it was said that we should not even step on the shadow of a teacher, but now you are reporting that you were slapped by a teacher. . ."

After scolding me in various ways and completely crushing my morale, he asked,

"Do you really want to punish your teacher?"

In this situation, I couldn't say that I wanted to punish him.   I therefore answered

"No"

like a dead mouse.   He then interrupted my statement and told me to go home.

The chief of the police branch may have desired this outcome and could have seized another chance to receive a bribe by bringing this statement to the institute, as was typical in Korean society during the 1970s. Subsequent to this event, I eschewed formal education and persevered with self-study. Ultimately, I self-taught myself and successfully passed the college entrance examination.

As a lawyer now, I realize that I had to return to the academy and demand a refund of the tuition fee as well as compensation for damages.

Sae Ongjima (塞翁之馬) - The Irony Of Fate

To enter society as a proper adult, Korean men believe they must first resolve their military service issues. In 1978, I applied to the Combat Police Force(CPF) with this in mind. At that time, there were many applicants for the CPF, as it was a way to avoid mandatory military service. Therefore, the competition was fierce, with three rounds of tests, including interviews. I passed through the second round of testing and while waiting for the third test being an interview, I wanted to get a haircut to look presentable. So, I asked my younger brother to help me cut my hair, but we ended up with many bald spots, so we had no other option but to shave our heads completely.

During the final interview for the third round, an interviewer asked me,

"Why did you shave your head?"

I responded by saying,

"I shaved my head to enter the Combat Police Force."

The interviewer told me to leave without any further questions. Although I was worried that shaving my head had given a negative impression, I later saw my name on the list of accepted candidates. I was convinced that the interviewer had been touched by my willingness to enter the CPF by shaving my head as a firm resolution.

In many cases, there have been events where an unfortunate incident led to a fortunate outcome like 'Sae Ongjima[6] (塞翁之馬)'. Looking

---

[6] Is a word derived from 'the horse of an old man living in the periphery'

back, many of the difficult experiences I had in the past are the foundation of my work as a lawyer today. I now believe that God has been testing me since I was young to make me the lawyer I am today.

Although I currently work as a lawyer in Australia, I have had many experiences in Korea that have been valuable in my work. For example, when I was involved in a software copyright dispute, I faced many difficulties and obstacles in Korea's legal system. However, those experiences have proved valuable in my current work.

Before entering the CPF, I did manual labor by putting up barbed wire fences on a mountain to earn money and train my body. Carrying heavy concrete pillars on our shoulders up a steep mountain at the age of 18 was very difficult, and it made me realize that slavery, as depicted in the movies, must have been just as hard.

After working one day, my body was sore and I was in pain, and I thought I wouldn't be able to work the next day. However, I realized that if I couldn't handle this kind of work, I would not be able to handle military training. So I persevered and worked hard for a week until my muscles developed, and the work became easier.

However, at that time, the supervisor who had been assigning us work informed us that he had to suspend work due to an issue with the company. He asked us to bring our work stamps to him in exchange for the outstanding wages owed to us. When we arrived at the designated location and waited with other workers, he came out and instructed us to follow him to the company office and receive our wages directly.

We entered the office and received in the name of Soo Yong YOON an amount twice the daily wage multiplied by the number of days when I first signed the contract. Later, I discovered that this supervisor

---

which means that one cannot hastily determine fortune or misfortune because the world is constantly changing.

had been inflating the daily wage reported to the company for the workers, and then personally paid reduced amounts to us in order to pocket the difference. However, the company discovered this fraudulent activity and decided to pay the workers directly, bypassing the supervisor, in order to protect their rights.

After receiving double the amount promised by the supervisor, I was overjoyed and planned to head straight home. However, as I approached the company entrance, the supervisor was waiting for us and invited all the workers to have one last drink together. Despite feeling hesitant, I noticed that there were also tough guys who appeared to be skilled at fighting, so I reluctantly agreed to join them.

"The supervisor pays us our daily wage and he also needs to use the remaining amount to support himself. It would be unfair to take all the money we received today as our own, as we owe gratitude to the supervisor who provided us with employment. I contracted for a daily wage of 4,000 won, so I will deduct that amount from the 8,000 won I received today and return the rest to the supervisor. If you have a conscience, you can choose to either return the supervisor's share or keep it for yourself."

Upon reflection, it appears that the individual in question was a member of the same team as the supervisor at the time. However, I was unaware of this fact and consequently deemed their words to be credible. As a result, I resolved to accept solely the sum that was originally agreed upon and subsequently returned the remaining funds.

There was a major incident in Australia a long time ago that was even featured in Korean news. An ethnic Korean businessman in Australia brought over Korean workers each month through the Human Resources Development Service of Korea[7] , offering them a certain

---

[7] Based on the National Technical Qualifications Act, it is a quasi-governmental organization under the Ministry of Employment and Labor

amount of allowance and salary in exchange for their cheap labor. The workers came to Australia with dreams of earning higher wages than in Korea, but in reality, after deductions for high taxes and living expenses, they ended up earning no more than they would have in Korea. When they found out that Australian workers under the same conditions were earning double their wages, they complained to their Korean employer. In response, the employer threatened to send the complaining workers back to Korea or fire them, prompting many workers with a strong sense of justice to petition and bring attention to the incident.

Some people criticized the situation, saying that if they had made a contract, they should have just received the money as agreed, and wondered why they were being so greedy. Others accused the Korean laborers of being exploited unfairly. This reminds me of my past experiences. In Korea, the approval for labor export came later than in Australia. Nowadays, private companies can legally supply labor to other companies, but when I was working, individuals were not allowed to do so. Strictly speaking, the supervisor had illegally registered people like me with the company and embezzled our salaries. However, we naively returned 50% of our wages to the supervisor.

After some time, I applied for the Combat Police Force and received basic training at Nonsan Training Center under the authority of the Police Headquarters. As someone who was experiencing military training for the first time, it was a harsh and challenging experience for me, to the point where I wondered if there could be another place like this under the sky. However, due to my previous experience with hard labor, I was able to feel that I had gained enough physical

---

of the Republic of Korea that was established to carry out projects related to lifelong learning support, vocational competency development training, qualification testing, skill promotion and employment promotion

strength to endure for a long time in the collective training. While gripping my fingers on the iron bar and stretching my body, many of my fellow trainees around me fell and got hit by fists, but I was able to withstand the pressure firmly. In my mind, I could comfort myself by saying,

'I did well to do the labor work before entering the military.'

**A collective punishment called
"Wonsan Bombing"**

Chapter 2: Days of Compulsory Combat Police

Gangjeong Post in Jeju Island

Nonsan Training Center

I was finally selected as the 56th Combat Police Officer and received training at the Nonsan Training Center under the Police Headquarters' commission.

The day before I enlisted, I had already finished the farewell party with my friends. On the day of departure, I casually left home after saying goodbye to my mother, who simply said, "Take care." She sent me off like she always did when I left for school or work.

When I arrived at Nonsan, many trainees had come with their parents and friends, and some even came with their girlfriends. But I was alone, not knowing that trainees should be sent off so grandly, as if

Nonsan Training Center in the 1970s

they were being sent to a faraway country. I confidently walked into the training center and registered myself. Then I was assigned to a platoon and stood in line at the barracks. Neatly dressed officers who seemed to be instructors were standing in a formal posture at the front.

We trainees exchanged jokes and laughs with the officers, in a happy mood, and some trainees waved goodbye to their families and friends who were watching us from behind. After the roll call was completed, trainees said "goodbyes" to their loved ones and lined up behind the sergeant who led us to march behind the building to the sound of his cadence.

As soon as we turned behind the building where we could no longer see our parents and friends, the leader of the squad and the surrounding officers stopped us and created a completely different and threatening atmosphere by shouting,

"Everyone who laughed earlier, come out now!"

Then, they pointed at some people in the middle of the line and ordered them to step forward, and started hitting and kicking them. We were taken aback and didn't know what to do in that moment. We wondered whether we should inform our parents and friends behind the building about this lawless behavior or just run away from the scene.

However, fleeing in such a manner would likely be perceived as an act of desertion, which could negatively impact our records. Furthermore, the prospect of being apprehended while attempting to escape would undoubtedly result in even greater distress. Consequently, we were compelled to comply with their directives, unable to voice any objections. We were required to remain alert and act expeditiously, akin to automatons, in response to their commands.

After receiving a collective punishment, we were escorted into the building. The first order of business was to strip off our civilian clothing and don the military uniforms we were issued. Unfortunately, the haphazard distribution of uniforms meant that none of them fit properly. When one brave trainee pointed out that his uniform was ill-fitting for his body, he was ordered to step forward and was berated with a flurry of fists for not knowing that his body must be fit to the military uniform issued, not vice versa.

While some trainees exchanged glances and quickly changed into better-fitting uniforms, I silently donned a slightly oversized one. The trainees were also given boxes to store their personal belongings, including any small amounts of money they had brought from home, along with their civilian clothes. They were instructed to write their home addresses on the boxes so that they could be sent home.

Subsequently, the training centre became a lawless place where instructors would beat trainees at will. If a trainee didn't want to be hit, they had to act quickly and obey their commands. However, the instructors often gave impossible commands, and inevitably, everyone was hit at least once. It was a living hell, one would think there was no such lawless land in the world.

For example, when the drill instructor shouted,

"Grenade on the bunk bed!"

we were all supposed to crawl under the bed, but since the space underneath was not big enough for all of us, it was impossible for us to comply with the command.   Those who were lucky enough to get under the bed first would avoid being hit while those who couldn't get under in time would be hit with shoe feet or sticks.

However, when the drill instructor shouted,

"Grenade under the bunk bed!"

we now had to climb on top of the bed. This time, those who had crawled under the bed first and avoided being hit with a stick were now the last ones to come out, and they were the ones who were going to be hit.

After receiving disciplinary punishment and being scolded throughout the afternoon, it was time for a meal.

"You, you!"

the instructor randomly designated someone to serve food. Fortunately, I was also selected as a food server. When we went to the cafeteria to get the food, they used a ladle to scoop rice into a bucket and filled another bucket with soup. I and other food servers then stood in line and used small ladles and rice paddles to serve the trainees in front of them with rice and soup.

After about a week had passed, I had grown somewhat accustomed to life in the Training Centre. During our free time in the evenings, some of the more financially fortunate trainees would indulge in buying delicious snacks and drinks from the PX[8]. However, I had no idea about this and had sent all the money I had brought with me back home, leaving me with nothing to eat.

One of the trainees took pity on me and shared some bread and a drink, which tasted divine. In gratitude, I gave him a generous amount of beef jerky during the next mealtime. As for the few unpleasant characters, I showed my displeasure by offering them only beef broth. Looking back now, it seems that extreme situations like these bring out the true nature of human beings, and it is a pity that I was no exception.

---

[8] PX stands for Post eXchange being a store at a military installation that sells merchandise and services to military personnel and authorized civilians

UDT Member

After completing the 8-week training at the Army Nonsan Training Center as the final selection of the 56th Combat Police, we were asked to submit our preferred work locations up to the 4th priority.

As Busan was obviously my hometown, I listed it as my first priority, followed by Gyeongnam as the second priority, and any other location for the third and fourth priorities.

However, unexpectedly, I was assigned to Jeju Island. Later, I found out that since there were no applicants who preferred Jeju Island, all first priority applicants for Busan were sent to Jeju Island, and all first priority applicants for Gyeongnam were sent to Busan, pushing everyone down one location.

A group of around twenty individuals received orders to go to Jeju Island, and three or four of them decided to travel together with me. The order stated that they had to report to the Jeju Island Police Department within 48 hours without any travel expenses provided. However, I, who had no money, cannot recall how I managed to arrange for transportation to Jeju Island. It is likely that I urgently requested my mother in Busan to send me money.

Some of the people who received the order to go to Jeju Island had the means to take a plane, while others dispersed to visit their homes. Among them, the three individuals who planned to travel to Jeju Island by ferry via Mokpo, including me, stuck together and boarded the train for Mokpo with their backpacks.

We had the opportunity to go up Mt Yudalsan[9] from Mokpo and enjoy a brief picnic. The world appeared exceptionally captivating after two months of rigorous training. The three of us relied on each other and moved forward, so there was nothing to be afraid of in the world.

During our waiting at the Mokpo port, we encountered a UDT (Underwater Demolition Team) member who had arrived on a different boat. The UDT[10] member had eyes that looked piercingly sharp and seemed ready to attack our group upon making eye contact, growling,

"You sons of bitches!"

One of my companions suggested,

"Hey, don't fight!"

and immediately calmed down the situation. Although our group had three people and the UDT member was alone, our group felt intimidated.

To avoid any confrontation with the UDT member, our group refrained from making eye contact with him, and the UDT member passed by without provoking us. It is probable that the UDT member had just finished his training on one of Mokpo's islands, and

---

[9] Mt Yudalsan is a 228-meter high mountain located in Mokpo, Jeollanam-do. As one of the eight scenic spots of Mokpo, it is the pride and symbol of Mokpo, and is known as Mokpo's spiritual mountain.

[10] UDT stands for Underwater Demolition Teams whose "frogmen" were trained to destroy obstacles on enemy-held beaches prior to amphibious landings.

despite our group having undergone harsh training themselves, they were subdued by the UDT member's spirit.

Served at Post in Jeju Island

It was reputed that the working conditions for the combat police were arduous, and the military presence on Jeju Island was substantial enough to have earned it the moniker "Devil's Island." Upon our arrival at Jeju Island Police Department, we were transported to the Jeju Island 1st Mobile Unit via an operational truck, with an assignment to be made at a designated coastal guard post.

However, we observed an individual performing squat jumps as a form of disciplinary action on an open field. We were puzzled as to why someone was engaging in such activity in a deserted area. As we investigated further, it became apparent that the individual was being punished for failure to provide adequate meals in front of a disciplinary lockup where a senior member was locked in. While we found it somewhat comical, we also expressed concern that the presence of such members could potentially make life on the island less than ideal.

Late that night, I and my colleague were assigned to the Kangjeong Coastal Guard Post ("Post") in Seogwipo, Jeju Island. We moved by an operational vehicle and arrived at the Post, and were greeted by the chief of Post who said

"It's your first day and too late, so go to sleep first!

Exhausted, my colleague and I went to the allocated bed and soon fell asleep.

In the early hours of the morning, my colleague woke me up by nudging me and

urgently asking me to come out. When I followed my colleague out, I found a bulky senior member in the kitchen. He punched me in the chest twice, attributing his violent behavior to my lack of discipline for oversleeping. This immediate senior member had been causing considerable trouble and harassment for me and my colleague. At one point of time, I even contemplated using the M16 rifle present at the Post to shoot him. However, I chose to exercise self-restraint and endure the situation, taking into account my future prospects. Given the circumstances at the time, it is not surprising to witness a rise in gun-related incidents in the United States. The proximity of a gun and the ease of its accessibility in moments of extreme anger can lead to unfortunate events.

One day, at around 2 o'clock in the morning, when it was not yet time for my shift change, the senior member woke me up.   In fact, he was asked by his senior to make him some instant noodles as a hangover cure.   But he woke me up from my sleep and ordered me to make the super senior member noodles and go to work.

Despite my shift not starting until 4 am, I quickly made the noodles for the drunken senior member and went back to catch a few more hours of sleep. However, my slumber was interrupted by a marine guard[11] who urged me to come outside. Upon facing the drunken senior member again, I was met with his furious punches to my chest and stomach, all because I had carelessly omitted the green onions from his noodles. He ordered me to make him another pot, leaving me speechless with a deep sense of resentment. Returning to the kitchen, I decided to take revenge by pouring the dirty dishwater into the pot and boiling a new batch of noodles, taking care to finely chop the scallions and adding eggs before serving it to him.

I waited and watched until the senior member finished eating his instant noodles, fearing that if the water I used to wash the dishes was discovered, I would be in trouble. Fortunately, he complimented my cooking skills and told me to go back. For this reason, even if the food is not delicious in the restaurant, I do not complain or ask for it to be remade, as I do not want to risk eating such food cooked by the unset chef with spoiled ingredients.

---

[11] A Marine Guard refers to short-term soldiers trained in the Jeju Marine Corps who commute to the coastal outpost in the evening, work, and then return home the next day. They are alternative service personnel.

An unfamiliar acquaintance whom I encountered while on vacation.

At any Coastal Guard Post in Jeju, an average of 7-8 soldiers served together with one chief of the Post. Our duty was to monitor the coastline for any signs of enemy infiltration or espionage. This required us to scan the sea with searchlights at night, but in reality, we also had to monitor the land behind us. This was due to the fact that any negligence in carrying out our duties during a surprise inspection would result in severe disciplinary action or punishment for all of us.

Around the time when I became accustomed to living at the Coastal Guard Post, news came that Wang Gocham, a super senior member, who was about to be discharged, had been assigned to our Post. I prepared a separate dinner for him in anticipation of his arrival. When a person with a rough voice entered the Post and greeted us, it turned out to be the same terrifying person, who was locked in the disciplinary detention facility, had been disciplining his subordinate for a failure to properly serve his meal.

Thinking to myself,

"Ah, I am dead now!"

I set up the meal with a strong military spirit. Surprisingly, this Wang Gocham treated me kindly. He seemed to be 4-5 years older than me, possibly due to having attended university, and as a result, he treated me like his own younger brother.

Just as life at the Post began to stabilize, I received a telephone message from the Police Department in the early hours of October 27, 1979, warning us of a Jindotgae One alarm.

With the members at the post (the author in the middle)

This is a step-by-step alarm measure issued when there is a local threat from North Korean armed spies or special forces infiltrating South Korea, or when there is a defection within the unit during such situations.   Normally, the "Jindotgae Three" alarm is issued, but when the possibility of a threat is high, the "Jindotgae Two" alarm is issued, and the military and police are put on high alert. When it is determined that a threat has actually occurred, the highest level of alert, the "Jindotgae One," is issued.

Upon receiving the early morning telephone message, my initial thought was,

"Could it be that there has been a conflict with North Korea at Panmunjom?"

I began to blame my luck, thinking to myself,

'Of all the times, a war breaks out between North and South Korea while I am serving my duty. It seems like I have such an unlucky life.'

My anxiety grew as we all watched the morning news, where President Choi Kyu-ha, the acting president, declared martial law. Later, we learned the devastating news that the then President Park Jung-hee had been assassinated by his subordinate, Kim Jae-kyu[12].

---

[12] Park Chung Hee, the third President of South Korea, was assassinated on October 26, 1979, during a dinner at the Korean Central Intelligence Agency safehouse inside the Blue House presidential compound in Jongno District, Seoul, South Korea.

Jeju Island Airport Guard

Following the passing of President Park Chung-hee, I was reassigned to the Jeju Airport Security Unit during the period of martial law. Given the airport's classification as a critical national facility, it was imperative to fortify security measures due to the imposition of martial law, which mandated that police officers be on duty. After bidding farewell to my superiors, I left the Post with my belongings. Notably, Jeju city buses waived fares for combat police officers on official duty, allowing me to ride for free by presenting my official credentials.

Upon arriving at Jeju Airport, I proceeded to the security office to register my transfer. The periphery of Jeju Airport featured a network of watchpoints scattered around the runway, where combat police officers maintained a 24-hour security presence. Going forward, I would also be assigned to one of these watchpoints.

Among the members of Combat Police Forces (CPF), those with influential family connections were assigned to serve inside the airport facilities, unlike myself who was tasked with guarding the perimeter. These individuals received preferential treatment and were separate from the regular airport security unit. However, the majority of CPF members resided together in the barracks and their primary responsibility was to be stationed at one of the watchpoints during their assigned shifts.

The area surrounding the airport runway was abundant with mandarin fields, so during night shifts, we could indulge in picking and eating them. During winter, we roasted mandarins in the fireplace and relished their warm and sweet flavor. Even today, I reminisce about those times by roasting and eating mandarins, which had a surprisingly less sour taste and a delightful flavor. I highly recommend trying this.

Regrettably, some wicked senior members in the barracks derived pleasure from harassing subordinates based on rank. To avoid these unpleasant senior members, it was more comfortable to stay in the watchpoint and eat mandarins. However, senior members who were well-intentioned and had a higher rank than the wicked members issued orders that no one should harass lower-ranked members in any way, and everyone should live together and set an example.

These individuals were deeply religious and were soon to be discharged from mandatory service. The problem was the middle-ranking members, between myself and the well-intentioned senior members, who secretly gathered lower-ranked members, and harassed us even more cunningly and maliciously, without the knowledge of the well-intentioned senior officials.

We couldn't even let the high-ranking members know about this fact. The high-ranking members will soon be discharged, but there is still enough time for the middle-ranking members to harass the lower-ranking members like me. Unaware of this, the high-ranking members thought that the atmosphere in the barracks was becoming peaceful thanks to their righteous policy(?).

Although I thought, "How foolish they are!", I had no choice but to endure the middle-ranking members' cunning harassment. Among their harassments, the most excruciating one for me was the punishment called "Gisu-batda [13]," where they make the lower-ranking members lie down and strike their buttocks hard with a stick.

---

[13] Inhumane punishment where if the top senior hits the buttocks of the junior right below him with a stick, the person who got hit must hit the junior right below him with the same stick as much as he got hit, otherwise, he would be hit again.

Then, the further lower-ranking members must hit their subordinate's buttocks as hard as they were hit by their senior members.

At the time, I had a boil on my buttocks, and even a single blow with a stick caused excruciating pain throughout my entire body. However, the senior members would dismiss my pain as exaggeration and hit me again.

The life of airport security guards was not all about suffering. Sometimes, they also had enjoyable moments such as partying. Moreover, Jeju Island is known for its famous black pork, and when someone caught a black pig in the area and gifted it to the police station, the station would send it as a care package to the airport security guards. This provided a pleasant surprise and allowed the security guards to indulge in delicious pork to their heart's content.

During night shifts at the watchpoint, we would sometimes joke around with the police station's switchboard operators over the phone. I even had the chance to go on a date with a girl I had been talking to frequently.

It seemed that many young Jeju women were intrigued by CPF members as potential marriage partners to leave the island, but their parents were often against their daughters leaving the island. Therefore, when CPF members were introduced as boyfriends, the parents were not pleased

I too had started to develop a closer relationship with one of the switchboard operators, but just as things were starting to progress, I received a reassignment to the 1st Mobile Unit of the Gyeongnam Provincial Police Department and had to bid farewell to Jeju Island.

The 1st Mobile Unit of the Gyeongnam Provincial Police Department

In the early 1980s, a notice was issued for those wishing to relocate their workplace to write down their preferred areas in order of priority from first to fourth.   I wrote down Gyeongnam as the first priority

Along with the CP members (Rightmost is the author)

and Busan as the second priority because I wanted to go to Busan, where my parents were.   Initially when I received orders to go to Jeju Island, those who had written down Gyeongnam as their first priority, like me, were sent to Jeju Island. That is why I had written down Gyeongnam as the first priority despite my desire to go to Busan.

However, this time, everyone was able to receive orders to the area as they wished in the first priority, so I ended up being sent to Gyeongnam, which in fact I did not want. I had already learned from experience that this is what happens when resorting to cheap tricks.

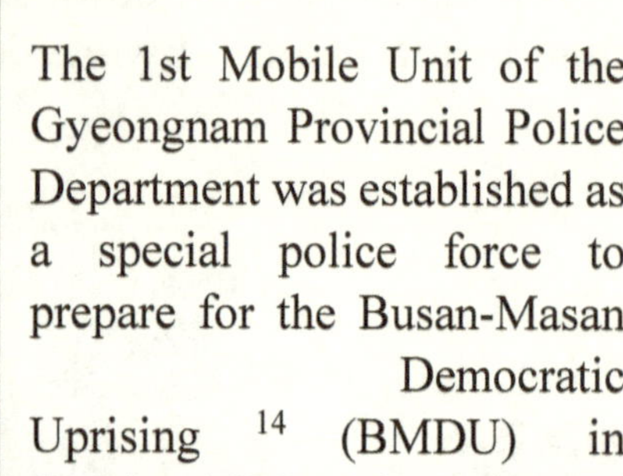

The 1st Mobile Unit of the Gyeongnam Provincial Police Department was established as a special police force to prepare for the Busan-Masan Democratic Uprising [14] (BMDU) in October 1979, and was housed in the office of a Bus Terminal in Masan. The unit consisted of founding members from across the country who applied for Gyeongnam area as their first priority, as well as police officers appointed as platoon and company commanders.

[14] The Busan-Masan Democratic Uprising, which occurred from October 16 to 20, 1979, was a significant "citizen protest" in Busan and Masan (now Masanhappo-gu and Howon-gu, Changwon-si) that lasted for five days. This event played a crucial role in bringing an end to Park Chung-hee's Yushin dictatorship and is regarded as one of the "four major democratization movements" along with the '4.19, 5.18, and 6.10 uprisings.'

This place was located beneath the sports field of Gyeongnam University, and students could overlook our training and preparation. Our mission was to monitor the activities of Gyeongnam University and Masan College students and suppress their demonstrations. Occasionally, we were also deployed to control the situation during crackdowns in Masan city.

Once, while being mobilized for a traffic crackdown in Masan, a taxi was caught violating a traffic signal while I was enforcing regulations on traffic violations such as illegal turns, lane changes, and signal violations. I stopped the taxi and asked the driver to present his license. At the time, licenses were designed to be folded in half and opened, and when the driver presented his license and unfolded it, I noticed that there was 5,000 won cash inside.

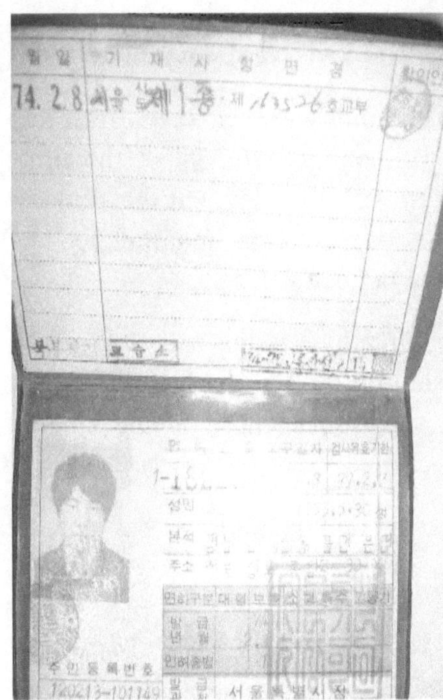

An old driver's license that could be folded

I took out 5,000 won and returned it to the driver, warning that such actions could be punishable under bribery laws, and followed the driver's request to let him go.

Suddenly, I heard applause from behind. It turned out that all the passengers in the bus waiting at the signal behind me were watching, and I could hear them saying,

"As expected, the Combat Police are more honest than current police officers."

Demonstration of the Airborne Special Forces

Our assignment was to train for a week-long operation to suppress multiple demonstrations. Some of us were selected as undercover agents and infiltrated Kyungnam University and Masan University to monitor and report on student movements.

During that time, my first cousin once removed[15], who was one year younger than me and a college student, participated in a student demonstration in Busan and became a fugitive. Her father was also taken to the Central Intelligence Agency for questioning due to his daughter's involvement. Currently, she has become an ardent supporter of Pastor Jeon Kwang-hoon, criticizing the Moon Jae-in government and advocating for the Yoon Seok-yeol government.

When I went to Busan on vacation and met with her, she delivered a speech about the injustice of the military government at the time. However, I was already indoctrinated with the idea that the students participating in the demonstrations were being manipulated by impure forces and, as a result, did not believe her.

At the time, the background for making such judgments was mixed with some resentment due to the strenuous training we had undergone every day, unable to even take a vacation because of the student demonstrations.

After months of training for suppressing demonstrations, we visited a

---

[15] "First cousin once removed" refers to the relationship between two people where one person is the first cousin of the other person's parent. In other words, the two individuals are from different generations, with one individual being a cousin of the other person's parent.

military base one day to observe a demonstration suppression in the Busan-Gyeongnam area.

It was thought to be a special forces unit, and we were given basic riot gear consisting of helmets with face shields, bamboo body armor, and shields. However, the special forces soldiers were only wearing their usual uniforms with helmets and equipped with M16 rifles.

As we watched with some awkwardness, their booming shouts and imposing actions were sufficient to subdue us as onlookers.

They created a formation and demonstrated how to advance with bayonets, stabbing people with their rifles in the process of suppressing the demonstrators. In retrospect, I suspect that they may have been special forces soldiers deployed during the Gwangju Uprising[16].

After a while, we heard the news that North Korean guerrillas had infiltrated Gwangju and that a war had broken out. Among the orders issued by the Police Headquarters to each mobile unit across the country was a directive to provide meals and accommodation to the members of the Gwangju Mobile Unit if they came to us. However, no one came to our Mobile Unit.

Members of the Airborne Special Forces arresting Gwangju citizens

---

[16] The Gwangju Uprising is widely regarded as a turning point in South Korean history, and is seen as a key moment in the struggle for democracy in the country.

Masan Provincial Hospital

One evening, I suddenly felt a chill all over my body and the cold was so severe that I shivered uncontrollably, and my body temperature fluctuated rapidly. I was urgently transported to the Masan Provincial Hospital and hospitalized.

Upon arrival at the emergency room, the nurse tried to check my body temperature by measuring it with a thermometer, but I was shaking so hard that she couldn't get a proper reading. She then exclaimed,

"Try to endure it! Can't a soldier even endure this?"

At her words, I did my best to endure, and miraculously, my shivering stopped and she was able to check my body temperature. Even now, I'm not sure why that worked, but the people around me at that time thought that the nurse's strength was able to calm me down.

Afterwards, the hospital performed various precision tests and diagnosed me with pleurisy. The doctor showed me an X-ray and told me that my lower right ribcage was filled with fluid, and that I needed to have the fluid drained with a syringe, which would cause some pain.

I respectfully expressed my disagreement with the diagnosis of pleurisy   as I believed that my symptoms indicated a cold or flu with chills, rather than a condition requiring a needle to be inserted into my ribcage. The mere thought of such a procedure caused me to shudder.

"I'll tough it out by only taking cold medicine and not seeking treatment for my pleurisy. But, if the same symptoms reoccur. I'll make an appointment to get treatment for my pleurisy."

I informed the doctor of my decision and departed from Masan Provincial Hospital.

I am grateful for the excellent medical care provided at this institution, which extends free treatment to public officials designated as national hospital patients. Although the hospital is government-funded, it remains a valuable resource for treating public officials.

I have received various forms of medical assistance at Masan Provincial Hospital, ranging from wisdom teeth removal to cavity treatment. However, I faced difficulties when I developed acne on my face and my skin became excessively rough. Despite numerous visits to the dermatology department at the hospital, the only treatment available at that time was an unknown comprehensive skin ointment that caused my skin to turn red and worsen over time. I was advised to wash my face more frequently and to continue using the ointment regularly. Unfortunately, this resulted in my skin developing a texture similar to that of a tangerine peel, which persists to this day.

Current state of Masan Provincial Hospital

During that period, my self-esteem was severely affected by my appearance and I was consumed by thoughts of self-pity, wondering whether anyone would ever want to marry me, a plain-looking, pastor's son with skin that resembled tangerine peel.

A Man Called Tarzan

The lump on my buttocks that appeared while I was on Jeju Island was causing discomfort and I was also tired of participating in demonstration suppression exercises, I decided to get treatment for the lump and went to Masan Provincial Hospital. After examining the lump, the hospital staff informed me that surgery was necessary. Therefore, I took advantage of this opportunity to take a sick leave and was admitted to Masan Provincial Hospital to undergo surgery.

In fact, when a member in the mobile unit said they wanted to go to the hospital because they were sick, the high-ranking members often gave them a hard time and accused them of faking illness, so it took a considerable amount of guts to take a sick leave. Therefore, I first asked the doctor to provide a diagnosis document explaining why surgery was necessary and submitted it to the administrative office of my unit.

With the diagnosis document indicating that surgery was necessary and my request for a sick leave, who would refuse it by accusing me of faking illness? With this, I was able to be admitted to Masan Provincial Hospital.

On the day of the surgery, they laid me down and gave me lower body anesthesia, and then inserted a needle into my spine. I experienced excruciating pain that was so intense that I couldn't even let out a sound of "ouch." It was like experiencing the extreme situation of a frog trembling all over when it is pricked in the back with a needle. The pain was so intense that I never wanted to experience it again. After the anesthesia finally took effect, the surgery began.

During that time, the medical technology at Masan Provincial Hospital was very low, so the pilonidal cyst was surgically removed and a small piece of gauze was packed into the wound. The gauze was changed daily until new tissue growth was observed.   At this time, the pain was indescribable because it was done without anesthesia.

The new gauze was replaced each morning when the nurses and doctors made rounds to my room.

When I assumed a position similar to that of a cat or dog, the doctor removed the packing gauze from the wound, disinfected the area, and repacked it with new gauze. Due to the excruciating pain experienced during the procedure, I could not help but scream out.

As days went by, my screams echoed through the hospital ward every morning, earning me a reputation as the "Tarzan" of Masan Provincial Hospital. Unbeknownst to me, other patients and nurses would discreetly smile at me as they passed, but upon noticing them, I felt utterly embarrassed.

Admission to Seoul Police Hospital

Although it may appear trivial now, at the time, my condition was beyond the capabilities of medical technology to treat. Despite enduring excruciating pain, I had to undergo daily dressing changes for an abscess on my buttock at the Masan Provincial Hospital. Unfortunately, before the wound could fully heal, the dressing became blocked, causing inflammation, and the thought of undergoing the same surgery again was dreadful. Consequently, I was transferred from Masan Provincial Hospital to the police hospital in Majang-dong, Seoul.

This transfer provided me with my first opportunity to visit Seoul. Although I had lived there briefly as a child, my only memory was losing my mother and being found crying in a police station this was my first actual sightseeing experience in the city. Prior to reaching the police hospital, I informed my parents in Busan and took an express bus to Seoul.

During that time, a tour guide like a female flight attendant boarded the express bus and sat at the front, providing a pleasant introduction to the history and specialties of each region as the bus passed through, with a beautiful voice. It felt like we were on a sightseeing tour bus. From time to time, the guide would come to the back to check if any passengers needed anything. Nowadays, even standing without a seatbelt on the highway is not

With younger cousin in Seoul

permitted due to safety concerns, but back then, no one thought about safety belts, and no one wore them.

As we approached Seoul, the song "Song of Seoul" began to play on the bus. The lyrics went,

"The bells are ringing,
flowers are blooming,
the birds sing and smile.
Oh my love, don't leave me.
On the beautiful streets of Seoul,
where we fell in love for the first time,
I live in Seoul."

Patti Kim[17]'s rendition of the song truly represented Seoul, and listening to it as we arrived made me feel excited.

When we got to Seoul, I first stayed overnight at my aunt's house before being admitted to the police hospital the next day. As I was the son of her younger sister, she treated me like her own child. At the time, my aunt ran a store selling foreign goods at the Namdaemun, now known as the Sungnyemun Market, and seemed to be doing well financially.

Pain is the level of medical technology

Finally, when I was admitted to the police hospital and taken into the operating room, they made me lie face down on the bed just as I had been during my surgery at Masan Provincial Hospital. As they pulled down my pants a bit to give me a spinal anesthesia injection, I was reminded of the pain I had experienced at Masan Hospital and I

---

[17] A South Korean singer who debuted in 1959 and "ruled the country's entertainment scene" in 1960s and 1970s.

immediately stood up and refused the lower body anesthesia injection. Instead, I asked for general anesthesia.

The doctors all looked at me with surprise and asked why.

"When I had the same surgery at Masan Provincial Hospital, they gave me a spinal injection and I felt a pain in my spine like it was being cut off. It was so intense that I couldn't even breathe."

Then, the anesthesiologist or the responsible doctor said,

"What a foolish way! This anesthesia injection doesn't hurt at all, so don't worry."

"But what if it hurts?"

"It's just a slight pain like getting pricked by a needle. You can bear that, can't you?"

"Really?"

"We'll be gentle, so if it hurts, let us know then."

To my relief, the anesthesia injection at the police hospital turned out to be only slightly uncomfortable, and it was over in a matter of seconds. The needle did not penetrate my spine, and the only sensation I felt was a mild tingling at the base of my spine.

"Are you going to have the wick inserted and removed daily starting from tomorrow following the surgery?"

"We don't use that method anymore these days."

"Then, do you not use a wick?"

"We do use a wick, but as the wound heals, the wick will dissolve on their own."

At that time, I realized how important medical technology is. When medical technology is outdated, the pain experienced by the patient is beyond words. ...

The power of 9 boiled eggs

At that time, my aunt was selling foreign goods at Namdaemun Market and was skilled at giving bribes to avoid being harassed by nearby police officers. So, without my knowledge, she gifted the responsible doctor who oversaw my surgery with a rare and expensive whiskey called Chivas Regal[18].

The power of bribery was immediately apparent as the doctor ensured that I could stay comfortably at the police hospital for a while without being discharged. This was because, upon being discharged, I could be subjected to relapse due to the demonstration suppressing training, and I would not be able to receive proper postoperative care.

As a young person with a hearty appetite, I went to the hospital convenience store during the day and found a package of ten boiled eggs. I bought them all and came back to my hospital room, where I devoured nine of them in one sitting. I offered eggs to other patients around me, but only one person took one, leaving me to eat the remaining nine eggs.

And that evening, I lost consciousness. How much time had passed? From a distant place in a painful, long, and dark tunnel with a small light, a faint voice was heard calling out,

"Soo Yong, wake up!"

---

[18] The reason why Chivas Regal became famous in Korea is because the late President Park Chung-hee enjoyed drinking it.

I, enduring the pain, moved towards the place where the faint sound was coming from. Gradually, the pain weakened and the light became brighter, and then the voice of a man was heard saying,

"You're finally awake! You're alive now!"

As it turned out, I had eaten nine eggs and suffered from food poisoning, causing me to lose consciousness. It was said that if that place had not been a hospital, I would have already died.

My aunt exclaimed,

" How can you have eaten 9 eggs when most people would get tired of them after one or two?"

And she went to the hospital convenience store and complained about the spoiled eggs for sale. Nowadays, she could have even filed for compensation.

<u>The little ladies I met at the hospital</u>

At the police hospital, there was a very attractive young girl in the neighboring room. She was well-behaved and her parents also held me in high esteem. Although I can't recall her name, we often visited each other's rooms and had a friendly relationship. Even though she had undergone surgery for acute appendicitis and was discharged shortly after, she continued to come to the hospital almost every day to see me.

I remember that the girl's house was probably near the police hospital.

The young girl and I spent a lot of time together, and one day a middle school student from the neighboring room expressed a desire to join us. The three of us hung out together and whenever my aunt brought me food, I shared it with the middle school girl, who usually kept to herself.

One day, when I went to share my aunt's food with the middle school girl, I saw someone who appeared to be her mother in the room. She started asking me about where I lived, which school I went to, and what my parents did. A few days later, the middle school girl was discharged from the hospital without saying goodbye to me.

After she left, both the middle school girl and the young girl came to see me together one day.   It was a pleasant surprise, and I said,

"You left without saying goodbye..."

The middle school girl explained that her mother had forbidden her from seeing me, but she came to meet me secretly. I believe she was the daughter of a school principal in Seoul, and it was the first time I had felt discriminated against. As we were not in a romantic relationship, her parents seemed to have gone too far and worried, but I had no other choice.

The cute little girl continued to visit me in my hospital room and play with me for a while even after that incident. On the day I was discharged, her

A middle school girl and a girl who came to see me

parents invited me to their home and treated me to delicious food. However, I cannot remember how we lost contact with each other.

One thing I remember is the girl's mother begging the doctor who was in charge of her daughter's surgery,

"Please make the scar from the operation as small as possible because our daughter will have to compete in Miss Korea Contest in the future."

It was a touching moment, but I couldn't find out whether the girl actually competed in the Contest for Miss Korea or not, even after closely following the Miss Korea Contests every year to date.

The little lady who came to see me every day

Chapter 3 During My Tenure at the Police Station

**At the first place of work,
Donggwang Police Box**

First-time Police Officer

In 1982, after being discharged from the military, I submitted job applications all over the place. First, I took the police officer exam, but while waiting for the results, I also took an employment exam for a place called Bechtel Corporation ("Bechtel") at the Kori Nuclear Power Plant.   On the same day, I received acceptance letters from both places, which created a lot of conflict for me. Bechtel, a foreign company, had interviewed me and the foreign boss who conducted the interview seemed to have a very positive impression of me, specifically offering to hire me in the HR department with a salary higher than that of a police officer.

Furthermore, according to some employees there, most of the employees at Bechtel left for the United States a few years after working there, which made it a very attractive job opportunity because at that time overseas travel was restricted in Korea under the dictatorship.

On the other hand, my parents strongly wished for me to become a police officer.   At the time, there was no one in our household working as a civil servant, and with the turbulent world where the Central Intelligence

With a Filipino friend

Agency seemed to control everything, I believed that some kind of power would be necessary to make it in this tough world.

In the end, I followed my parents' advice and became a police officer. After receiving basic education at the Bupyeong Police Academy, I was assigned to the Donggwang Police Substation in Busan. Ironically, this was the very same place where I had been reunited with my mother when I was a child after losing her on the streets.

Behind the Donggwang Police Box, there was a small alley where a red-light district was located. After passing through the red-light district, a major road emerged that led to the Jungbu Police Station. As part of the routine process of handing over a suspect to the police station, I had to navigate through this alley lined with brothels multiple times a day.

A woman, notorious as a brothel pimp, would often visit our police box and offer complimentary beverages like yogurt. Despite her efforts to befriend me, being a new addition to the team, I didn't feel inclined to drink any of the beverages provided by the pimp lady due to the disturbing visuals described in the book 'Children of the Dark[19]' that I had read prior to joining the police force.

One day, a young man entered the police box, engaged in a heated argument with the pimp lady. According to him, he had paid for the services of a girl but wasn't satisfied and requested a refund. When his request was refused, he threatened to sue the establishment for violating the law prohibiting prostitution. The pimp lady, however, claimed that the young man had spent the agreed-upon time with the girl and then requested a refund, which she couldn't provide, and was prepared to dispute his allegations.

---

[19] A Korean novel in 1980s that accuses the shocking reality of a dark back alley through a vivid description of the scene in which my experience and coverage are melted.

The senior police officer on duty at the time took charge of the case, but instead of sympathizing with the young man, he scolded him for causing trouble at the police box.

"You already had a good time with the girl. How can you ask for a refund?"

He threatened him without respect, and never mentioned the pimp's illegal activities.

"It's okay not to receive a refund, but shouldn't the owner of the prostitution be punished?"

"Dude, you, the person involved in prostitution, should be punished first!"

Following negotiations mediated by a senior police officer, both parties agreed to settle the matter as if nothing had occurred, and the case was resolved through mutual agreement. Later, as the young man departed, I observed the pimp lady purchasing beverages before returning to the police box. To my shock, I then saw the senior police officer receive cash from her palm via a handshake, confirming the rumors I had heard about police corruption and leaving me with a sinking feeling in my heart.

'If something like this happens again, I must handle it myself,'

I resolved in my mind.

Not long after, while I was on duty at the police box, the pimp lady came to the police box after fighting with a customer. I quickly prepared the paper to prosecute her under the laws on preventing prostitution and Misdemeanor Punishment Act. Knowing I was preparing the paper, the pimp lady put something in her mouth, choked, and collapsed with foam in her mouth. Then, a tall man appeared, claiming to be the pimp lady's son, and caused a scene at the police box, arguing that the police officer had caused his mother's death. As a rookie police officer, I was very confused, but I calmly asked the security guard to take the pimp lady to the nearby hospital emergency. The security guard had received favors from the pimp lady before, so they quickly took her to a nearby hospital by taxi. After some time, I heard from the doctor that there was nothing wrong with her, and she was brought back to me.

Despite the pimp lady's feigned confusion and disorientation, I proceeded with my earlier decision to file a report and submit it to the criminal division of the central police station. However, to my dismay, less than an hour later, the investigator in charge shockingly released the pimp lady.

She came back to the police box, confidently saying to me,

"Officer Yoon! even if you try to lock me up, you can't because I know everyone in the central police station."

I was utterly stunned when I discovered that the notorious female pimp had already managed to corrupt all the detectives in the Jungbu Police Station, leaving no one capable of bringing her to justice. I can't help but wonder about her current whereabouts and situation, considering she must be a grandmother by now.

Two Perspectives On Prostitution

One day, while studying law in Australia and observing the implementation of special laws to eradicate prostitution in Korea, I found myself comparing the two countries in terms of prostitution. In Korea, the Special Law on Prostitution punishes not only those who engage in sexual acts but also those who buy sex, with the aim of eradicating prostitution itself and establishing a human rights protection and self-reliance system for women who have been victimized by prostitution, ultimately fostering a healthy society.

However, according to the statistics of the Korean National Police Agency, which marked the 2nd anniversary of the enforcement of the Special Act on Prostitution, the number of prostitution establishments decreased by 34.6%, and the number of employees decreased by 52%. However, there is a concern that a new form of perverted prostitution has taken the place of the old one, and secret prostitution in private homes may be more worrisome from a public health and hygiene perspective.

On the other hand, in Australia, prostitution is allowed in certain areas with proper business licenses in light of the respect for women's sexual autonomy. There is no legal means to prevent such activities between adult individuals, but unlicensed prostitution in residential areas is subject to crackdowns for tax evasion or other private interests. By allowing prostitution business owners to gather and manage in designated areas, this approach appears to efficiently promote public health and hygiene management.

The prioritization of women's sexual autonomy versus sexual

protection can give rise to many debates. However, the following humor on the view of sex leaves a bitter aftertaste.

In court, the judge harshly scolded the woman who was arrested for adultery[20]. Then the woman responded,

"I don't know when my body started being controlled by the state."

Recently, a client approached me with a case regarding an unlicensed operation of a massage parlor that resulted in prosecution by the authorities in Perth, Australia. Despite being marketed as a healthy massage, it was in fact an illegal sex work venue. In Australian newspapers, there are entire sections dedicated to blatantly advertising prostitution services under the title "Personal."

My client had advertised their business in such sections, operating in a residential area instead of a commercial one, and was subsequently reported by local residents and charged with violating section 218 of the Planning Act. The maximum penalty for this offense was a fine of AUD 50,000 (approx. KRW 45 million) and a daily fine of AUD 5,000 (approx. KRW 4.5 million). The prosecution sought the maximum penalty, which was a challenging situation for my client due to their limited English proficiency and unfamiliarity with Australian law.

Nevertheless, I pleaded for a nominal fine to be imposed, citing mitigating factors such as their client's admission of guilt, lack of prior convictions, difficulty adapting to Australian society due to language barriers, and lack of knowledge about proper business operations. Furthermore, the defendant had dutifully paid taxes to the Australian Taxation Office, even though they did not have a permit from the city government. In the end, the judge considered the

---

[20] In South Korea, on 26 February 2015, the crime of adultery lost its effect due to the decision of the Constitutional Court to be unconstitutional.

defense's arguments and imposed a total fine of AUD 5,000 (approx. KRW 4.5 million), concluding the case.

Notably, Australian society does not view prostitution with the same level of contempt as in South Korea. In this particular case, the illegality of the defendant's actions was the issue, rather than the nature of their business. Unlike some other regions of Australia, there is no specific licensing scheme for sex work establishments in Western Australia, but certain areas are designated as commercial zones where such businesses are permitted. Police periodically conduct operations to prevent illegal activities and prevent crimes in such establishments.

During a stroll in Korea, one may notice that most shops occupy sections of roads where pedestrians walk to display their products. However, this is a violation of Korea's Road Traffic Act. Despite this, it is challenging to strictly enforce such violations, possibly due to the phenomenon in Korean society that emphasizes flexibility. Furthermore, it is questionable whether many vehicles adhere to the speed limit on Han River bridges and roads without speed cameras because in that case, the driver is considered not flexible.

In my opinion, laws that cannot be enforced or have no meaningful purpose should be abolished. Instead, laws that can be realistically enforced should be developed.

Unfortunately, most Koreans, when they are caught for an illegal act, rather than self-reflection on the illegal act, tend to think that it's not their day as there are many other violators. This phenomenon echoes the Korean proverb " There is no one who does not shake off dust.[21]" reflecting the reality of Korean society where survival according to the law seems impossible.

---

[21] Equivalent to the English proverb "Everyone has a skeleton in the closet"

Perhaps in a Korean society where Christianity has a high following, the tolerance of illegal activities may stem from the biblical insight that "one cannot live according to the law but only by the grace of Christ." This insight could be heard in the context that one cannot live by the law, therefore, one should live with flexibility or bribery. When a suspect is prosecuted and enters the escort car, they should never proudly show a "V" sign with their fingers and smile, but rather feel ashamed in front of reporters.

Sacrifice of the Homeless

The police box's primary responsibilities include patrolling, handling minor criminal offenses, searching for lost children, and receiving reports of lost items. In some cases, when beggars who have collapsed on the street due to illness come to the police box with a report from a passerby, they are immediately transported to the City Hospital for treatment.

If the beggars were deemed to be healthy, they were not sent to the City Hospital but instead directed to a vagrant camp. Each police box was equipped with contact information for the City Hospital and a homeless children's facility, so if reported, a transport vehicle from the facility would arrive within an hour to collect the reported individual. I later learned that during this time, the Busan Brothers Welfare Center was responsible for taking in street children from each police box.

**The appearance of
the old Brothers Welfare Center**

At the time, I believed that the orphanage was a government-run welfare center for the poor. So, when the orphans were taken to the police box, I immediately contacted this facility and handed them over. Although they begged me not to send them there, I persuaded them by saying,

"The state provides accommodations for free, so why not go?"

Only a few people were sent to the Brother Welfare Center, but when

I later learned about the incident, I was shocked to my core.

Later, it was discovered by me that the Brother Welfare Center, established by a former army sergeant named Park In-geun, had obtained a license as a shelter for beggars from Busan City. However, over a span of 12 years, from 1976 until the end of 1987, the center had committed various heinous crimes such as labor exploitation, assault, rape, and embezzlement of national funds, leading to the deaths of at least 513 children. The center has since been dubbed the "Korean version of Auschwitz."

It's important to note that sick beggars or unclaimed bodies are usually sent to the City Hospital, not the Brother Welfare Center. These individuals suffered from various illnesses, ranging from serious diseases to the common cold. From my   experience, it appeared that there were more mentally ill patients than others.

If any homeless without family or relatives dies after being sent to the City Hospital, the police officer who sent them is responsible for his/her simple funeral procedure. Ironically, it was rumored among police officers at the time that these patients sent to the City Hospital had a higher chance of dying than recovering from their illness. Some even speculated that they were being used as subjects for clinical trials.

According to a senior police officer at the time, the homeless with mental disorders who were sent to the City Hospital were frequently used as test subjects for clinical trials. It was a terrifying story that I had only ever seen in movies. I recall hearing that medicine made tremendous progress after wars because of cruel clinical trials conducted on prisoners of war. However, in modern society without wars, patients like the unidentified homeless who were sent to the City Hospital might have been the most suitable candidates for clinical trials because they could not undergo risky clinical trials on healthy people.

I cannot say for sure whether secret clinical trials were actually conducted on these homeless patients in Korean City Hospitals, but in a society where power prevailed in the past, such allegations seem probable. Police officers who received notifications of even healthy people dying six months to a year later might have thought,

"Oh, another person was sacrificed for clinical trials."

Homeless patients themselves, despite coughing and trembling, often preferred death over being admitted to municipal hospitals or government protection facilities.

On one occasion, a beggar was waiting for a municipal hospital transport van at a police box. He was shivering and trembling, and begged me to give him medicine so he wouldn't have to go to the hospital. I kindly sent him to the hospital, as if performing a good deed. However, I did not hear any news about the patient's fate until retiring in 1987. I now wonder if the beggar died as a result of being sent to the hospital, and is curious about his fate.

Smuggler Crackdown Anecdote

During my time working at Dongkwang Police Box, I received a report while on duty that a suspicious individual had entered a motel carrying two large travel bags. The behavior of the individual seemed questionable, prompting an experienced senior officer to advise me to investigate the situation. Despite the cold nighttime weather and lack of concrete evidence, I heeded the senior officer's request and proceeded to the motel alone.

Although I cannot recall the name of the motel, I remember it was located in Jungang-dong. Upon arriving at the motel's entrance, an individual who appeared to be the motel's owner whispered to me that the suspect was staying in room 307. I acknowledged this information and proceeded to knock on the door of room 307.

"Who is it?" a voice from inside asked.

"I am from the motel front desk," I replied.

Although I wasn't a motel employee, since I came based on the report of the motel owner at the front desk, it was correct to say that I was from the front desk. As the suspect opened the door, his reaction was one of extreme surprise upon making eye contact with me.

"I am a police officer and will conduct a brief search,"

I said politely as I entered the room and requested his identification. The suspect claimed to have no national ID card and offered only a passport, which revealed multiple entries and exits to Japan. Two large, immigration-sized bags were discovered in a corner of the room, prompting the narrator to inquire about their contents.

"Oh, these are gifts I bought during my trip to Japan to give to my family and friends," he replied.

"Is that so? Can you please open the bags for me?"

The male suspect hesitated to show the contents of the bags and requested me to listen to his explanation.

"I am a trader who travels to Japan to support my family by bringing back gifts to give to my relatives and friends. Can you just let me off this once?"

At that time, "trader" referred to smuggling. It was a time when ordinary people could not easily travel abroad, so crew members or overseas permanent residents would bring in duty-free goods from overseas and sell them domestically for profit.

At the time, I adhered strictly to the belief of upholding all laws and regulations, with the man's financial situation being of no consideration.

"Understood, let's examine the contents of the bag first."

I was personally curious about its contents. Upon opening it, I was astounded to find high-end products such as Rolex watches, gold and silver bracelets, and cameras, which were beyond my   wildest imagination at the time.

The man then discreetly handed me a bundle of Japanese Yen and implored me to turn a blind eye and let him leave. At the time, the value of 1 Yen was ten times that of Korean 1 Won, and a stack of ten-thousand Yen notes was worth approximately ten million Won in total. This was a significant sum for me, whose monthly salary was around 180,000 Won. The money would have been a windfall, a sudden stroke of luck like winning the lottery. The man knew that if he were prosecuted through me, all his possessions would be confiscated, he would be fined, and categorized as a frequent traveler, making it impossible to sustain his livelihood. Therefore, he tempted me with a considerable amount of money that I could not refuse.

However, I held a personal conviction that "even if I have nothing, I will never yield to the temptation of money," and thus, bravely resisted the temptation and handed the man over to the Central Police Station. In retrospect, I deeply regret my action towards this man.

As per NewsTapa's special project, "Who Rules This Country," which has been under continuous reporting since August 2018, it was confirmed that two months after the Lee Myung-bak government's inauguration, the list of emergency measures rulings and judges was deleted from the government website.

This was done to appease the military dictatorship government led by Park Chung-hee, which involved deleting the names of loyal judges who handed down death sentences for violating emergency measures. The deleted content also included information regarding Yang Seung-tae, the judge sentenced defendants to 10 years in prison for distributing subversive materials demanding the abolition of the Yusin[22]. It is disconcerting to note that most of the loyal judges who followed the dictator's wishes, including Yang Seung-tae, went on to become Chief Justices and even lawmakers, leading dignified lives. In contrast, it is regrettable that I could not overlook the smuggling offender, who was only struggling to make ends meet at the time.

---

[22] On 17 October, 1972, President Park Chung-hee issued a special presidential declaration on martial law, dissolution of the National Assembly, and suspension of the constitution. The dictator called it "the Revitalizing Reform".

The Sneaky Detective's Double Play

In Australia, it would be unthinkable due to the issue of conflicts of interest, but at the time in Korea, it was common to first inquire if anyone had connections within law enforcement when dealing with criminal incidents, and to solve the problem through those connections. From the perspective of my in-laws, who had a daughter and son-in-law both employed as police officers, it seemed that I was also seen as a kind of connection.

Once, my wife's aunt became aware of her acquaintance, a young man who wanted to marry a woman she considered promiscuous and unreliable. The aunt warned the man about the woman's previous marriage, causing the engagement to be broken off. The woman then accused the aunt and the man of defamation by truth[23], resulting in a criminal lawsuit.

My wife's aunt turned to me for help and asked,

"What crime did I commit by speaking the truth?"

I went to the Southern Police Station, which was investigating the case, to inquire about the case.

While it was impossible for police officers to share information with each other in Australia, in Korea at that time, this was a common practice. The detective leading the case was cunning and sly, and emphasized the severity of the offense. He also pointed out that the

---

[23] The United Nations recommended that South Korea abolish the criminal defamation law in 2011 and 2015. Despite repeated recommendations from the UN, the Constitutional Court of Korea ruled twice in 2016 and 2021 that the law was not unconstitutional.

victim's marriage had been strained by the words made by my wife's aunt and advised me to await the decision of his senior officer, who held the authority to determine the outcome of the case.

However, the individual who was jointly sued at the time happened to be the son of a prominent CEO in the tourism industry in Busan who wielded significant influence in the region. Upon sharing the details of the case as relayed by the detective in charge, the aforementioned individual claimed to have heard a different account from the same detective, that is, the detective pledged to use his sway to convince the complainant to retract the charges. When I cross-checked this information with the detective, he confirmed that it was untrue and explained that the head of the investigation department was out of town, necessitating a wait for his return before any further action could be taken.

When I next encountered the man and my wife's aunt, I recounted my conversation with the detective, whereupon the former promptly informed his father of my statements. The father reacted angrily, alleging that the detective had already promised to resolve the case for a sum of money. Upon bringing this to the detective's attention, he became irate, accusing me of disrupting a case that he had already handled deftly. However, it transpired that the detective had attempted to manipulate his position and accept bribes, only to be thwarted by my intervention. Consequently, the CEO of the travel agency also expressed his dissatisfaction with the detective's actions, severing all communication and accusing him of misconduct.

Upon reflection, several legal issues become apparent when assessing the case in light of current Australian law.

Firstly, it is worth noting that even in South Korea in 2023, speaking the truth can still constitute defamation and result in criminal charges.

Secondly, as a police officer handling the case on behalf of my wife's aunt, there was a clear conflict of interest that went unnoticed at the time.

Finally, the detective in charge's conduct, including attempting to accept bribes while providing inconsistent information, would undoubtedly have resulted in his dismissal if the case had occurred in the present day.

Gochugaru Myungdo

The place where I was first assigned was Donggwang Police Box, Busan Central Police Station, and the area I was in charge of was where Busan's famous Cheolhakgwan[24] and Myungdo[25] gathered.

I, who have always been very interested in the afterlife, took this opportunity to conduct a survey to see if Cheolhakgwan and Myeongdo can really predict the future.

At the time, law enforcement officials possessed the legal authority to conduct lawful investigations within their jurisdiction, including conducting census inquiries. As such, I took every opportunity to conduct census inquiries by visiting each household.

The typical appearance of Myungdo

---

[24] Literally meaning "Philosophy Hall" but not related to any philosophy. It is a place where divination is performed using the four pillars of destiny.

[25] Myeongdo refers to a person who acts as a mediator between the god of ancestors and the human descendant.

Initially, I visited a Cheolhakgwan, where I conversed with the inhabitants to glean insights into their way of life and income structure. Cheolhakgwan is a Korean fortuneteller's house where divination is conducted using the four pillars of destiny and zodiac signs.

Upon listening to the fortuneteller's analysis of the four pillars of my destiny, his commentary proved to be quite cogent. Among his observations, I distinctly recall him saying, "I lack my parents' virtues," "However, I will encounter a noble person in the future," and "My later years will be prosperous."

In retrospect, I realize that these predictions are quite general in nature and likely applicable to a wide range of individuals.

During another visit to a Philosophy Hall [26], the fortuneteller interpreted my fortune and warned me that there was a risk of losing an arm or a leg in my fate, but claimed that by possessing his talisman, I could prevent such danger at a low cost. Although I was unhappy with this proposition, I could not allow myself to fall prey to this scam artist by giving him any money.

So, armed with that fortune-telling, I went to a place called Gochugaru Myeongdo. Myeongdo (明圖) is a term that can be interpreted as a sacred mirror or the face of a god, but it also refers to a person who practices divination, or specifically, a woman who practices divination and is possessed by the soul of a dead child.

I said that I had come out to do a census, and in the midst of conversing on various topics, I asked if it was true that the next-door neighbor said that there was a risk of having my hand or arm amputated due to my four pillars of destiny.   Then, as the Myungdo lady shook the rattle, her voice changed to play a role of a baby boy and said that the guy at the Philosophy Hall next door had committed

---

[26] See Cheolhakgwan above

fraud to me, and that I was not destined to have my limbs amputated.

As we continued talking, the daughter of the house entered. It is probably remembered that it was a house that was renovated from a family home to do a business of Myungdo.   A girl my age came in and I stayed there a bit more out of curiosity and talked a lot with the Myungdo lady as well.   According to the daughter, she couldn't lie to her mom because her mother was possessed by a baby boy. It was so strange and amazing that while we were having various conversations, the lady suddenly told me to go back quickly, saying that the chief of the police box was looking for me.

After thanking the fortuneteller for the magical experience, I promptly returned to the police box to inquire if the chief was looking for me. However, he responded with a curt "never." It became clear that the fortuneteller had tricked me, as she had likely been annoyed by the presence of a uniformed policeman at her business for an extended period of time.

How annoying I must have been when I interfered with the sales without any consideration!   Perhaps the person at the Philosophy Hall who predicted that my hand or arm would be severed also had an unfavorable feeling against a cop.

Falsely Accused of Bribery

During my   tenure as a novice police officer, a colleague was discovered to have received a cash envelope from an unlicensed arcade operator within the jurisdiction. It is worth noting that the operation of an unlicensed arcade business can yield significant profits, even after accounting for potential fines incurred during a few months of operation.

Consequently, my   superior at the time, the chief of the police box, devised a strategy to set up an unlicensed arcade under his wife's ownership and conducted personal crackdowns on neighboring arcades to maximize profits for his wife's business. The chief directed his subordinates to conduct comprehensive crackdowns on all unlicensed arcades in the vicinity.

However, one officer disobeyed this directive and accepted money from an unlicensed arcade operator, thereby allowing the business to operate unencumbered. Upon discovering this fact, the chief vehemently threatened to publicly reprimand the officer during the morning roll call, attended by all officers of the police box, if the officer failed to voluntarily report the acceptance of the cash envelope.

During that time, Officer Choi, a close colleague with whom I often discussed personal matters, proposed to have a private conversation in a tranquil location. Choi was renowned for being well-liked and having amicable relationships with his peers and subordinates. Hence, it seemed peculiar for him to seek assistance from me when he could have approached several other individuals in his circle.

We proceeded to a nearby tea shop to hear Choi's story.

"Officer Yoon!   To be honest, I received an envelope with money as a reward for turning a blind eye to an unlicensed arcade's illegal activities."

It dawned on me why the chief displayed such ire during the morning briefing. Given that the arcade owner, who was in competition with his wife's arcade, had offered money to one of his subordinates to overlook their unlawful operations, the chief must have felt threatened.

"So, what course of action do you intend to take now?"

Choi had a difficult time opening his mouth.

"Well, it's difficult, but can't you say that you received the bribe instead of me?"

As Choi tightly grasped my hands, tears streaming down his face, he made a heartfelt plea. He spoke of his wife's pregnancy and the potential shock she would face if he were dismissed from his position. While I held reservations towards Christianity, I remained rooted in my core belief of living according to God's teachings.

I thought to myself, 'Jesus said to love our neighbors as ourselves and even to love our enemies, and He gave His life for them. Shouldn't I help my neighbor, Choi, who is not even an enemy, according to His will?'

With hesitation, I asked,

"What if I get fired for reporting that I received the envelope instead?"

Choi responded,

"Officer Yoon is known for being honest at our police station, so it is highly probable that the chief will view your infraction as a mere inadvertent mistake and consequently, choose to overlook it. If in the unlikely event that her dismissal becomes imminent, I am prepared to intervene and provide factual testimony to prevent any unwarranted repercussions."

Choi successfully persuaded me that my help would rescue him from an ongoing crisis, while I would face a temporary tarnish to my reputation, which would eventually recover. Encouraged by Choi's reasoning, I ultimately acquiesced to his request to report that I had received the envelope.

The chief at the police box appeared surprised as he widened his eyes. Given that I did not fit the profile of someone who would commit such an act, he likely inferred that it was an inadvertent error. As predicted by Officer Choi, the issue was resolved without any punitive measures taken against me.

However, following the incident, Choi's demeanor towards me shifted,  as he began to keep his distance and avoided any form of interaction during staff meetings. He appeared to be ashamed, almost reluctant, to make eye contact. Consequently, our relationship remained strained until our respective job postings resulted in our separation, and we never crossed paths again.

Upon reflection, I have come to understand that while Choi had requested my assistance, he had already taken possession of the envelope he had received. Regrettably, I had been unaware of the exact amount he had taken, and had simply acknowledged receiving the envelope. Consequently, Choi was able to fully reap the rewards of his unlawful actions.

The End of a Fellow Police Criticizing Jesus

As a child, I was reprimanded by my father for not praying before meals, which ingrained the habit of saying grace whenever I ate. Even during my shifts at the police box, when having breakfast with my fellow officers, I couldn't shake the habit of praying. One morning, my colleague Jo, who had noticed my regular habit of praying, asked me a question.

"What's so good about believing in Jesus?"

"It's not about good or bad, it's just natural for me to believe in my savior."

"I heard that Jesus himself didn't pray before eating..."

"I've never heard that before."

Officer Jo was a fellow police officer graduated from the Policy Academy at the same time, but he was a few years older than me. He had been disappointed by many Christian extremists in his life and did not like Christians, so he criticized Christianity a lot that morning.

At that time, being young and having faith in Jesus, I reacted by directly criticizing Officer Jo instead of humbly accepting his criticism of Christianity, as I felt it was a personal attack on me.

"The actions of your criticizing Jesus today will have consequences someday. It would be wise to repent now."

Officer Jo did not criticize anymore, saying that my words, "The actions of your criticizing Jesus today will have consequences someday" were offensive. Officer Jo, who usually drinks well at the team dinners and fawns over his senior police officers, is also popular with the local residents.

Especially noteworthy was an elderly woman who delivered yogurt and milk to the police box every morning and held Officer Jo in high regard. However, when I witnessed their interactions, I felt that they were crossing a line. Later on, the yogurt lady's husband pressed charges against both his wife and Officer Jo for adultery, which resulted in Officer Jo's dismissal from his position due to violating the dignity of a public official.

After Officer Jo was fired, it was later discovered that he began living with the elderly woman, who was over 10 years older than him and had children. It is unclear how his life progressed and whether he found happiness, but I feel remorseful that his words, "The actions of your criticizing Jesus today will have consequences someday," which he uttered at the police box breakfast table, may not have been the cause of what happened to Officer Jo.

A Thug Out Of Prison

Throughout my life, I have had many truly unique experiences. When I was young, I lost my parents on the street and wandered until I found protection at the Dongkwang Police Box in Busan, where I was finally reunited with my mother.   When I devoted myself to becoming a frontline police officer, my first assignment was back at the Dongkwang Police Box.

During a late night shift, before any other staff had arrived, a robust middle-aged man arrived at the Dongkwang Police Box, a jurisdictional police station, at around 8:00 am. He handed me a note, which upon closer inspection revealed that he was a repeat offender with seven prior convictions for robbery and violence. He had just been released from prison and was en route to his residence in Dongkwangdong, intending to report to the Dongkwang Police Box first thing in the morning. I was deeply concerned for his well-being and hoped that he would successfully reintegrate into society following his release from incarceration. In an effort to extend kindness and support, I offered him a warm glass of milk and held his hand, urging him to take care of himself.

"You have done well to date. Please feel free to approach me for assistance whenever necessary. Although I may not possess immense strength, I am committed to doing everything within my capacity to support you."

After bowing his head deeply and expressing his gratitude, he left. The incident slowly faded from my memory until about six months later when I was on a night patrol in Changseong-dong, Busan with a senior police officer. Suddenly, I heard someone calling out to me from a distance. I turned to see a man gesturing for me to come over from about 30 meters away. As I approached him, I realized that I didn't recognize his face. Curious, I asked him,

"Who are you?"

He smiled and replied,

"Did you ever work at Donggwang Police Box?"

"Yes, I did," I said.

"Do you remember when someone was released from custody one morning?" he asked.

"Yes, I do," I said,

Oh, now I remember! Wasn't this man the one who came to report his release that morning? But what is he doing here? He was running a restaurant in an alley in Changseon-dong's downtown area. He explained that the first person he met after his release was me. I warmly welcomed him, and the glass of milk I gave him that morning was so touching that he decided he would treat me to a meal if we ever met again. He invited me to his restaurant anytime and said he would serve me for free.

I didn't do anything for him and I had no memory of the minor incident, but I was grateful that he remembered it vividly and had started a new, healthy life. It was a message for me to be faithful in even the smallest things.

An Old Woman Selling Udon on the Street

This is a story from when I was working at the Changseon Police Box in Busan around 1985.   At that time, the police box was open 24 hours a day and I was assigned to work the late shift, which meant I worked from 1AM until the next morning.

One morning, when I went down to the police box, I found an elderly woman who was heavily drunk and looking for a police officer named Officer Lee. However, Officer Lee was not working that day and another officer had taken her complaint. Despite the woman causing a disturbance and making a mess, nobody had dealt with her and she was left for me to handle during my shift.

To proceed with a summary judgment for the elderly woman, I needed to understand the details of the situation. Therefore, I first calmed her down and patiently listened to her story. She explained that she runs a food stall selling noodles to make ends meet. However, Officer Lee had cracked down on her stall and she had to spend three days in detention. She was now struggling financially, and in despair, she even asked us to kill her. It was a difficult situation, and since no one else knew how to handle it, they left the matter for me to deal with in the second half of the shift.

When I heard the woman's story, I empathized with her and offered her comfort and reassurance. I also took the time to explain the role and limitations of a low-ranking police officer like myself. I told her that if I were ordered to crack down on her business, I would have to do it, but that I would try to help her as much as possible while on duty. After encouraging her to stay strong, I sent her home. While I could have immediately referred her for summary judgement, I didn't want to add to the lady's distress. Though I'm not sure if she fully understood my intentions, she did calm down and leave peacefully.

Two days later, I was on duty again and a security guard approached me, saying that someone was looking for me outside. Curious, I went to the back of the police box and found the same lady from before. She had brought a cup of coffee for me, carefully presented on a pretty tray. Even though I wasn't a fan of coffee at the time, I couldn't refuse her sincerity and drank it quickly, urging her to leave in case anyone saw her. When I asked where she was doing business, she told me she ran a stall in an alley in Gwangbok-dong, where she was trying to avoid police crackdowns. Before she left, I made a promise to visit her stall during my next patrol.

After some time had passed, I made good on my promise and visited the stall where the woman was selling udon. I ordered a bowl of udon to eat, purposely doing so while wearing my police uniform, as a means of sending a message to any potential blackmailers or other troublemakers in the area that this woman was under my protection. The woman appeared to be very pleased and proud that a police officer was eating udon from her stall.

When I asked the woman when her stall would close, she said that I was her last customer. I offered to help her pack up and close the stall to ensure she had some assistance. Together we pushed the cart from the back while she pulled it from the front to take it to the nearby storage. People around us were wide-eyed at the sight of a police officer helping the woman. They must have been amazed to see a police officer pushing the cart as they thought that the woman had great power. Later on, the woman told me that she felt proud as if she had the strongest connection in the world. She had been facing persecution from the surrounding merchants due to her stall, but after witnessing a police officer coming to her aid, the merchants did not persecute her as much after that day.

Afterwards, the lady at the food stall went to the taxi stand and I headed for the police box. The two of us were walking for a while, and suddenly the lady spoke to me in English.

"Can you speak English?"

I hesitated for a while, but since I was preparing to study abroad at the time, despite being a little awkward, I replied in English,

"Yes I can"

Afterwards, we were surprised to see each other and had a short conversation in English. The lady was delighted to say that she saw the person properly and briefly introduced herself, but I was very surprised.

She pointed to a three-story building on the street in Gwangbok-dong where she runs a food stall and shared that she used to be the owner of the building. Her husband was a hospital director there, but after fighting cancer for over 10 years, they lost all their property. Sadly, her husband passed away, and she lost everything, including her fortune[27]. Now, she is barely surviving by running a food stall with her daughter, who is a university student currently studying English.

On one hand, it was a deeply sad situation, but on the other hand, the woman's life was so filled with drama that she seemed almost like a character in a play, rather than a normal person.

In the aftermath, the woman would occasionally deliver a comforting bowl of udon to the police box, maintaining a close relationship with me for a while.   After bidding me farewell and announcing her plans to open a food stall in bustling Seoul, where business was booming, in order to earn money for her daughter's college tuition, I lost touch with the lady and have not heard any news about her since.

It's hoped that by now, the woman is able to spend the rest of her days happily alongside her daughter.

---

[27] In the past, when there was no medical insurance system, people lost almost all of their assets on cancer treatment.

Meet Jejus

On a winter night, while I was on duty at the police box, an elderly and disheveled man knocked on the door seeking assistance.

"What can I help you?"

"eh - h"

The elderly man was struggling to articulate his words, appearing hesitant and unsure of how to communicate effectively.

"It's cold outside, so please come inside first and talk to me."

Despite my invitation, I couldn't help but notice that the person's clothes were in a state of disrepair and emanated a strong odor of fish. It was clear that he had likely been wandering around Jagalchi Market[28] in Nampo-dong.

"Goodness, I'm not sure what's happening, but would you mind stepping outside with me for a moment to talk?"

I decided to take the conversation outside, thinking it would be more appropriate. The person followed me willingly without any resistance, as if understanding my decision.

"What's up?"

"Uhm, actually I'm so hungry"

The person's disheveled appearance and strong odor gave me a glimpse into his current situation. Despite this, the way he spoke conveyed a sense of decency. I couldn't help but wonder what events

---

[28] Korea's largest fish market representing Busan

led him to beg for a meal on a winter night.

"If you're hungry, wouldn't it be quicker to go to the restaurant and beg?"

"I went to the restaurant, but they wouldn't even let me in because I smelled."

The situation was incredibly embarrassing for the person. Despite his hunger, no one showed any sympathy due to his dirty and malodorous clothes. It was as if he was being judged and rejected without a chance to explain his circumstances.

"Sir, in that case, you should take a bath first. I am currently in a uniform and only have 10,000 won in emergency funds. So, please use this to go to a nearby public bath and take a bath. After that, I will guide you to a restaurant where you can have a meal."

This person took the 10,000 won money I handed over and said "thank you so much" and bowed his head several times to me, younger than him.

"Sir, the public bath is in this direction. After taking a bath, please come back, and I will guide you to a restaurant."

"Thank you, no one even wanted to come close to me because of my smell . . ."

This person expressed his gratitude and headed in the direction of the public bath that I had pointed out. As I watched him walk away, I was reminded of the image of Jesus.

"Whatever you did for one of the least of these brothers and sisters of mine, you did for me." (Matt 25:40, NIV)

Why Is a Medical Report So Expensive?

Victims of assault cases are encouraged to seek medical attention following an assault, as medical evidence can be useful in supporting their case. A doctor's opinion can be obtained free of charge, but if the victim requires an injury diagnosis or medical report, they may incur substantial expenses.

In the past, obtaining a medical report for injury was costly, with prices ranging from 70,000 to 90,000 won in the early 1980s in Korea. However, it is unclear how much it costs currently.   Considering that my   monthly salary was around 220,000 won at the time, it was incredibly expensive when converted to the cost of living at that time. If you complained about an unfair loss with a police station, a kind police officer would kindly inform you to attach an injury diagnosis and guide you directly to the hospital.

In many cases, victims followed the police officer's recommendation and sought medical attention at a specific hospital. It was not widely known that a portion of the cost of the injury diagnosis might be reimbursed to the police officer, and it is possible that some officers took advantage of this system for personal gain. While the prevalence of such practices in the present day is uncertain, it is worth noting that during that time, the income earned by police officers through injury diagnoses was substantial.

To illustrate, when the cost of the injury diagnosis is 70,000 won, the police officer would typically receive a reimbursement of 20,000 won. If there is a security guard accompanying the victim, the hospital would then return an additional 10,000 won from the remaining 50,000 won to the security guard. Thus, the income generated from the 70,000 won injury diagnosis would be allocated as follows: 40,000 won to the hospital, 20,000 won to the police officer, and

10,000 won to the security guard.

If there were many assault cases where medical reports were attached on the days when they were working, the corresponding income was high. Such income was pooled by the team leader among the personnel on duty that day. The next day, 50% of the total amount was taken and offered to the chief of the police box, while the remaining amount was divided equally among the personnel on duty that day. Moreover, this additional income was often legally directed towards one side while playing a social game called "Gostop[29]" on specific days.

The income collected, which amounted to 50%, was received by the chief of the police box who subsequently distributed it to each department or section chief at the police station. The section chief, in turn, forwarded a portion of it to the headquarters, which was then the National Police Agency. While it is believed that these corrupt practices and bribery schemes have been eradicated, and a transparent and ethical police organization now exists, at the time, I observed a police organization that was characterized by corruption, low standards, and self-serving behavior. The police organization has often been likened to a venomous snake, as it was believed that to secure a promotion, one had to punish the corrupt activities of subordinates, similar to how a snake devours its offspring to climb the ladder of success.

A senior police officer who had served in the 1960s had more vivid memories of the corrupt practices at that time. He placed a small empty pot in front of the police station, and drivers passing by would toss money into it as if paying a toll. The next day, he would collect the money and go home to count it with his wife, enjoying the thrill

---

[29] GoStop is a type of gambling or game using Hwatu, which is widely practiced in Korea.   Hwatu is Korean playing cards engraved with flower pictures in the meaning of flower fight.

of the ill-gotten gains. This was a clear indication of how corrupt things had become.

However, it appears that the police force has undergone a significant transformation since then. While my experience with the police organization was unsatisfactory, he believes that it has now evolved into an honest and friendly force. If given another chance, I feel he can fulfill a magnificent and genuine role as a police officer.

Is GoStop a crime of gambling?

I learned about a game called "GoStop" for the first time after joining the police force.   One team consisted of four officers, and if they were not busy, they would leave only one officer at the reception desk and gather in a dormitory on the second floor, pooling the pocket money distributed by the team leader the day before. They often played GoStop, but I was unable to participate, so the other members tempted him to learn by saying that they could not play "kwang" (a scoring rule in the game) without him.

So I started learning how to play GoStop, but I did it purely based on luck.   I realized that GoStop required some skill because I always lost my money as if legally robbed.   Since I was playing with the pocket money distributed by the team leader, I had no regrets. Shroud has no pockets!

My GoStop skills were not so good that even if I played for just 100 won per point, sometimes losing 20-30 thousand won or even 100,000 won. On rare occasions when we had a lot of money, we would play for 1,000 won per point, which was a considerable sum considering

that police officers' monthly salaries were only around 200,000 won at the time.

One day while we were gathered in the dormitory on the second floor playing GoStop, we received a report that a group of people in our jurisdiction were involved in illegal gambling with the same game. We immediately agreed not to disturb anything and left the game in place before rushing to the scene of the report.

Upon arrival, we discovered a mixed group of men and women actively gambling with GoStop, and we had collected an amount of money totaling around 7 million won. We took them all into custody and brought them to the police box for further investigation. During questioning, they claimed that they were only playing a 1,000 won per point game for entertainment purposes[30].

When an incident was reported to the police box, senior officials from different areas would begin calling, pretending to be relatives of the suspects in custody and using their influence to apply pressure. In some cases, even the military security agency and the central intelligence agency would contact us. To prepare for future requests, we always made sure to gather the personal information of the person they were inquiring about. This was necessary because in 1980s Korea, building connections like these was often essential for survival.

An acquaintance came to visit me and while having a drink, she told me that she wanted to take drastic action due to her husband's gambling problem and asked for my help. Her request was to raid her husband's gambling place, take everyone into custody, and give them a stern warning without pressing any criminal charges. It would be

---

[30] Article 246(1) of the Criminal Act (Korea) provides "A person who gambles or bets for the purpose of gaining property shall be punished by a fine of not more than five million won or a minor fine: Provided, That gambling which is just for momentary pleasure is exempted."

unthinkable in today's society, but it was possible back then.

At a later time, my acquaintance contacted me again, informing me that her husband was engaging in gambling activities with a group of individuals in an apartment. As her husband was familiar with my appearance, I was unable to personally respond to the situation. Instead, I dispatched a team of fellow officers and security personnel to the location.

Upon arrival, we discovered that the group had participated in a significant gambling operation with wagers totaling several tens of millions of won. Subsequently, we apprehended the group and escorted them to the police box for processing. During our investigation, the individuals pleaded with us to forgo criminal charges and simply issue a warning. They also pledged to abstain from further gambling activities.

As per our conversation, the officer who had priorly agreed upon our terms gave a stern warning and required them to sign a written commitment, pledging not to engage in gambling activities again, in lieu of being referred to headquarters. Though the husband of my acquaintance involved in the incident claimed that he had refrained from gambling since then, the veracity of his statement remains unknown.

Several decades later, as a lawyer, I met the acquaintance at a restaurant in Seoul's Gangnam district, where we nostalgically reminisced about the past and relished a delightful meal.

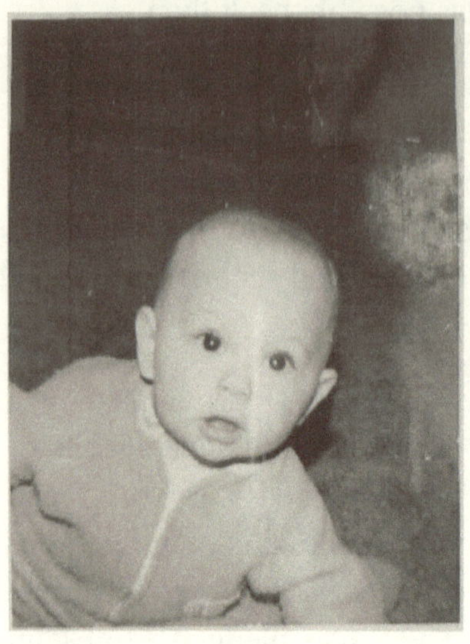

Shane

Foreign Friends

To enhance my English language proficiency, I used to strike up conversations with foreigners I came across on the street. Back then, it was quite challenging to find English speakers in public places, so they would express their delight when I initiated an English conversation with them. Through these interactions, I developed a great number of friendships with people from diverse cultural backgrounds. Unfortunately, I lost all their contact details when a fire broke out in my house, and only the recollection of our cherished moments together remains. Therefore, I would like to introduce some of my foreign acquaintances from my fond memories here.

U.S. Soldier "George"

The memory of George, a sergeant in the US Army during my time at the Gyeongnam Police Force, comes to mind. He stands out as someone who treated me exceptionally well, taking me to learn Korean archery and introducing me to his friends because of his deep affection for Korea.

George had a two-year-old son named Shane, and he would employ a Korean nanny to take care of him. On occasion, when I brought this blue-eyed child to the police station or my home, we would attract the attention of the entire neighborhood. The memories of those days remain vivid in my mind.

After George returned to the States, I lost contact with him, but I was later able to hear from Shane's Korean nanny. Unfortunately, it was revealed that George had developed mental illness, divorced his wife, and passed away while living alone.

Philippine Band "Mild Coffee" in 1983

Musical Band "Mild Coffee"

The jurisdiction of the Donggwang Police Box, Busan Central Police Station includes the Commodore Hotel, a prominent 5-star hotel in Busan that is known for its luxury accommodations. While on patrol, I came across a mixed band from the Philippines called "Mild Coffee" who were frequent visitors to the

George and his Korean friend couple

area. After striking up a conversation with them, they mentioned that they were performing at the hotel._

Their lifestyle appeared to be quite appealing, as they were able to travel the world while performing and earning a living. However, they also faced their own challenges. One of the band members lived with

Carlos and his girlfriend

his girlfriend from England, but she was only allowed to stay in Korea for up to three months. The prospect of having to apply for a tourist visa again and bear the expenses of airfare and accommodation was a significant source of concern for them.

In order to address the visa issue of his girlfriend, I accompanied her to the immigration office in Busan and introduced her as my own girlfriend, requesting an extension of her visa. As international marriages were not yet prevalent at the time, when the police officer said he would marry a foreign woman in the near future, the immigration officials readily granted her tourism visa extension, making the process as convenient as possible. Those were the days.

In appreciation, they extended an invitation for me to visit the night club where they performed at the Comodo Hotel. Sitting at the front table, I watched as they sang and even introduced me on stage as their close Korean friend. I was deeply moved when they dedicated a song called "Anak," which I loved at the time, to me by saying, "This one is for our dear friend Soo Yong."

It felt like I had chartered the entire nightclub at the Comodo Hotel to myself.

I later heard through the grapevine that the couple, for whom I had even pretended to be a fake boyfriend to extend her visa, eventually split up.

**Taekwondo international student - Anthony**

With Anthony (middle) and his girlfriend underneath (the one with glasses) at my wedding ceremony

During my time working at the Changseon Police Box, I encountered an individual of mixed-race and black ethnicity seeking assistance from the police after an altercation with a taxi driver. The individual arrived with a Korean woman, and due to language barriers, explained the situation in English, leaving the officers unsure of how to proceed.

In response, I intervened and conducted an interview in both English and Korean, which revealed that the taxi driver claimed the foreigner hadn't paid the full fare, but the foreigner argued that the fare was inflated because the driver took a longer route. Accompanying the foreigner was a beautiful woman who identified herself as his girlfriend. She was also engaged in a heated argument with her boyfriend over his role in causing the situation, admonishing him in English. The whole situation was quite tense.

Due to a disagreement between the individuals, the environment within the police box became disordered.　I advised the taxi driver to exercise leniency towards the foreign national. Additionally, I recommended that the mixed-race black individual come to an agreeable resolution. Ultimately, they reached a consensus independently and ratified the agreement I had prepared before departing.

Several days after the incident, the mixed-race black individual and his girlfriend visited me to express their gratitude. They generously invited me to lunch at B&C Bakery, located in the now-defunct Gwangbok-dong neighborhood. During our meal, I discovered that the woman was a Daeyeon Middle School teacher while her boyfriend, who hailed from the United States, had arrived in Korea to study Taekwondo as a professional athlete. I was also impressed by his fluency in the Busan dialect of the Korean language.

While socializing with Anthony's girlfriend, I was reminded of a story she shared about inviting him to teach English with a native accent to her students. However, a few days after the class, she was called to the principal's office and accused of negatively impacting her students' education by inviting a black man during school hours.

As a consequence, she was forced to resign from her teaching position. Despite making a case for the purely educational purpose of the visit and questioning why living with a black man was deemed problematic, the principal remained firm in his belief that a young teacher cohabiting with a black man was morally wrong.

After her dismissal from the teaching position, she confided in me about the incident, which provided insight into the social and moral standards of Korea at the time. Although Anthony and his girlfriend had become close enough to attend my wedding, I lost contact with them after they returned to the United States and I moved to Australia. If anyone who is acquainted with Anthony happens to come across this message, I sincerely request that you reach out to me.

Napoleon – The Relative of Marcos in Philippine

I have one unforgettable friend whom I met during my time as a detective in Gimhae Airport. His name is Napoleon, and he hails from the Philippines. As the relative of the former President of the Philippines, Marcos, Napoleon came to Korea and Japan with his daughter to start a new life after Marcos stepped down. I remember his daughter as a cute, doll-like child. Although Napoleon was staying in Japan when I was about to marry, I later introduced him and his daughter Jenny to my wife, and she got to know Jenny well.

Napoleon had a keen interest in trade, and I helped him as an interpreter when he visited various production companies in Busan to negotiate for export. I remember only his first name, and I'm uncertain about his surname. As for Jenny, it has been about 35 years since we last met, and she may have started her own family by now. If anyone recognizes Napoleon or Jenny based on the photo, please contact me.

With Napoleon and his daughter Jenny

Special Friend Eddie

I have a very dear and cherished friend in my life, whom I had the privilege of getting to know during my younger years. His Korean name is Lee Jong-bae, but I fondly remember him introducing himself as Epaphroditus from the New Testament's Philippians, and everyone called him "Eddie." Despite being a few years older than me, he became a great mentor and friend, sharing his vast knowledge and experiences through in-depth discussions with me.

Eddie's humility and unassertive nature have always stood out to me, and I consider him to be one of the most honest and genuine individuals I have ever met. Currently, he serves as a senior pastor at the Church of Christ in Seomyeon, Busan, where he brings his spiritual guidance to his congregation with passion and dedication.

What sets Eddie apart is his unwavering dedication to his faith and principles, as he always refrains from using the title of "pastor" and instead humbly refers to himself as "the evangelist." From the moment we met, he has always addressed me as "Brother Yoon," showcasing his genuine love and respect towards me as a friend and a fellow believer.

I noticed a unique trait in this friend that set him apart from other believers who tend to become more talkative and dogmatic as their biblical knowledge expands. This friend remained steadfast in his commitment to live by the principles he gleaned from the Bible.

My first encounter with this exceptional friend occurred during his stint as a clerk at "Esperanto," a bookstore located in the bustling Bosu-dong Bookstore Street in Busan. The owner of the bookstore trusted this friend so much that he handed over the entire bookstore's management to him. During my days off, I would often seek out this friend to discuss faith matters and seek his wise counsel. I recalled a conversation where he approached his friend, saying:

Evangelist Jongbae Lee

Seomyeon Church of Christ

"They say it is harder for a camel to go through the eye of a needle than for a rich man to enter the kingdom of heaven."

He then said,

"The Bible should always be read to the end. The next verse says, 'Man cannot, but God can', doesn't it?"

It really was.

In Matthew 19:26, it is impossible for a rich person to enter the kingdom of heaven, so the disciples were surprised and asked,

"Then, who can be saved?"

Jesus looked at them and said,

"With man this is impossible, but with God all things are possible."

The way of life of this friend, who has lived without coveting wealth for the rest of his life, is strange to me and sad at the same time. I hope that his life after death will never be in vain.

Airport Room No. 100

During my tenure as a police officer, I was constantly preparing to study abroad, and as a result, I made it a habit to always have English books with me. This image of me as a person with a strong command of the English language led to my superiors selecting me to join the foreign affairs section. I was fortunate to rank first in the national police English exam, which enabled me to secure a highly sought-after position at the time, as a member of the Airport Room No. 100. Even with connections to members of parliament, this position was notoriously difficult to obtain.

The Room No. 100 is a workplace for undercover detectives stationed at the international terminal of Gimhae Airport in Busan (similar to the current Incheon Airport). Their department is responsible for

At the police academy for

foreign affairs training (Leftmost is the author)

investigating crimes related to foreigners, so it was necessary for each member to have expertise in at least one foreign language. However, since it was a place where those with connections to higher-ups tended to gather, there were more people with connections than language specialists at the time.

I met and married a female detective who worked next to me here, and I have been living with one son and one daughter.

During my time as a combat police officer, I was stationed at the Jeju Coastal Guard Post. Under the

The Author's Spouse

orders of my senior member, I was responsible for monitoring the inland instead of watching for enemy invasions from the coast. Similarly, when I worked at the Airport Room No. 100, the abilities of the foreign affairs detectives who worked there were measured not by their ability to monitor and crack down on foreign criminal cases such as foreign currency control laws and surveillance of terrorist suspects, but rather by their ability to profit from smuggling and collusion.

Some police officials from the police headquarters who traveled on business to other provinces, even stopped by the airport room No. 100 to receive allowances from the chief of Room No. 100. While it may now be a legendary story that no longer occurs, at the time, to secure such funds, detectives of the Room No. 100 had to contribute certain amounts of money for that purpose.   Some detectives even colluded with customs officials to engage in numerous cases of tax evasion in order to gather the necessary funds. Such stories are now nothing but fond memories of the past.

Working as a detective

at Room No. 100

As someone who worked in the Room 100 in my early twenties, I could not turn a blind eye to the illegal activities happening around me. At that time, all individuals who entered and exited the country as VIPs through Room No. 100 or the National Security Agency were suspected to be involved in tax evasion and other illegal activities. As a result, all individuals who did not go through official channels were subject to thorough body searches without exception.

Once, a plane flying from the United States to Seoul had to make an emergency landing at Gimhae Airport due to bad weather. At that time, the head of the Gimhae Airport branch of Korean Air asked me to treat a young couple around my age as VIPs. Naively, I ignored his request and thoroughly searched the couple's belongings.

Despite the unremarkable nature of the couple's belongings, I decided to conduct a thorough search of their possessions due to my curiosity about their identity. As part of the police search procedure, I meticulously checked their identification documents, revealing the man's name to be "Jeon 00," while the woman possessed an identification card indicating her to be a top secretary working at the United Nations office in the United States.

Following the search, I inquired with the branch head regarding his favorable treatment of the couple, but he was unable to divulge any information due to orders from higher authorities.

Later, I prepared a intelligence report about their movements. The chief of Room No. 100, who was reviewing my report, found out through rumors that "Jeon 00" was the son of then-President Chun Doo-hwan. I finally understood why the airport manager was so flustered.

Also, one day I noticed a group of inbound travelers bypassing customs inspection and took immediate action to investigate their actions. Through the Passenger Inspection Section (PIS) of the customs office, numerous foreign goods were intended to be exempt from customs duties.   In order to conduct my investigation discreetly, I moved the group to a separate room and thoroughly examined their possessions.

Unfortunately, my investigation caused some disturbance at Gimhae Airport. I later learned that the head of PIS had granted the individuals in question exemption from customs duties at the request of the Director of the Gimhae branch of the National Security Agency, but the people that the head of PIS passed through did not exit the airport as expected.

After concluding the investigation, I proceeded to prepare a report for my superiors and brought the individuals in question to Room No. 100. Upon encountering the chief of Room No. 100, I noticed an air of discomfort and hesitancy. The chief then advised me, saying,

"While I appreciate your enthusiastic and thorough approach, I suggest that we overlook this incident for the sake of our relations with other agencies."

As a public official, I was aware that I was not obligated to follow any instructions that would go against the law. Therefore, they are sometimes referred to as "individual responsibility system" officials. However, I understood that, despite the ideal of being a responsible individual, the reality of working within a hierarchical system often requires one to consider the potential consequences of defying a direct superior's orders. As the chief of Room No. 100 was my immediate superior, I was unable to ignore his suggestion and ultimately released the individuals without taking any further action.

After the aforementioned incident, it appears that the director of Customs at Gimhae Airport and the director of the National Intelligence Service's Gimhae branch recognized the value of a young detective's skills and separately invited me for a drink, affording me the opportunity to personally greet them.

Subsequently, a customs section chief, who allowed smuggled goods to pass through customs upon the request of the director of the NIS's Gimhae branch, approached me with a complaint about his receiving disciplinary action and being transferred to another location due to this event. In addition, he left a curious comment, stating that one cannot survive alone in this world. This encounter was quite uncomfortable for me. I came to realize that the true VIPs who bypass official tax inspections while entering and leaving the country were the ones involved in large-scale tax evasion. Consequently, I ended up turning a blind eye to minor violators of Foreign Currency Control Act (FCCA) who were small-time offenders.

One day, a colleague detective who shared a similar sense of justice as me was preparing a warrant to detain someone who was trying to study in Japan in violation of FCCA. At that moment, Detective Lee, a detective who we were relatively friendly with, walked in and made eye contact with the suspect being investigated, recognizing each other as high school classmates.

My Friend Detective Kim

One day, Detective Kim who shared a similar sense of justice as myself was preparing a warrant to apprehend someone who was trying to study in Japan in violation of the foreign exchange regulations. At that moment, a detective named Lee, whom we were relatively close with, entered the room and recognized the suspect, whom he was interrogating, as a fellow high school classmate simply by making eye contact.

After understanding the situation, Detective Lee immediately instructed the colleague detective to halt the warrant preparation and asked if the flight to Japan was still waiting for takeoff. Upon looking out the window, they noticed that the plane had already left the gate and was slowly taxiing towards the runway. Detective Lee contacted the airport operations center and urgently requested that the plane be brought back since it had not yet taken off. As a result of their efforts, the plane returned and Detective Lee's high school classmate was able to safely depart for Japan on the same flight.

Twenty years later, when I started a venture business in Seoul, I met Detective Lee again. While reminiscing about the past, he revealed that the friend he had sent to Japan was currently a professor at a prestigious university in Seoul. He emphasized that without their friendship, his friend would have never gone to Japan and achieved such success. We both acknowledged the fickle nature of life. Nevertheless, this incident became an ironic tale that highlights the importance of connections for survival in Korean society. Many individuals without connections and financial resources were detained under the FCCA during their overseas trips, had all of their hard-earned money seized, and were unable to leave the country. I am left pondering how they managed to endure their lives thereafter.

Detective Kim was a close associate of mine during my foreign affairs training, with whom I shared a particularly close friendship. Although he was a few years older than me, he was characterized by his humility and bright personality, which allowed us to forgo linguistic formality distinctions in conversation[31].

During our shared training experiences, we forged numerous memories, such as accompanying our U.S. military friend to a missile base and being treated to a meal there.

At one point, Detective Kim shared an anecdote with me about teasing his own wife's name, a tale which has remained etched in my memory.

His wife's name is Kim Gilnyeon, which is written using the characters 'Gil' for 'luck' and 'Nyeon' for 'year'. This friend once teased his wife, suggesting that she change her surname to Ju. Initially, I didn't grasp the meaning behind his words, but when I tried changing her surname to Ju and pronouncing it, it sounded like 'Juk-ilnyeon[32]' or a very bad girl. This caused me to laugh my head off.

However, what made me laugh even more was when he told me that the name of his older sister-in-law was 'Gaenyeon', which took me by surprise. I asked,

"What kind of name is that?"

------

[31] In Korean culture, using specific language forms based on social hierarchy is the norm. However, forgoing such linguistic formalities in conversation is seen as a sign of intimacy between individuals.

[32] Literally it means "a girl to kill" but it is used as a profanity in Korean and is a very insulting word used when swearing or belittling other people. Commonly used interchangeably with "a damn/wretched person" or "a person I want to kill"

He explained that it is written using the characters 'Gye' for 'cassia' and 'Nyeon' for 'year', but when pronounced, it sounds the same as a highly derogatory term, 'Gaenyeon' or a bitch.

As such, he is a valuable friend to me, with whom I share a hobby of enjoying humor, and I have many cherished memories with him due to our strong similarities in this regard.

My friend and I were both assigned to work in Room 100 of Gimhae Airport, and we were known for our commitment to following protocol without exception. Perhaps as a result of this reputation, my friend was reassigned to the Southern Police Station after completing a two-year term, while I left for Australia to pursue my studies.

Later, I heard a story after returning from studying abroad that my friend left the police force because he failed to properly monitor a suspect who committed suicide by hanging himself while in custody at the Southern Police Station, where he was on duty.

When I visited Korea several years ago, he was suffering from leukemia, and I couldn't help feeling sorry for him when he came to meet me looking weak and sickly. Nonetheless, seeing him still enjoying humor and living optimistically gave me a little bit of relief. Observing his wife, who he used to tease with the nickname "Jukil-nyeon," diligently taking care of him also put my mind at ease. I sincerely hope that this couple will be full of health and happiness, and I hope that one day they can visit Australia in good health.

Bar Exam Preparation Proposal

At the airport, a CEO of a certain company was en route to a business trip in Japan when we met at the departure lounge and had a brief conversation. The CEO seemed to take a liking to me and promised to treat me to a meal after returning from Japan.

I had a positive impression of him as an older person who treated me humbly and thought it would be advantageous to know someone in the business world. After exchanging pleasantries, I parted ways with the CEO saying,

"Please contact me when you come back."

A week later, he followed through on his promise and we met at a Japanese restaurant called Angel Hotel in Seomyeon, Busan. Though not much of a drinker, I had a sake to set the tone and engaged in a conversation over dinner and drinks. When I inquired about his business, he mentioned that he imported golf-related products.

At the time, golf was considered a sport beyond the reach of commoners, and seeing someone who actually did business in the field made me feel envious and impressed with the luxurious lifestyle of the upper class.

Once my inquiries were concluded, I was inundated with a barrage of questions about myself. The line of inquiry began with my family background and gradually transitioned into topics such as law enforcement. Eventually, the questioning turned to my academic background, and I candidly revealed that my secondary education had been acquired via self-study due to my family's financial limitations.

Suddenly, he began posing his inquiries in English, to which I responded without hesitation. At the time, I had been dedicatedly studying English, regularly interacting with foreign individuals, and managing numerous interactions with Japanese tourists at the airport, which bolstered my confidence in both English and Japanese communication skills.

After briefly conversing in English, the person remarked to me,

"I've found a rare talent"

and advised me to study for the judicial exam[33]. I explained that I had already achieved a great accomplishment by self-studying through middle and high school due to my family's financial situation, and that I currently provide 100% of my salary to support my parents. As a result, I didn't have the financial means to study for the exam.

However, the person made an offer to provide financial support for all my living expenses and exam fees until I pass the exam. This individual had a son who was the same age as me. He suggested that I should become good friends with his son, so we could learn from one another through close association.

During the conversation, the person introduced himself again and gave me another business card. I noticed that he was Mr Han Eejo, held the position of the Chief Director of a university in Busan, and that his original profession was in higher education, while his golf business was a hobby.

Although the proposal came unexpectedly, I did not give an answer on the spot and said I would consider it. After pondering for about a month, I finally made a decision.

At the time, I found the process of studying for the judicial examination to be arduous, given my lack of formal education in the

---

[33] A national examination that tests qualifications to become a lawyer, abolished on 31 Dec 2017, consisted of three rounds: 1st (multiple choice), 2nd (descriptive subjective), and 3rd (interview).

subject matter and the competitive landscape of Korea. The bulk of successful candidates hailed from Seoul National University, and even if I were to pass the first exam, the probability of failing the second exam remained significant. Consequently, resigning from my position with the police force to prepare for the judicial examination was a challenging decision that defied logic.

Furthermore, during my preparation for the exam, there existed no assurances that the individual who had offered to assist me would honor his commitment. The prospect of losing my job and exposing myself as a fool if the promise were broken weighed heavily on my mind. Consequently, I respectfully declined his offer, expressing my gratitude but opting to proceed with self-directed study. Then the person said,

"If you change your mind, feel free to talk to me."

It seemed that our relationship ended there.

However, during my studies in Australia, I encountered financial difficulties and struggled to afford the tuition fees. However, with the help of Mr Han, the Chief Director, I was able to cover the cost of one semester. Regrettably, we lost touch thereafter. This left me wondering,

"Had I accepted their offer to study for the bar exam, would I have ended up in this same situation, receiving occasional financial assistance before losing touch?"

Upon reflection, I came to believe that declining his offer had been a prudent decision.

After completing my studies in Australia, I paid a visit to the benefactor's university to offer my respects.

"I have come to see Mr Han,"

I announced.   The response took me by surprise:

"Mr Han has passed away, and his son now serves as the Chief Director."

Shocked, I asked,

"When did he pass away?"

It turned out that Mr Han had generously sent me the funds to cover one semester's tuition before passing away from a heart attack a few months later. Tragically, I was unaware of his passing.

Despite this, I believed it would be courteous to meet his son and share some stories about his father. When I met the son, he appeared visibly intoxicated, but nonetheless said to me,

"I've heard about you from my father. Please don't feel indebted to my father and live your life in peace."

With that, my connection with Mr Han came to a close.

Chapter 4 Poor Life of Overseas Student

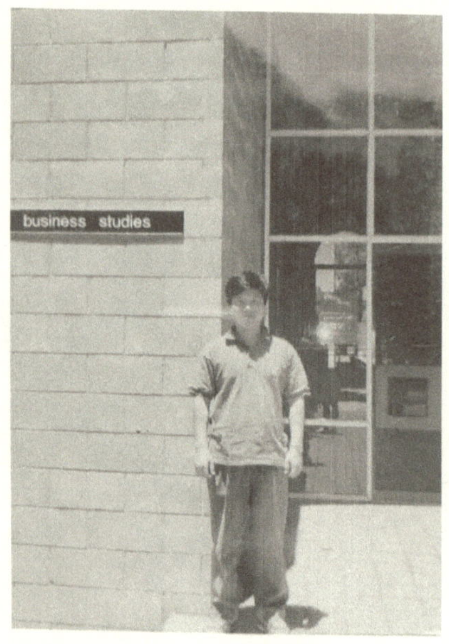

**At Churchlands Campus of
Edith Cowan University in 1988**

Preparation for Overseas Study

At the time, I disliked the corruption and injustice prevalent in Korean society, as well as my father's biblical teaching that

"Everything under the sun is meaningless."

I wanted to live a meaningful life under the sun while I still had it, and the reason why I pursued self-study of English during my spare time was driven by my desire to break free from the confines of my life circumstances. I believed that knowing English was key to escaping Korea.

However, despite his efforts, the church founded by my father was not financially sustainable and, as a result, my parents became increasingly reliant on me.   All of my salary had to go to supporting them, and any extra money I had from my work as a police officer had to be used as my allowance.   The idea of living a meaningless, disposable life with no future prospects was personally agonizing to me. While I wanted to save up my salary for my own future, I felt a strong sense of responsibility towards my parents and younger siblings as the eldest son, and I knew I couldn't abandon them.

Despite these feelings of resignation, I gathered my courage and decided to seek help from foreign universities directly, hoping to find a way out of my situation.

To begin with, I sent letters to the National University of the Philippines and the University of Giessen in Germany. In these letters, I explained my background and the economic challenges that I faced, while expressing my strong desire to study abroad at their esteemed institutions.

My decision to choose the University of the Philippines was partly influenced by my fondness for the Philippines, having been impressed by my Filipino friends who had come to Korea. Additionally, during the 1980s, the economic situation in the Philippines was not as dire as in Korea. Moreover, I had heard that competition in dental schools in the Philippines was less intense than in Korea, and I envisioned returning to Korea as a qualified dentist after graduating from a Filipino dental school.

Despite initial skepticism about whether these universities would take notice of my letter, I received responses from both institutions. The National University of the Philippines commended me for my hard work but suggested that studying in Korea might be a better option for me, while wishing me the best of luck in my future endeavors.

I also received a response from the President of the University of Giessen in Germany. In his letter, written in English, he offered me conditional admission as a fully-funded scholarship student at the University of Giessen. The university also pledged to fully support my living expenses.   However, the only condition was that I pass the German language proficiency test prior to arriving in Germany.

At the time, I was studying French Language and Literature at the Korea National Open University and had confidence in my language skills after winning first place in the French language contest for new students in my first semester.   Therefore, I replied that I would study German and go to the University of Giessen. However, studying German on my own proved to be a challenge, especially while simultaneously studying French literature and working as a police officer. Moreover, finding a German tutor in Busan was difficult, as none of the foreigners around me spoke German - they all spoke English.

Despite my efforts to study German, I eventually concluded that it would be better to prepare for the TOEFL exam and study in an English-speaking country instead of pursuing my dream of studying at the University of Giessen. It was disappointing, but I ultimately discontinued my studies at the Korea National Open University during the second semester of my first year to prepare for studying abroad at an English-speaking university. However, when I investigated the eligibility requirements for studying abroad, I discovered that the minimum academic requirement was completion of at least one year of university education. As I was one semester short, I enrolled in any university to make up for the missing semester before I could start studying abroad at a foreign university the following year.

As a result, I found Busan Theological Seminary(BTS) as an option for enrolling in the second semester. With completion of one semester at the Korea National Open University, I was able to transfer to BTS for the second semester. Although the theology students with whom I studied were all individuals with a strong religious faith aspiring to become pastors, I enrolled in theology out of mere curiosity as I needed to complete only one semester in order to qualify for studying abroad.

I had only casual interactions with my fellow students, mostly during occasional meals together. However, their behavior was somewhat questionable. In particular, I found philosophy lectures interesting, but they showed little interest in them due to the fact that they were not religious in nature. They even criticized the philosophy professor for not having a strong religious faith.

Moreover, during final exams, some students did not study hard but instead went to a mountain oratory to pray for success in their exams. In any case, having successfully completed my final exams, I decided to take the TOEFL test as I deemed myself eligible for studying abroad. I received admission offers from several universities in the UK, the US, and Australia after submitting my applications, and I chose Australia purely for the sake of its legal status.

During that time, international students were not permitted to work legally in the United States and the United Kingdom, but this was not the case in Australia. As a former police officer with a strong sense of compliance, being caught working illegally overseas would have been a serious breach of my personal values. Therefore, I accepted an offer of admission from the University of Curtin in Western Australia.

In addition to this, I had to successfully complete the first-ever Self-Funded Overseas Study Qualifying Examination (SOSQE) to obtain my passport. However, this examination was later discontinued after the liberalization of overseas travel. Pursuing my studies abroad was a rigorous process, as I had to fulfill multiple requirements, such as completing one year of university, taking the TOEFL exam, passing the SOSQE, and completing the Overseas Traveler Education Course.

Despite these challenges, I successfully completed all the necessary requirements. Subsequently, there were rumors that the first SOSQE was created as a temporary measure by former President Chun Doo-hwan to legally send his son overseas, but this remains an unverified hypothesis.

Corruption at the Australian Embassy

In 1987, at the time of President Roh Tae-woo's June 29th Declaration[34], I was preparing to study in Australia. My wife and I were preparing together for our study abroad, and we received our passports together. However, when we applied for visas at the Australian Embassy, the visa officer informed us that only my visa had been granted, and my wife would have to apply for her visa next time. I was not aware of the convention of making a request by discreetly handing over a bribery envelope to the visa officer, and I naively believed the visa officer's explanation. Therefore, after discussing with my wife, we decided that I would go to Australia first, and we would apply for her visa through the university later.

My decision to study in Perth, Australia was driven solely by the desire to immerse myself in academia without encountering other Koreans. However, upon arrival, I discovered the presence of a Korean church and dozens of Korean residents in Perth. Promptly after my enrollment at Curtin University, I discussed the visa refusal of my wife with the school officials, who were taken aback by the discrepancy in visa issuance between spouses. Consequently, they promptly contacted the Australian embassy in Korea to request a reconsideration of my wife's visa application.

However, in response to the inquiry, the embassy stated in their

---

[34] On June 29, 1987, Roh Tae-woo, a prominent figure of the Democratic Justice Party and a presidential candidate, responded to the popular demand for democratization and constitutional amendment through direct elections by making a special declaration aimed at stabilizing the situation.

facsimile to the university that my wife's visa had been declined at her request, leading to the cancellation of her visa. Subsequently, I was informed later that night by my wife that her visa had been approved and she was required to collect her visa from the embassy. Despite the positive outcome of my wife's visa being eventually granted, I couldn't help feeling somewhat discomfited at having been deemed an atypical student, as the university official placed greater credence in the embassy's communication than my own account.

Subsequently, I became aware of a visa scandal at the Australian Embassy in Korea, leading to the removal of all implicated personnel. As a legal practitioner in Australia specializing in immigration law, I am highly cognizant of the imperative for transparency in the visa application handling procedures at the Australian Department of Home Affairs. However, I have observed some Korean clients being swindled by certain immigration agencies that purport to have links with the Department. This underscores the continued impact of the "backdoor" or "connection" culture, which had previously been prevalent in Korea, in perpetuating fraudulent activities.

Most Expensive Banana

Upon informing numerous deacons who regularly attend my father's church that I would be pursuing my studies overseas, they expressed their deep disappointment and sadness. Even my parents expressed regret, given that their son and daughter-in-law are both police officers who could lead comfortable lives in Korea. In a similar vein, my wife's parents also shared their apprehension, saying, "We heard that going abroad is challenging. . ."

In hindsight, my decision to pursue my studies overseas appeared like a risky and daring challenge. Deciding to leave our stable government jobs as a couple to pursue expensive overseas education was not a simple choice. Moreover, even upon returning to Korea, there was no guarantee of securing a job, and we would most likely have exhausted our savings by then.   To be frank, stating that we were completely devoid of any sense of unease would be a disingenuous portrayal of our emotions.

Back in 1987, the idea of traveling abroad was a daunting prospect for most people, especially given the limited options available for obtaining visas and the high costs associated with international travel. Nowadays, the availability of working holiday visas makes it much easier to live and work abroad before making a long-term commitment.

After submitting a resignation letter stating that I would resign to pursue overseas studies, I received a call from the HR department instructing me to revise the content. They advised me to simply state that I was resigning for "personal reasons."   In the past, I might have caused a fuss over this, but since I'm resigning anyway, it doesn't really matter what they say or do.   I submitted my resignation letter with the revised content of "resignation due to personal reasons" as the personnel at the HR department requested.

After a combined seven years of service in the combat police, the severance pay I received amounted to a mere 2.5 million won, equivalent to AUD $3,000. Although I felt a twinge of regret knowing that I could have received a superannuation had I worked for 13 more years, I was able to overcome this lingering feeling with a strong conviction to break free from the constraints of my environment.

In addition, I also had a thought of

'Now that we are married, we should ensure that our future children will grow up in a good environment...'

Although our couple applied for a visa together, my visa was issued first, so I planned to travel alone to Hong Kong on 9 August 1987 via Korean Air, and then enter Perth, Australia via Qantas Airways. On the evening of 8 August 1987, I took a night train from Busan and arrived in Seoul, where I had to go to Gimpo Airport in time for the morning flight. Before taking the night train from Busan, my wife's aunt came to see me and gave me a bunch of bananas, which were considered very expensive at the time. She gave them to me to eat on the way to Australia, and I really filled my stomach with bananas for the first time in my life.

I arrived at Hong Kong at approximately 10:00 am via Korean Air. Given that the connecting flight to Perth on Qantas Airways was scheduled for 10:00 PM, a waiting period of nearly 10 hours ensued. Prior to departing Korea, I had consulted with frequent travelers to gain insight on how to occupy my time in Hong Kong, thereby enabling me to head directly to the Kowloon city center upon disembarking the Hong Kong airport. Rather than being burdened by the compulsion to converse exclusively in English, I found it intriguing and amusing to immerse myself in an English-only environment.

While strolling through the streets, a fruit vendor caught my attention by offering ripe and succulent bananas. Although I had received a generous gift of costly bananas from my wife's aunt in Korea, I did not procure these bananas with the intent of consuming them, but rather to acquaint myself with the local pricing of bananas. It is noteworthy that a single row of bananas was priced below 1,000 Korean won, equivalent to AUD $1.2 at the time. This revelation took me by surprise, given that bananas were regarded as a commodity of considerable value in Korea, with individual bananas being priced at approximately 5,000 won, equivalent to AUD $6. Later, I learned that the Korean government had implemented a prohibition on the importation of bananas in order to safeguard domestic growers located in Jeju Island, consequently rendering bananas in Korea prohibitively expensive.. .

First Impression of Australia

When deciding where to study, I chose Perth, Western Australia with a focus on my academic success. Despite not being as well-known as cities like Sydney or Melbourne, Perth's quieter environment offered fewer distractions and a better chance to concentrate on my studies.

Perth View Drawn by Artificial Intelligence

Another consideration was the large Korean community in those cities, which could potentially distract me from my studies. Therefore, I believed that choosing a lesser-known destination like Perth would

allow me to stay focused on my academic priorities.

While making my decision, I was also influenced by the popular Australian movie, Crocodile Dundee. The film's depiction of Western Australia as a wild and rugged place with crocodiles and vast deserts caught my attention. I was convinced that studying in such an unusual environment would provide a unique life experience while also being conducive to academic success.

Shocking First News in Australia

On 10 August 1987, at 5 AM, Qantas Airways announced the arrival at Perth Airport, Western Australia.   As I looked out the window, I couldn't help but imagine the desolate, rugged scene depicted in Crocodile Dundee. However, to my surprise, the view was quite different from what I expected. The city was well-lit and bustling, just like any other urban city. Though it didn't meet my expectations, I found the urban atmosphere appealing and silently congratulated Perth on its development.

The first place I stayed when I arrived was a small motel next to Gloucester Park, behind the current Royal Perth Hospital. It was reserved for me by the university officials and, although it no longer exists, it was a reasonably clean and decent place at the time.

As I arrived in the early morning and had some time before the university officials came to pick me up, I went outside to explore Perth. The first thing that caught my eye was a store selling newspapers and basic food items. Since there was no internet at the time, newspapers were the only source of information available. I think the price was around 20 cents, but the thickness of the newspaper was no joke, and it felt like I got a big item for free as if I had just taken advantage of a big bargain sale.

The article that appeared on the front page at the time was "Rambo Style massacre." This was a shooting incident that occurred on Sunday evening, 9 August 1987, in Hoddle Street, Clifton Hill, a suburb of Melbourne, Victoria, Australia. Seven people were killed and 19 others were injured in the shooting incident, and after a police chase lasting over 30 minutes, Julian Knight, a 19-year-old former Australian Army officer cadet, was arrested in nearby Fitzroy North on charges of shooting.

Upon reading this newspaper article, I felt that Australia was not a safe place like the United States and immediately went back to the accommodation to wait for the university representative to arrive.

Later, when I told the university staff about the newspaper article, they reassured me that Australia was generally safe as long as I didn't go to strange places at night. This put me at ease. Anyway, I needed a place to live with my soon-to-arrive wife, so with the help of the university, we paid $20 per week to live in a room on the first floor of an Australian man's house in a neighborhood called Applecross in Perth, and shared the kitchen with him.

My Wife's First Impression of Australia

Unlike me, my wife had her visa issued a month later due to manipulation by the consulate staff, and she had a different first impression of Australia. When she heard that consumer goods were expensive in Australia, she brought a box of notebooks and stationery, and even brought a package of kimchi because there were no Korean markets. At the airport, when she tried to check in her luggage, it was overweight, and she had to pay tens of thousands of won in excess baggage fees to bring the heavy luggage for me.

She said everything looked beautiful because she was excited to meet her husband, and she even thought the view of Perth from the sky before landing was incredibly clean and beautiful.

Prior to my wife's arrival, I resided with an Australian landlord who was a retired engineer, with whom I shared dinner every night while learning both the English language and Australian culture. The experience was both enjoyable and educational. However, after my wife's arrival, we faced several challenges. As most Korean students resided in or around Wembley, our choice to reside in Applecross made it difficult to socialize with them. I persuaded my wife that residing further away from other Korean students would enhance our focus on our studies, especially considering that we were paying a modest $20 per week for our accommodations, compared to the $70 per week rent for apartments in Wembley. Thus, it was prudent to save expenses and continue residing in our current abode.

Aussie Landlord

Despite my persuasive efforts, my wife soon came up with an additional reason to move. Sharing the kitchen with the Australian landlord posed a challenge when it came to cooking Korean food such as soybean paste stew or kimchi stew, which was a beloved dish of hers. Our living space, while distinct from the kitchen situated on the first floor, was not conducive to cooking due to the kitchen sharing arrangements.

One evening, I proposed to the Australian landlord the idea of trying Korean cuisine, which he readily accepted. I decided to make a traditional Korean dish, soybean paste stew, to challenge the preconceived notions that my wife had about the smell and taste of Korean food. I believed that it was

With Aussie Landlord Neil

important to demonstrate that it was possible to cook and consume Korean food while living with an Australian without any discomfort.

After preparing a delicious meal of soybean paste stew, rice, and kimchi, we sat down with the Australian landlord to enjoy the traditional Korean dish. To our delight, he complimented the dish and finished it all.   I therefore believed that this experience would have given my wife the confidence to continue cooking Korean cuisine in our shared living space and as a result, we would no longer have any reservations about living in close proximity to an Australian and our decision to stay in Applecross would be reaffirmed.

Despite the successful dinner with the Australian landlord, my wife's discomfort with the living situation persisted. She brought up her concerns again, citing the inconvenience of having to use the bathroom on the ground floor when the landlord was on the upstairs. While I understood her point, we were unable to move immediately due to financial constraints. We agreed to start looking for a new apartment in the Wembley area to address her concerns and provide a more comfortable living situation.

In due course, a dispute arose between the Australian landlord and ourselves. Although I cannot recollect the specific grounds of the disagreement, it might have been due to our excessive water consumption or a failure to adhere to his instructions. Admittedly, the issue of our water usage is reasonable, considering Australia's scarcity of water and exorbitant water rates.

However, it was perplexing that the landlord accused us of not listening to him. It is possible that his directives were culturally different or unclear, leading to a misunderstanding. Regrettably, our rapport with the Australian landlord, who lacked cultural sensitivity, came to an abrupt end.

Memories of the Korean Uniting Church

When I visited Curtin University's campus, I encountered a fellow Korean overseas student named Yoon Bu-kyung, who coincidentally shared the same surname as mine. He had come to Australia not to study, but to seek an opportunity for a better life after working as a journalist in Korea. Consequently, he had little interest in academics and instead focused on socializing with female students on campus. Despite his poor command of English, he often relied on me for assistance, and one day he introduced me to a Japanese overseas student who also struggled with the language. I was curious as to how they were able to communicate with each other effectively.

At one point, they even found themselves waiting for each other in different places, and I had to relay their respective locations. I am unaware of what became of this journalist-turned-student after our time at Curtin. If this book could help us reconnect, it would be a pleasant opportunity to reminisce about our shared memories.

The most memorable experience during my study in Australia was at the Korean Uniting Church. At the time, there were only about 10 or so Korean families living in Perth, and on Sundays, they would all come together to socialize at the church. As the restrictions on overseas travel were gradually lifted, more and more international students began to come to Perth, which revitalized the church.

My wife and I attended the church every week, teaching Sunday school and participating in the choir, activities that we had never done before at my father's church in Korea. At the time, we believed that it was God's will for us to be there. Although the Korean Uniting Church later split into 4-5 separate churches, the relationships between the international students and Korean residents were still strong and genuine.

The minister who led the Korean Uniting Church at the time was Elder Ji, who was studying theology to become the pastor of the church in the future. He had worked at the YMCA in Korea before coming to Australia and was a very sociable person. I felt that he would have been successful in any business venture, not just ministry.

This individual, out of concern for newly arrived international students, strongly advised them against visiting the casinos in Perth and spending their tuition money on gambling. However, many international students who were unaware of this warning ended up being led to the casinos by hearsay about their existence, rather than being guided towards the church. Despite this, the weekly influx of international students brought a new energy to the church, and we had the opportunity to exchange information and interact with them.

International Student Pastor J

In 1987, while studying in Australia, I had a close relationship with a fellow Korean student, Reverend J, who was my age. While I was living with my wife, Reverend J was living alone as his wife had not yet arrived in Australia. To accommodate him, I would invite him to my home almost every mealtime so we could share meals together, which brought us even closer as friends.

Reverend J and I became fast friends once we discovered that both our fathers were pastors and that I too had studied theology in Korea before coming to Australia. He was popular among people of all ages as he held the title of pastor at a young age.

The residence of Pastor J was situated in close proximity to our own abode, and given his lack of personal transportation, I extended the gracious gesture of utilizing my own vehicle to ferry him to and from various destinations. Additionally, on a weekly basis, I would offer to retrieve him from his domicile and provide a ride to the Korean church, where we would participate in communal religious observances together.

Nonetheless, it was noteworthy that despite accompanying each other to church, Pastor J would always request that I precede him during the return journey, citing an invitation to dine at another congregant's residence. While the limited size of our church community meant that the host was someone familiar to us, and the pastor's social affability made him a highly sought-after guest, it was nonetheless disconcerting to observe that Pastor J was being singled out for special treatment. As human beings, it is not uncommon to experience feelings of disquiet in situations like this, despite understanding the reasons behind it.

Upon further reflection, I came to realize the profound significance of

Jesus' teachings, specifically His words regarding the treatment of the meek and lowly,

"Truly I tell you, whatever you did for one of the least of these brothers and sisters of mine, you did for me."

However, the church, unfortunately, did not provide an inclusive and welcoming environment for those who were modest and unpretentious.

In hindsight, it is evident that Pastor J possessed a remarkable shrewdness. As the offspring of a prestigious senior pastor of a large church in Korea, he undoubtedly enjoyed a degree of wealth that surpassed my own. Yet, he did not allow his status to dictate his lifestyle, as evidenced by his reluctance to purchase a car. Unaware of his background, I presumed him to be a young and destitute pastor, and thus endeavored to assist him in every way possible, including accompanying him on job-hunting endeavors, demonstrating the use of cleaning equipment, and imparting interview skills to boost his chances of landing a job.

One fateful day, I received a frantic phone call from Pastor J, who had been involved in a car accident while returning home from his part-time cleaning job. To complicate matters further, he had falsely identified himself as myself and provided my name and address to the police. Consequently, he implored me to accept responsibility for the accident on his behalf. It transpired that Pastor J had acquired a used vehicle solely to facilitate his cleaning job, but he had not yet obtained a driver's license. Had he revealed the truth to the police, he would have jeopardized his academic prospects and potentially faced deportation to Korea.

I once made a selfless sacrifice for Officer Choi by taking the blame for a bribe he had received during my tenure in the police force. In light of this past act, it seemed only natural to extend my help to Pastor J when he implored me for assistance. Though, in hindsight, my decision was unwise and hasty from a legal perspective, I believed it to be God's will, and thus, considered it a noble deed to sacrifice myself out of love for my neighbor.

During my involvement in the case related to Pastor J's car accident, I made the decision to acquire a different vehicle. Given the intense heat in Perth, I desired a vehicle that offered air conditioning. Fortunately, another international student, who generated supplementary income by repairing cars, proposed a deal to swap his own car, equipped with air conditioning, for my car, which lacked this feature. As part of this agreement, I agreed to provide an additional $1,000 in compensation. Following the transaction, I completed the transfer of ownership for the new vehicle on my part.

A car with air conditioning

However, the mechanic failed to complete the registration process on his part for the transfer of ownership of the car received from me, and attempted to sell it to a third party. Later on, the mechanic lent the same car to a fellow international student, who caused a major accident and fled to Korea, abandoning the vehicle.

As a result, officially I was involved in two car accidents. I was able to navigate these situations effectively with my training and expertise acquired during my time as a police officer in Korea. I understand that without my professional experience, handling such incidents could have been much more difficult.

Pastor J's wife arrived in Perth and briefly stayed in Perth. They moved to Sydney after she returned a collection book of pop songs that she had previously borrowed from us. Unfortunately, the collection book was damaged and torn.   Although she was not aware of the car accident I had experienced, she expressed remorse for the condition of the collection book and offered to replace it. While I declined her offer, I appreciated her concern and gesture of kindness.

After he left Perth, I have unfortunately experienced a break in my relationship with Pastor J.   Despite sending several letters of regards to him, I have not received a reply and remain unsure of the reason for our falling out.

A few years later while I was studying theology in Australia, Pastor J held a key position in the Uniting Church and even visited the Korean Uniting Church in Perth without contacting me.   I believe that a person's true character is revealed through their actions, particularly when there is an opportunity to extend kindness and generosity to others. I believe that voluntarily bearing a loss for the sake of one's neighbor is a noble and compassionate act.

Drawing upon the film "Secret Sunshine[35]," it is possible that Pastor J has already sought repentance and received forgiveness from his God.   The loss of my relationship with Pastor J has been a source of sadness in my life, and I deeply regret any misunderstandings or conflicts that may have contributed to this situation.

---

[35] A Korean film about a poignant example of forgiveness where a mother who lost her son to a kidnapper believed in the power of her faith and visited the perpetrator in prison to extend her forgiveness. However, it was discovered that the kidnapper had already been absolved by her God prior to her attempt to forgive him.

Car Accident and Dream

As I continued my service within the church during my time studying in Australia, I found that the demands on my time and energy continued to grow. While serving in the choir, an international student was identified as a valuable asset by the pastor and many church members. As he was entrusted with more volunteer work, he ultimately chose to return to Korea without completing his academic studies.

This individual had the financial resources to be able to make such a decision and was praised by the church for his contributions. However, as an international student with a specific period of time in which to complete my studies due to the limited financial resources, I found it challenging to balance the demands of church service with my academic obligations.

I had hoped that the church would take into consideration the unique challenges faced by international students such as myself, but unfortunately this did not happen. The difficulties I encountered during this time were beyond what I had initially anticipated.

During that period, I spent all the funds of our severance payment and savings brought from Korea in order to pay for one year of tuition. The following year, I would have been required to return to Korea if I did not earn enough money. As a result, my spouse worked full-time at a tent-making plant during the week while I worked full-time at a now-defunct company named Microforms in East Perth.

Since my schedule allowed for all lectures to be attended at nighttime, I had the flexibility to work full-time during the day and study full-time at night. Thus, it was imprudent for me to spend the entirety of Sunday at church. Additionally, I was required to prepare for Sunday School on Saturdays or even during the week, in order to fulfill my obligations as a Sunday School teacher.

Therefore, when I proposed to my wife saying,

"We prioritize our academic studies and discontinue our church responsibilities."

my wife, who initially converted to Christianity through my influence, expressed discontent with my passive approach. Her commitment to church service was akin to that of a newly skilled thief, unsure of when dawn would break. She maintained that if I had to forgo church service due to academic pursuits, she would attend and serve the church alone. As a result, frequent disagreements arose between us.

In the meantime, my wife became pregnant with our first child. As the delivery date approached, the Korean Uniting Church had planned a three-day, two-night group church camp in Busselton WA. I made the decision not to attend the camp in order to support my wife during this important time, but my wife expressed disappointment with my decision. Coincidentally, a kind-hearted friend named Kim, who my spouse and I were close with, also opted out of the church event and suggested that we take a two-night, three-day trip to catch abalone. Unlike me, Kim had permanent residency and a stable income, and his car was reliable enough for long-distance travel.

The three of us opted out of attending the church camp due to personal reasons and instead decided to travel on our own to a lodging that was distant from the church camp area. During our two-night and three-day trip, we had a fruitful time catching and consuming an abundance of abalone, and were able to rest well before returning to Perth.

My pregnant wife occupied the back seat of the vehicle while Kim drove, and I sat beside him. After driving for 1-2 hours, I offered to take over driving when I noticed Kim struggling.

"Would you like me to take over driving if you feel tired?"

Assured by my offer, I took the wheel and reassured him that he could rest. As everyone slept, I silently drove down the dimly lit street, evoking the ambiance of late-night countryside roads. Suddenly, a thunderous blast shook the surroundings, and our car began to veer uncontrollably, eventually turning around several times. I cried out instinctively, causing my wife to awaken from the commotion.

At that moment when the car was rolling, I was consumed with a sense of dread, fearing the worst for my wife who was seated in the back. I thought, in the aftermath of the accident, my in-laws would accuse me of being responsible for their daughter's death, citing her decision to follow me to Australia as the reason for her untimely demise. The thought of my poor parents, particularly my mother, grieving over the tragic loss filled me with deep sadness. Despite holding police positions, my wife and I had left our jobs to pursue studies in Australia and had been struggling to make ends meet through self-education. As the reality of the situation sunk in, I couldn't help but think that perhaps our decision to skip the church camp and embark on the trip on our own had somehow angered God, leading to this unfortunate event. In a moment of desperation, I called out to God for help, making a vow to dedicate the rest of my life to serving Him if I survived. Looking back, it's amazing how many thoughts could occur in that brief moment of the accident.

Fortunately, our car did not cross the center line and stopped turning at the side of the road in the direction of travel. My immediate concern was for the safety of my wife, who was sitting in the back seat with a full-term body. Upon hearing my cries, she woke up and looked at me with a bewildered expression. Overwhelmed with relief, I attempted to express my gratitude by kissing her cheek, but she recoiled and turned away. Meanwhile, the occupants of the vehicle that struck ours from behind quickly emerged and approached our car to ensure our safety.

"Are you guys alright?"

"Yeh, we are alright but my wife is pregnant!"

"Shit! He said she is pregnant!"

In due course, the commotion subsided and shortly thereafter, a police vehicle, an ambulance, and a few tow trucks arrived on the scene, transforming the area into a bustling thoroughfare. Our vehicle was then towed away and we managed to arrive safely home via taxi.

I found out that the driver of the vehicle trailing ours inadvertently collided with the rear of our car while experiencing drowsiness. The impact resulted in the complete destruction of the rear portion, causing my wife, who was seated in the back, to narrowly avoid injury. However, both my wife and our first child emerged unscathed from the incident.

Later on, I experienced discomfort in my neck during sleep, which persisted for several weeks. At the time, I was unaware that it was a repercussion of the car accident and attributed it to poor sleeping posture.

At daybreak, reports of yet another automobile collision surfaced. Specifically, news emerged regarding a mishap in which a deacon's vehicle overturned while returning from the church camp in the company of her two daughters. Regrettably, a deaconess succumbed to the injuries sustained at the scene, leading to the tragic loss of a considerate deaconess who had been very instrumental in caring for us as international students. The incident was undoubtedly an unfortunate turn of events.

An incident of greater magnitude overshadowed our own misfortune, rendering it inconsequential. Nonetheless, during a private encounter with an elder couple whom I hold in high regard, I shared details of our ordeal, stating that we too had been involved in a significant accident on the same day. It was at this point that the elder's wife recounted a dream she had had about the late deaconess.

During a church function, while sitting in front of the church congregation, a member of the crowd hurled a stone in our direction. Fortunately, the projectile missed its intended target and struck someone else. In response, the individual hit by the accidental throw became enraged and attempted to retrieve the stone to target our couple deliberately. However, the elder's wife intervened and dissuaded him from doing so by pointing out that Mr Yoon had not thrown the stone, thereby making it unwarranted to target our couple.

Upon hearing the account, I experienced an inexplicable sensation of shivers. The elder and his spouse are individuals whom I deeply appreciate for the support they provided to our children during my attendance at an Australian Baptist church and theological pursuits. Despite their immense kindness, I have not been able to reciprocate their graciousness.

Baby Delivery in Australia and Korea

My first child was born whilst my studying in Australia and subsequently, while staying in Korea for a period after completing my studies in Australia, my second child was born. Having undergone childbirth in both Australia and Korea, I am well positioned to provide an informed comparison of the obstetric environments in both countries.

In Australia, there is no medical charge for childbirth as all associated expenses are covered under the Medicare program. Unlike in Korea, individuals are not required to bear any personal financial burden. Historically, a lump sum payment of approximately 5,000 USD (equivalent to 4.4 million KRW) was provided for each child. However, as of March 2023, a fortnightly payment of $1,785.42 (equivalent to KRW 520,000) is disbursed for the first child for a period of 13 weeks, and $596.05 (equivalent to KRW 520,000) is

After the birth of the first child

provided for each subsequent child over a similar period.

The majority of Korean nationals residing in Australia prefer to give birth within the Australian healthcare system, given its robust obstetrics and gynecology framework. The general practitioner, referred to as the home doctor, who initially evaluates the pregnancy, subsequently refers the expectant mother to a larger hospital equipped with delivery facilities. In Australia, unless the situation constitutes an emergency, it is necessary to obtain a recommendation from the home doctor before directly accessing a specialized hospital. Once admitted to a large hospital, pregnant women are required to undergo monthly check-ups until the time of childbirth, and participate in various programs related to childbirth and infant care.

On 1 February 1990, my wife reported experiencing discomfort, and I promptly took her to the hospital. Since it was a facility where she had previously undergone regular check-ups, her personal information and medical history were meticulously recorded. Consequently, my wife was able to complete the admission process with minimal explanation at the entrance. Following a brief wait, a nurse approached us with a cheerful smile and offered a wheelchair to my wife. However, she declined, citing her condition as only a mild stomachache that didn't warrant a wheelchair. Nonetheless, the nurse insisted that my wife comply with the hospital's regulations, which prohibit patients from walking within the premises.

The nurse escorted my wife in a wheelchair to the examination room, and I followed behind enviously looking at my wife sitting in the wheelchair. From the sidelines, I observed how she meticulously assessed the position and condition of the baby. The nurse was thorough in her explanations to me, providing detailed reasons for each step of the process. Additionally, a trainee nurse who had recently graduated introduced herself and requested permission to practice on my wife. Her compassionate care for my wife left a positive impression on me, and despite my initial reluctance, I acquiesced to her request.

The nurse informed us that the child was in a normal position, and advised us to wait until the pain persisted. We were directed to a private room, where we waited, passing time by watching television and reading newspapers while eagerly anticipating the arrival of our newborn. The room was stocked with complimentary biscuits and coffee, providing us with ample refreshment. At thirty-minute intervals, nurses and doctors attended to my wife's condition, and took the opportunity to explain various aspects of childbirth to me, as her spouse.

Finally, when my wife's pain intensified, she was escorted to the delivery room, which was spacious and equipped with a large bed in the center and a breathing apparatus on the right side. There, my wife was half-lying there like a queen being served by maids she was surrounded by a team of medical professionals including two obstetricians and gynecologists, two surgeons, two nurses, and two trainees, all dedicated to ensuring her safe delivery.

Despite my wife's prolonged discomfort, the fetus remained unyielding, prompting the medical staff to monitor the fetal movements at ten-minute intervals by assessing the wife's pulse. During this time, the attentive nurses offered me refreshments, while the physicians provided detailed explanations of my wife's condition and the childbirth process. Such compassionate care and informative guidance were so thorough that I felt as though I could deliver my second child myself in the future.

The memory of the birth of my first child in this manner remains deeply ingrained in my mind, and I hold profound gratitude towards the Australian medical staff who were involved in the childbirth process at the time.

In contrast to my experience in Australia, the birth of my second child in Korea was vastly different. The obstetrics and gynecology facilities in Korea felt impersonal, almost akin to a veterinary hospital. However, I have heard that in recent times, some hospitals in Korea have started providing comfortable delivery facilities similar to those in Australia, and have also become more considerate of mothers and their families. Nevertheless, it was disappointing to note that in Korea at that time, the hospital prohibited husbands and family members from entering the ward right from the entrance.

When my wife was admitted to the delivery room, I recalled my experience with obstetrics in Australia and attempted to follow her in, but the nurse reprimanded me saying

"Husbands should not come in!".

Feeling tired from waiting outside, I grew increasingly restless and my four-year-old child expressed his impatience by squirming around. I approached the nurse to inquire about the waiting time for the delivery,

"My child wants to fall asleep here, but is there no place for the patient's family to wait comfortably?"

"If you are waiting at home, we will contact you right before giving birth"

"Ok, thank you my home phone is 678-1234"

After being reassured by the nurse, I left the hospital with my first child. It was already late, and we were both exhausted, quickly falling asleep upon arrival at home. I was unsure of how much time had passed when my wife called me early the next morning to inform me that she had given birth to our daughter and asked me to come to the hospital as soon as possible. Despite the nurse's promise to call before the delivery, I did not receive any notification from her. While it is possible that I missed the call due to falling asleep, I am confident that the nurse never contacted me, given my tendency to wake up easily. My wife expressed disappointment in me, claiming that I was the only father who was not present for the birth of their child, and that my actions were irresponsible.

When I first laid eyes on my second child, born under these circumstances, I didn't feel any instant attachment or affection. Instead of being able to hold my child, the nurse led me to a viewing area where babies were kept in small beds. After sifting through the various infants, the nurse pointed out which one was ours through a window. It was a vastly different experience from the emotional and physical connection I felt with my first child. I couldn't help but worry about the possibility of infants being mixed up in the sea of baskets, and I was left with the unsettling thought that perhaps the nurse had not confirmed if the child shown to us was truly ours. With the first child, it felt like we were both giving birth together, but with the second child, it felt like we were adopting. I couldn't shake off the anxiety that our daughter might be mistaken for another child.

My Thoughts On Children

During the time leading up to the birth of my first child, I had a delightful dream. In the dream, I was fishing in the sea, catching a massive fish and reeling it in with my fishing rod. The water in the ocean was crystal-clear and the fish swimming beneath the surface were visible in their entirety. Nevertheless, the size of the fish was not to be underestimated, as it was so colossal that it could have covered the entire sea with its girth.

Afterwards, I briefly pondered over the issue of naming the child. I considered asking my parents to come up with a name, but I felt that since they had already named their own children, including myself, it would be more meaningful for me to choose a name for my own child.

Although I secretly hoped for a daughter to be born, a baby boy was delivered instead . Since I wanted him to be treated well and not be intimidated by other children throughout his life, at one point, I thought about naming him "Hyungnim," which means "big brother" in Korean. I thought it would be nice for his friends to naturally call him that, but later I realized the situations that we as the parents would also have to call our child "Hyungnim", which made me think that this name wouldn't work.

And another name that came to mind was "Hotan[36]," as he was to be born in Australia, but my wife opposed it as it sounded too humorous. Admitting my lack of naming skills, I purchased a book on naming for my wife to study and choose a name herself. She eventually decided on the Chinese character "炫(현)," which means bright and

---

[36] "Hotan" is a combination of "ho" meaning Australia and "tan" meaning "birth"

shining.

When we had our second child, my wife chose the name "Sohyeon" for her. In Korean, it means "small hyeon," while in Chinese characters, it's made up of the characters for "white and gentle" - combining white "소(素)" and virtuous "현(賢)." This beautiful combination symbolizes a white, pure, and kind-hearted individual, which perfectly describes our little one. The name was lovingly chosen by my wife.

Interestingly, my wife and I had actually discussed not having children before we got married, as we were aware of the many orphans in the world who struggle without parents and knew that many of them would benefit from having a family.

In addition to these reasons, there was a deeper personal conviction that drove me. It stemmed from my religious faith at the time, as I had observed that many people were more concerned with avoiding hell than striving for heaven when taught about the concepts of both in church. Believing in the dreadful hypothesis of eternal punishment for fleeting actions in this world, I couldn't help but feel that having children was akin to throwing them into the crossroads of heaven and hell. When I confided these thoughts to someone, they saw me as an oddball because they viewed children as "a gift from God." Consequently, I refrained from sharing these sentiments with anyone else.

However, upon deeper reflection, having children is undoubtedly a gift from an ancient and anthropological perspective. Even in agricultural societies where labor was scarce, having more children would have been essential, and in today's world, it is a fact that those with children are more likely to succeed in running their own businesses, as evidenced by observing self-employed individuals.

Current policies that increase benefits for families with multiple children are also based on viewing children as "assets" for the future, but fail to consider the perspective of the child who is yet to be born.

My point is not to advocate intentionally avoiding childbirth. Indeed, natural childbirth should be celebrated and embraced as a joyous event. However, I cannot understand why many infertile couples persist in trying to have their own biological child, often wasting significant time and resources on infertility treatments. If there is a genuine desire to have a child, I believe that adopting an orphan in need of parents would be a more selfless and morally upright option.

Insisting on one's own bloodline is, in fact, a selfish act.

Chapter 5 The Trials of My Life

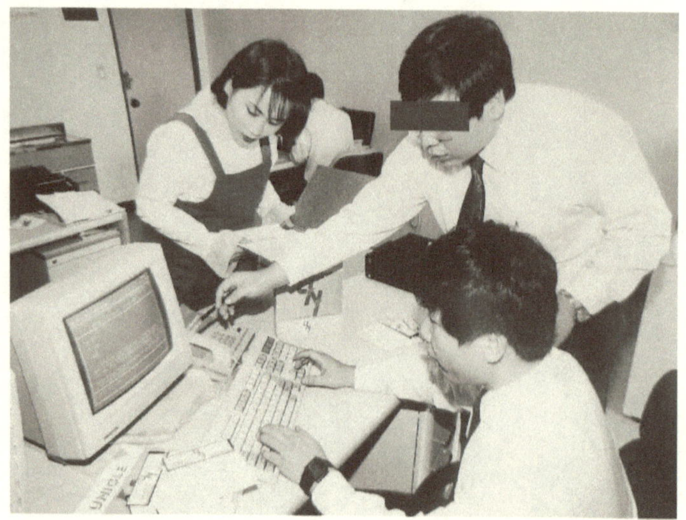

Working in the office with the partner L

Violation of the Reserve Forces Act

After completing my studies at an Australian university in January 1991, I was residing in Korea when the police arrived with an arrest warrant for violating the Reserve Forces Act. Specifically, I was accused of failing to undergo reserve forces training[37] while studying in Australia. This was a clear administrative error on the part of the village office, as I had fulfilled my obligation to report for overseas travel prior to leaving for my studies in 1987. At the time, it was mandatory to obtain written permission from either the Military Manpower Administration or the village office before traveling abroad.

Following my studies in Australia, I was arrested under the Reserve Forces Act. I explained the situation to a detective at the police station which both my wife and I had once belonged to, and I was overcome with anger and embarrassment upon seeing my former colleague detectives. Fortunately, the case was ultimately dismissed upon providing evidence of my immigration record. Despite this outcome, I couldn't help but feel disheartened by the experience.

Following my return to Korea, a gas explosion caused a devastating fire at my residence. Moreover, I endured human rights abuses at the hands of a prosecutor, in relation to copyright law issues. Despite my deep ties to Korea, the absence of power and resources left me feeling compelled to seek a better life in Australia. Hence, I applied for immigration through the Australian Embassy, with the hope of securing a more humane and fulfilling future.

---

[37] Prior to 2016, all individuals discharged from compulsory military service had to undergo reserve forces training for four hours a year.

During my immigration application process, I received a family relationship certificate, which included a resident registration record. Upon reviewing the document, I discovered a criminal record attributed to me for violating the Reserve Forces Act. However, this was an administrative error, as I had previously been acquitted of the charge. It was disheartening to see that the mistake had been included in my certified copy, and I felt a sense of injustice and frustration. My concern was that the Australian Immigration Case Officer, who may not have been aware of this mistake, could have misconstrued me as a convicted offender based solely on the documents, potentially resulting in my application being rejected.

In Korean society, regardless of the nature of one's affairs, a copy of resident registration is typically required. Upon realizing that this record could potentially tarnish my reputation, I promptly visited the village office and requested a meeting with the manager. During the meeting, I explained the situation and urged the manager to remove the erroneous record, warning that I would not hesitate to pursue legal action if necessary. While the manager apologized for the error, they explained that administrative records could not be deleted at their discretion. When I inquired whether the matter could be resolved through administrative litigation, the manager earnestly implored me, suggeting

"Are there any other options available to address this matter without resorting to administrative litigation?"

After expressing my concerns to the manager, I felt reassured by their professional and courteous demeanor. Encouraged by this positive interaction, I inquired whether it was possible to include the phrase "administrative mistake" alongside the record of my violation of the Reserve Forces Act. To my relief, the manager indicated that they had the authority to make such a modification at their discretion. As a result, my Resident Registration Certificate included a notation that read "Administrative Mistake in Violation of the Veterans Affairs Act." While the revised civil law precludes the issuance of such a certification, the negative impact of the earlier error on my life remains significant and not to be dismissed lightly.

100 million won in Compensation

After completing my studies at an Australian university in early 1991, I returned to Korea with a sense of ambition. Despite my family's financial struggles, I had a strong desire to make a meaningful impact in Korea. Having spent four years in Australia, I developed a deep appreciation for anything related to Korean culture and felt a sense of familiarity upon returning.

A grandchild was also born in Australia, and our parents were very happy to see the face of their grandson who was less than a year old. In anticipation of the grandchild's stay with them, they opted to replace their outdated boiler with a new one.

During the night that the gas boiler was being replaced, I experienced a particularly distressing dream. In the dream, a monstrous creature with a dark blue face, human body, and snake-like head attacked me by flicking its tongue. In response, I wielded a long sword and successfully severed its head. Despite waking up immediately after the nightmare, it was still the middle of the night, so I decided to share the dream with my wife in the morning.

As a person of Christian faith, I had always been skeptical of dreams. However, a childhood experience had left a deep impression on me. I dreamt that I had lost my younger brother, and the next day, the exact same situation played out in real life. Fortunately, because of my dream, I was able to take action and prevent a tragic outcome.

On the following morning, amid the hustle and bustle of a typical Korean morning, I left for work, completely disregarding the dream I had the previous night. However, I received an urgent phone call from my younger brother during work hours. It prompted me to recall the dream, and I immediately asked him what was happening.

"Older brother! It was a big deal."

"What's the matter, tell me quickly."

"Our house caught fire and burned down."

After receiving an urgent phone call from my younger brother, I hung up the phone without saying a word, thinking to myself, 'It must have been a dream from last night' and ran home, as I didn't want to hear any more bad news just in case. I refrained from asking any further questions, such as "Is your sister-in-law all right?" or "What about Hyun?", out of fear. While on my way home, a plethora of thoughts plagued my mind, including 'were my son and wife at home safe?', 'If everyone was burned to death, how should I live from now on?', 'How much did they suffer the moment they were burned to death?', 'What should I tell my in-laws?' and so on, relentlessly troubling me.

As I approached my home, I noticed the roads in the vicinity were damp and disheveled, while the windows of our apartment building appeared burnt from a distance. It was apparent that multiple fire trucks had been deployed, and the neighborhood was bustling with activity.

Upon my arrival, I immediately searched for my loved ones - my son Hyun and my wife. Fortunately, my brother was able to direct me towards their location. The relief I felt was immense. Our family had a close call with a traffic accident in Australia, and yet here we are in Korea, alive and unscathed. In that moment, I silently expressed my gratitude and appreciation to the divine power in my heart.

Upon learning what had happened, I was informed by my wife that she had taken our son to the public bath to comfort him when he woke up crying. After that, they went to the conventional market, where our son insisted on riding the merry-go-round. Unfortunately, the water that the firefighters were using to extinguish the fire in our home ended up soaking my wife's shoes, causing her to grumble to herself,

"Who is pouring water like this?"

The fact that our child woke up before the explosion and that my wife decided to take him to the market was a stroke of luck. Had it happened in a different order, the outcome could have been much worse. It made me realize how truly blessed my family is.

Upon arriving at the scene, we observed the firefighters putting the finishing touches on the house while plain-clothed individuals, who appeared to be police officers, instructed us to visit the police station once we regained our composure. The apartment's residents, meanwhile, gathered donations and offered them to us, with the district office also providing a blanket featuring the Korean Red Cross logo, sweatpants, and a small amount of condolence money. I couldn't help but wonder if this was the first time I received welfare benefits in Korea, albeit not from the government but from the Red Cross, a charitable organization funded by people's donations.

Meanwhile, the police investigation proceeded in a rather erratic manner. It appears that the investigation was focused on determining any potential negligence on our part, such as whether the fire was caused by someone in the house or whether the house was covered by fire insurance, and whether it was a crime committed for the purpose of obtaining insurance money. I found this approach offensive. Additionally, their statement that

"You should be grateful that you are not being punished for a crime of fire caused by negligence when a fire occurs"

made me question the impartiality of the investigation.

The fire was caused by an explosion in the boiler tank, which had been replaced the day before by an unlicensed installer. However, the attitude of the police, who shifted the focus of the investigation towards our side, was excessively biased. I was deeply concerned about this situation and wanted to bring it to the attention of the media. I first reached out to a producer at a certain broadcasting station to express my grievances but was met with resistance due to concerns over accusing government agencies. Undeterred, I then sought assistance from a well-known newspaper, but encountered arrogance and indifference to my plea.

I had no choice but to seek assistance from my acquaintances and contacted a newspaper reporter from Busan. During the interaction, the young reporter demonstrated a commendable sense of justice by meticulously noting down my complaints and ensuring that the article would be published extensively. However, he candidly informed me that his power was limited, and there was nothing he could do if the editor-in-chief of the newspaper decided not to publish the article due to a cordial relationship with the relevant organizations.

Remarkably, the next day, an article about the police's biased investigation appeared in the social section of the newspaper, which was unexpected. Following this, the police station contacted us immediately, and their demeanor was entirely different from their previous demeanor. They treated us politely and courteously, but unfortunately, the nature of the investigation remained the same.

During the course of investigating the cause of the fire at the scene, a professor at a university in Busan alluded to us indirectly, saying,

"To ensure that this case is handled properly, you need the power of a government agency higher than that of the police. Unfortunately, there is nothing we can do about it."

I naively believed that a new fair system had been implemented in Korea as it was a civilian government, which played a vital role in reforming Korea to be a livable society. However, the investigation conducted by the police gave the impression that there was no discernible difference from when I and his wife were serving as police officers in the past.   Since the university professor investigating the cause of the fire expressed concern about reporting the cause of the fire conscientiously, my family and I realized that we could not sit back and let the situation be.

To ensure an accurate cause of the fire, my family mobilized all our connections and sought the help of a competent person from the

National Security Agency. With the objective of rectifying the partiality of the police investigation, we sought the support of the National Security Agency's personnel. As a result, we were informed that the police had promised the competent person from the National Security Agency to do their best to obtain an accurate cause of the fire.

Following the incident, the police's attitude towards us became more polite, and they conducted three to four additional investigations to eliminate any doubts regarding our involvement. It was confirmed that there was no short circuit or negligence on our part, and the focus shifted to proving the unlicensed gas boiler installer's negligence.

Now, the police must prove the fault of the unlicensed gas boiler installer. However, the police maintain a biased stance by stating,

"Although the Gas Safety Corporation is required to pay 100 million won in compensation for gas-related fire accidents, not a single person in South Korea has received this compensation."

They advise us to give up on receiving compensation from the outset.

The reality of the situation was difficult to accept, and I struggled to come to terms with it. Instead of receiving compensation for the damages or rebuilding the interior of our house, which was now reduced to ashes, I was left feeling a deep sense of sadness when I confronted the realities of living in Korea.

In an effort to seek justice, my father sought legal advice from multiple lawyers. Eventually, we were advised to file for damages from the gas installer through a separate civil lawsuit.   Upon hearing this, my father paid the lawsuit fee of 2.8 million won, which was the sum of condolences we had received from various sources at the time.

However, at that time, the lawyer received the sum of 2.8 million won from us delayed commencing the civil lawsuit advising that because the criminal case was still pending, we needed to wait until the verdict was delivered in the criminal case. He said if the gas installer was found to be at fault in the criminal case, it would be much more advantageous to file the civil lawsuit.

As the lawyer had advised us that in order to seek damages, it was necessary for the gas installer to be found negligent in the criminal trial, the entire family attended the criminal trial with the hope of a favorable outcome. Unfortunately, the verdict was ironic - the unlicensed gas supplier was acquitted. The judge's rationale was that if the gas boiler had been installed improperly, it would have leaked and exploded immediately. Despite clear evidence that the gas boiler installer was unlicensed and a university professor's testimony stating that the fire was caused by gas, the judge still acquitted the accused.

In contrast to Australia, Korean judges have the authority to conduct a fact-finding investigation ex officio to uncover the substantial truth of the matter. However, to our surprise, the judges in this case sided with the unlicensed gas supplier, using a perplexing logic that was difficult to comprehend.

The words of the police officers left a deep impression on me,

"No one in Korea has ever received 100 million won in compensation insurance for a gas accident."

It was clear that holding the gas company criminally liable for negligence could have resulted in adequate compensation from either the Gas Safety Corporation or the installer. However, if the installer was acquitted, the government agency responsible for gas safety would be absolved of any liability.

This case went to the High Court of Korea as the prosecutor appealed due to our opposition, but even the High Court ruled not guilty due to the uncertain cause of the fire. It was an incomprehensible event that the unlicensed installer who installed the gas boiler, which exploded, was acquitted. The whole process was misguided from the beginning by the police, who investigated in the wrong direction, and past events passed by like a fleeting memory, including the painful confession of the university professor in charge of the fire investigation. There is still a suspicion that there may be some reason that cannot be overcome by individual efforts. Moreover, in the midst of such difficulties, there are still memories of bad lawyers who took advantage of the plaintiff without any action, sucking the blood of the poor person who paid the litigation costs of 2.8 million won.

Neighborhood in the Apartment

When the fire broke out in our apartment, fortunately only our unit was destroyed, and all the other units in the apartment building were unharmed. However, in order to put out the fire in our unit, the water sprayed by the firefighters seeped down the walls and flowed into the apartment unit directly below ours, where an elementary school teacher lived.

One day, she kindly asked us to come to her apartment. We thought that she was inviting us to comfort us as we were suffering from the fire, or to offer us a warm cup of tea. With gratitude, we visited her apartment.

As soon as we entered the apartment, we could see that it was a complete mess, and the living room with the door wide open was also left in a state of disarray. We had a gut feeling that the teacher did not invite us over to treat us kindly.

The elementary school teacher said,

"I understand that you are going through a difficult time due to the fire, but we also need to survive, so I'm swallowing my pride and asking for this favor. As you can see, the walls in our apartment have been stained and ruined. We can't just leave it like this and need to redo the wallpaper. So I was wondering if you could cover the cost of the wallpaper."

I was truly dumbfounded. While it was true that the water sprayed by the firefighters had soaked the wallpaper in the house and left stains, upon seeing the walls covered in children's scribbles and tears, it was obvious that her unit needed to be repapered anyway.

And yet, the elementary school teacher had the audacity to suggest that we take responsibility for the free papering of her unit in exchange for the cost of the repapering. It was astounding to see a person with such a conscience. Witnessing this person's sense of ethics, I was even afraid to send my children to school.

"Excuse me, from what I heard, you are a schoolteacher, and you know that we are currently suffering from the fire in our unit, having lost all our household contents and not having any money for repairs. And yet you as our neighbor. . ."

"What does being a teacher have to do with this? If you don't want to help, you should just say so. How can you say so from the pastor's house?"

At the time, my   father was a pastor serving at a small church, so the local residents called my home the "pastor's house".

"No, just because some water got on the already damaged wallpaper, do we have to fully compensate for the cost of new wallpaper since we are from in the pastor's house? How can a schoolteacher have such a conscience?"

"What did you say? Looks like a young person who is not that old..."

The schoolteacher's conduct was brazen and audacious. Despite my reluctance, my wife compelled me to leave her abode. Subsequently, this individual met with my parents and denigrated my character, accusing me of callousness and self-interest, exploiting my parents' sense of morality to coerce them into agreeing to finance a new wallpaper installation for her dwelling, thus effectively concluding the matter.

In due course, my parents completed the wallpaper installation on her entire unit without my knowledge. To this day, I remain perplexed as to whether I was leading an overly stringent existence.

Tragedy of Partnership

There is a painful memory that I cannot forget in my life. It is a representative example of how powerless people like myself can easily become victims of the abuse of power, demonstrating how high the power of the Korean prosecution was at one time, to the extent of being called the "Prosecution Republic."

During a difficult time when a fire had broken out in my apartment, causing me great distress, my direct supervisor at work, Mr L, suggested that we start a business together to make big money in the midst of our troubles. We decided to rent an officetel[38] in Busan and begin our business venture according to Mr L's proposal. I had no money, but I had the ability to develop software and provide system consulting. As Mr L was well aware of the software I had developed and deemed it to have sufficient marketability, he proposed that we start the business with a 50-50 equity split, with him providing the funds and me handling the technical side.

However, I thought that dividing the equity 50-50 when he was providing the capital wouldn't be fair, so instead, as the investor, he would own 90% and I would own 10%. However, since I was currently experiencing financial difficulties due to the fire at my home, we agreed that I would take a certain amount of living expenses from the capital, even if there were no immediate profits.

---

[38] An officetel is designed to be a partially self-contained building, such that its occupants can live and work in the same building, minimizing commute time.

Seed of Unhappiness

We decided to name the software, which I developed in Australia, "Unicle" and wanted to register the software copyright.

"Unicle" is a combination of "You and I," which means us, and "Miracle," which means a miracle, creating the meaning of "our miracle."

At that time, Mr L asked me to register his name as a joint author when registering the copyright for Unicle. Since we planned to work together in the future and sail on the same boat, it was not difficult for me to include his name as a joint author in the registration of the software. I later faced significant difficulties by including Mr L as a joint author in the software registration.

Despite the joint registration, Mr L broke the promise to invest a certain amount of capital, and as a result, I was unable to receive my living expenses on time and found myself in a difficult situation. It turned out that L was actually a person without any money, and his apologetic face as he hung his head low made me feel rather sympathetic.

Given the irreparable circumstances, the only course of action was to maximize business operations and generate profit. At the time, the software developed by I was a Computer-Aided Software

Engineering (CASE) tool [39], which allowed programming to be automatically performed by the computer with minimal instructions. This revolutionary product was recognized as highly valuable, and upon its market release, a company immediately appeared offering to become the Seoul distributor, paying a deposit of 100 million won without delay.

However, L took all the profits home under the pretext of managing the funds, and when I later inquired about the whereabouts of the funds, it was revealed that he had used them all to pay off his personal

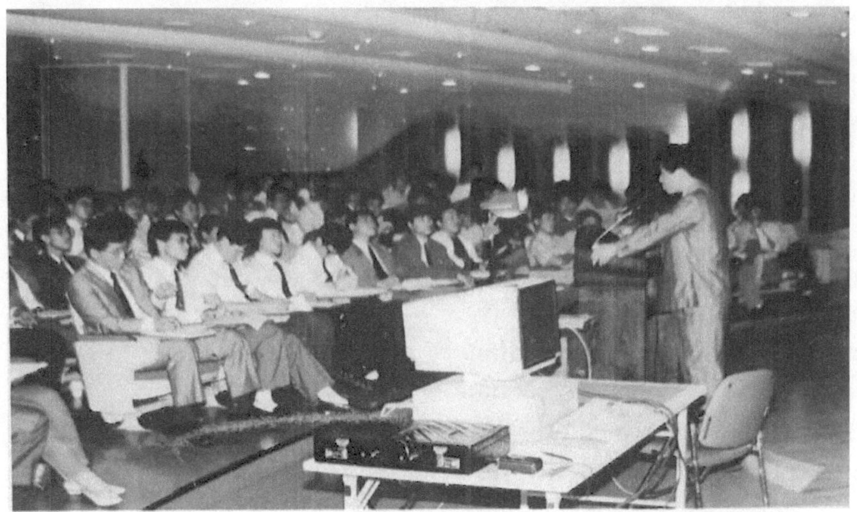

Education Seminar for Forner at Daewoo Group

debts. Such irresponsible and inadequate management made it impossible for me to continue working with him as a business partner. After only a few months of partnership, I declared a separation from him and became independent.

---

[39] A computer-aided software engineering (CASE) tool is a software package that provides support for the design and implementation of information systems

My Own Business

During a three-month preparation period, I developed software that was much more powerful than "Unicle," which I had sold while working with L. To differentiate it from "Unicle," I registered the software copyright under the name "Forner," combining the Korean word "너" (meaning "you") with the English word "For" to create a word meaning "for you." I chose a different name for the software because I had parted ways with L, and I didn't want to cause confusion among consumers if L were to sell "Unicle," for which he was a joint copyright holder.

Initially, I secured a capital of 2 million won by borrowing from my younger sibling and procured an office on a monthly rental basis. By minimizing costs, I embarked on establishing my own enterprise. Subsequently, I proceeded to hire freelancers aspiring to venture into the software development business using my proprietary software. The recruited personnel were mandated to acquire the software and acquaint themselves with its usage. The venture witnessed a prosperous start with a net profit of 1.5 million won within the first month. Furthermore, we were able to obtain software development contracts and simultaneously expand the market reach by enlisting regional distributors. As a result, the market recognition of Forner observed an organic increase.

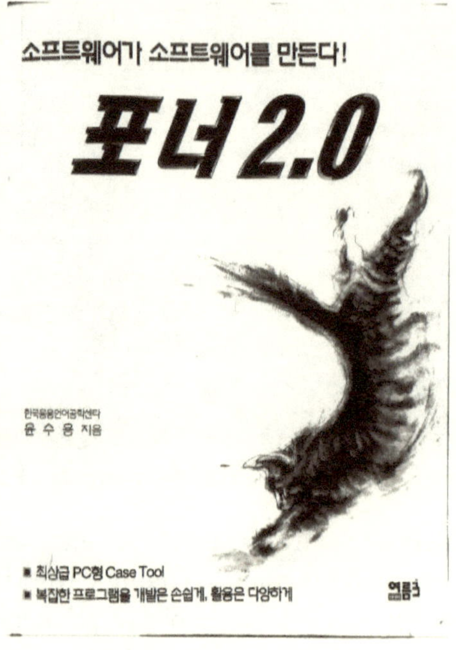

Forner 2.0 with a CD

Nonetheless, I received a concerning report about a product closely resembling my software being sold at bookstores. Hence, I visited a nearby bookstore and uncovered that my software and accompanying literature were published and marketed under the name of an unfamiliar individual. Upon seeking clarification from the publisher, it was disclosed that the author in question was the former colleague, Mr L's spouse.

Book in question – Unicle

After receiving a report of my software and accompanying literature being sold under the name of an unknown person, I immediately reached out to Mr L to ascertain the circumstances. He disclosed that he had instructed his spouse to aid in the publication of my manuscript, but a mistake by the publisher resulted in her being credited as the author. Although I forgave the error with regard to the already-published work, I made it clear to him that there could be no further publishing of my work under any unauthorized names.

To prevent any future incidents, I drafted a written document containing the pertinent details and obtained his signature, which I had officially notarized.

It was later revealed that Mr L had unlawfully accessed my computer and copied the source code of the program I had developed during our collaboration. When registering the copyright of the program, he requested to be added as a joint author for life, and in retrospect, it all felt like part of Mr L's calculated scheme.

I firmly declared in front of Mr L, "Let's make sure we never meet again," and we parted ways on cold terms. About a month later, when my program was gaining recognition and establishing a foothold in the market, I received a summons from the Dongnae Police Station in Busan. Upon

On a business trip with Mr L

investigating the matter, I learned that Mr L had filed a criminal complaint, claiming that my program, which I had previously registered him as a joint copyright holder, was in violation of his copyright and was being sold illegally.

He was truly an unscrupulous and incomprehensible person. My name was also included as a joint copyright owner... And he was just listed as a collaborator, not an actual developer. Moreover, didn't he apologize to me with his head bowed and even create a memorandum of understanding based on that certificate and have it notarized? It's unbelievable how someone who confessed to their wrongdoing could suddenly turn around and file a lawsuit with a hostile attitude like this...

During the police investigation, I presented the notarized document

Author introduced in The Segye Times in 1994

that L had written for me, explaining in detail that the original creator was me and that the one who violated the copyright law was actually L. I also provided additional explanation about his lack of ethics that I had experienced during our collaboration. After learning all the facts, the investigating police officer told me that L was truly a bad person and advised me to go home and rest.

Copyright Litigation 1

After about a month, the result of the case was released from the Eastern Branch of Busan District Prosecutor's Office. The result of the investigation was "no suspicion." In fact, I found the expression "no suspicion" itself very unpleasant. When a complaint is filed, it is customary to investigate and prosecute if there is suspicion, or dismiss the case if there is no suspicion. However, I disliked the expression because it gave the impression that the innocent person had previously been suspected, and I greatly disliked L, who made me accept such an expression unilaterally. However, since the incident has already ended with this, I have made a promise to put the past behind me and focus only on business, and have been trying to forget about the unpleasant relationship with L.

Re-investigation

However, about a month later, I received a summons from Prosecutor L in Busan Eastern District Prosecutor's Office. When I looked into the matter, it turned out that L's wife had sued me for violating the program copyright law. I couldn't understand it at all. If it was a violation of the program copyright law, then L's wife was the perpetrator and I was the victim. Moreover, wasn't this case already settled as a past incident? Also, it was highly unusual for the same prosecutor's office to conduct a reinvestigation on a case that had already been cleared of suspicion, unless there was a special lead for investigation.

The prosecutor in charge of the reinvestigation had the same surname as L, and the prosecutor watched with interest every situation where the investigator questioned me.

"Mr Soo Yong Yoon"

"Yes"

"You know Mr Y, right?"

"I don't know."

". . ."

The investigator looked puzzled and glanced at the prosecutor as if to report, "He doesn't seem to know?" The prosecutor then stepped forward and spoke up.

"Ah, don't you know Mr L?"

"Yes, I know Mr L."

"Ms. Y is Mr L's wife."

"On what legal basis did Ms. Y sue me?"

"You don't need to say that, and we will investigate whether Ms Y has the authority or not."

As I explained that this case had already been resolved and showed the notification of the processing result that I received from the same prosecutor's office previously, I said that this was a closed case. In response, the prosecutor appeared surprised and asked me to wait outside while he called Ms Y to find out more about the situation. After a while, he called me back in and said,

"Although the case has already been concluded, Ms Y is feeling very unfairly treated and wants us to conduct another investigation. Could you please cooperate with us? If you are innocent, there's nothing to worry about and you can go through the investigation with dignity, right?"

They told me to go back home for the time being. From that point on,

I experienced firsthand the biased investigation by the prosecution in South Korea and was able to understand the true meaning of the word "unfairness."

Commencement of the Ordeal

When I was summoned for the second time, L's wife, Y, was present. Her face was unpleasant to look at, but she chatted amiably with the prosecutor and investigator. The investigator and prosecutor made me sit in the middle in front of Y, and treated me as if I were a criminal who had committed a murder. They loudly complained about my sitting posture being incorrect and nitpicked at every small detail. Even worse, they created extreme anxiety for me by saying all kinds of unbearable abusive words. It seemed as if they were trying to appease Y by belittling me in front of her. The investigator and prosecutor took turns soothing and calming me for a while, but eventually revealed their true colors.

"Mr Yoon, don't tire yourself out like this. Why don't you just hand over the program you're working on to Y? You're smart enough to develop it again if needed, right? If not, this case will become a headache for all of us and we want to resolve it quickly."

"How can you make me so unjust and make such a demand? I cannot make any concessions to the person sitting here, even if I can to anyone else."

I spoke firmly. Then the lead prosecutor and investigator's attitude changed again.

"Well, there's nothing else we can do. Let's investigate once again."

They showed no interest in uncovering the truth, such as who was being unfairly treated and what the real nature of the case was, and seemed to conduct the investigation solely as a way to vent their frustration over not being able to hand over the program to Y. From then on, the prosecutor had nothing to do but keep me waiting at the prosecutor's office for 4-5 hours at a time, and even when I went home, I was warned to always be on standby for a 24-hour call from the prosecutor's office and not to go to another province.

One day, the prosecutor called me and asked if there was an institution that could compare the source codes of the two programs I developed and confirm whether they were the same program or not in order to resolve this case as early as possible. When I suggested the Copyright Association in Seoul, the prosecutor told me to go there with Y the next day to obtain a verification certificate. The prosecutor insisted that I and Y must go together to prevent the possibility of my manipulating the presented documents if alone. They informed me that they would ask Y to meet me at the entrance of the Copyright Association at 3 PM the next day.

Setting aside all personal matters, the next day I hurriedly went to Seoul and had no choice but to wait for Y at 3 p.m. on the first floor of the Copyright Association. However, even after 5 o'clock, Y did not show up. The next day, when I complained to the prosecutor in charge,

"Why didn't you send Y and make me go all the way to Seoul for nothing?"

the prosecutor and investigator scolded me instead. The reason was that I should have persuaded and taken Y with me to meet at the Seoul Copyright Association, but I went there alone irresponsibly. Afterward, this prosecutor had harassed me in such an unreasonable way that I wanted to jump out of the prosecutor's office window and die in front of him.

I have seen many people who committed suicide during the investigation by the prosecution such as Chairman Chung Mong-hun of Hyundai Group during the investigation by the prosecution into the North Korean money transfer case and former President Roh Moo-hyun during the investigation of the Park Yeon-cha gate. Even though

I am not a celebrity of that level, I could understand their minds well enough.

Extreme Abuse of Power

One day, the investigator and the prosecutor had a big argument in front of me regarding my case, and it was quite a spectacle to see them shouting and bickering at each other.

The investigator, despite being a subordinate of the prosecutor in terms of job position, appeared to be over ten years older than the prosecutor at first glance. For some reason, if I as a suspect had behaved like that towards the prosecutor, the prosecutor could have detained me on the spot for an offense of obstruction of official duties.

Nevertheless, the investigator, who acted like a senior, was arguing with the prosecutor, using informal language with each other, even in front of me who was their suspect. At the time, I was also uneasy about watching them fight like that because they might be directing their anger towards me, the innocent. As if that wasn't enough, the investigator shouted at me and told me to leave the office and wait in the hallway immediately. And then, I waited in the hallway until the end of working hours, trembling with anxiety, and only then did the investigator tell me to go home.

When I was exhausted from extreme fatigue due to being summoned almost every day without any reason at the Prosecutor's Office, L and Y, a couple, applied for an injunction to ban the sale of "Forner" my program and filed a civil lawsuit for 1 billion won in damages for copyright infringement at the Eastern Branch of the Busan District Court. The judge in charge of the case found the content of the *ex-parte* application for an injunction to ban the sale of the program suspicious and immediately summoned me as the defendant. I stayed up all night to prepare a response letter and submitted it to the court.

I returned to my home country of Korea from Australia to start a new life, but the experience was tainted by my perception of the Korean prosecution office as a group of ruthless demons. At the time, I didn't understand the intricacies of the legal system, but I knew enough about the logic of law to feel that something was deeply wrong. From that point on, I gave up my business pursuits and began to study criminal procedure, criminal law, copyright law, and other legal subjects with the fervor of a law school applicant. My sense of injustice was so strong that I studied as if I were preparing for the bar exam.

However, my conviction that the truth will always prevail was crumbling as I was summoned back and forth to the courts and prosecution office, and I came to the conclusion that I couldn't trust the purity of the courts or the prosecution, seeking external help in every possible way. One law school student advised me that the best defense is a good offense, and even though I had a good understanding of the law, they suggested that engaging a lawyer is desirable in legal battles.

My Counterattack

As such, I lodged a formal complaint with the Busan District Prosecutor's Office, citing L's infringement of copyright law and charges of theft and fraud. I also accused L and Y of making false allegations against me. My intention was to demonstrate a strong stance, hoping that the authorities would investigate the case centered on me. However, to my surprise, the prosecutor assigned to my case was hostile and unhelpful. As a naive person at the time, I didn't realize that prosecutors could collaborate with each other.

"A person who worked together in the past is making such a messy complaint like this, so can't you come to an agreement? Oh, this is messy!"

He treated me in such a way that he was annoyed by adding even trivial things like my complaint when he already had a lot of other work. The unfairness of the situation was so overwhelming that it drove me to the brink of insanity.

"They were the first to sue me, but why are you blaming only me?"

I spoke cautiously, choosing my words carefully, as though I were a child complaining. This was because I had heard that the prosecutor's authority is extremely powerful in Korea, and I couldn't risk them finding any fault with me. As the Korean prosecutor's office has exclusive rights to prosecute, .

David, My Australian Friend

During a period when I was facing considerable hardship from the prosecutor in Korea, David, an Australian friend, and his family made a visit to the country. Presently, David is retired and touring all across Australia with his wife in a caravan, relishing the leisurely life of a retiree. However, during my   days as a student in Perth, David served as a pastor at an Australian Baptist church and had adopted and nurtured two Korean children.

With a desire to continue passing on Korean culture to their children, David's wife, Debbie, took it upon herself to study the Korean alphabet and seek out interactions with Korean international students. In the course of these endeavors, she visited the Korean Uniting Church where I was in attendance, and thus, the two became acquainted.

With David at Busan Tower

David hospitably treated us to a lavish meal while entertaining us in his home, with the intention of acquainting us with the Australian household culture.   As we engaged in conversation, I was struck by David's exceptional nature. He possessed a keen intellect and extensive knowledge about computers, having spent much of his time programming and studying independently. As a result, I, who was also studying computer programming at the time, found it effortless to associate with David.

On the day I left Australia after completing my studies in Australia, I made a promise to David that I would take care of everything if he visited while I was in Korea. For David, visiting Korea with his wife and two young children held great significance beyond just meeting my family, and this prompted him to make the trip to Korea.

At the time, I was going through a difficult period. My apartment had caught fire, resulting in the loss of all my possessions, and I had also recently parted ways with my business partner to start my own

With David's Family in Jeju Island

venture. Additionally, I was struggling with a corrupted prosecutor and this took a toll on me emotionally. Despite this, I welcomed David without showing any signs of my personal turmoil. In particular, I felt a strong sense of responsibility towards his two adopted children and resolved to take care of them better than their biological parents would have when they came to Korea.

Upon the arrival of David's family in Seoul, I borrowed a van from a distributor in Seoul to transport them to Busan. I then had them stay at a motel in Busan that was close to my home. I had notified to the prosecutor in advance that I would not be able to receive an investigation during their stay.

During the time that David's family stayed in Busan, we also traveled to Jeju Island together. I generously spent the 5 million won (equivalent to $6,000AUD) for David's family that I received from the Seoul branch as my software royalty. David recorded videos during our trip, and showed them to his adopted children as they grew so that they would never forget their memories of Korea.

At the time, my apartment caught fire, and we had to temporarily reside in a small studio unit. However, the humble living quarters made it difficult for me to extend an invitation to David's family while they stayed in Busan. This decision was made because David wished to show his two adopted Korean children only the positive aspects of Korean culture.

Thanks to this relationship, David had always invited me to his home in Melbourne several times, but for one reason or another, I never found the time to visit him to date. I had hoped to retire someday and have the time to visit his home, but David retired before I did

Nonetheless, every time David visits Perth, he never forgets to call me and continue our friendship, for which I am grateful. In fact, I have had many white friends before, but most of them were not comfortable enough to the point where I could feel the cultural differences. However, David seemed to understand the Eastern culture well, having adopted and raised two Korean children.

David's flawless logic and expertise in various aspects are giving me a lot of lessons.

Copyright Litigation 2

It appears that the prosecutors of the Republic of Korea have held the belief that they possess the authority to manipulate the fate of individuals at their whim. Some argue that this approach is necessary when dealing with criminals. However, it begs the question whether this treatment would extend to parliamentarians or individuals with social affiliations. Furthermore, the fundamental principle of criminal law, which upholds the presumption of innocence until proven guilty, must be considered.

As the plaintiff, I question whether it is appropriate to treat plaintiffs with the same level of scrutiny and suspicion as criminals. When Park Cheol-eon [40] underwent investigation by the prosecution, I scrutinized a newspaper article that presented a detailed account of the investigative process. However, it did not seem that he was being subjected to the harsh treatment afforded to suspected criminals; instead, it appeared that the prosecution was extending the utmost courtesy to him.

---

[40] A former prosecutor, he was called the Crown Prince of the 6th Republic as a cousin of former President Roh Tae-woo's wife, Kim Ok-sook. After Kim Young-sam came to power in 1990, he was arrested for a slot machine case and then released.

The prosecution of the Republic of Korea's unfair behavior appears to be never-ending. During the impeachment investigation of Park Geun-hye in the past, the media widely reported on the scene of Woo Byung-woo, chief of civil affairs, being treated like an emperor, and this fact is well-known throughout the entire nation.

Upon my experience in Korea, I've come to realize that my previous belief in the universal equality of all individuals before the law may have been overly idealistic and not fully reflective of the reality in the country.

Failure of Counterattack

Anyway, when I expressed my frustration about their unfair treatment, the prosecutor instructed the assigned investigator to investigate and

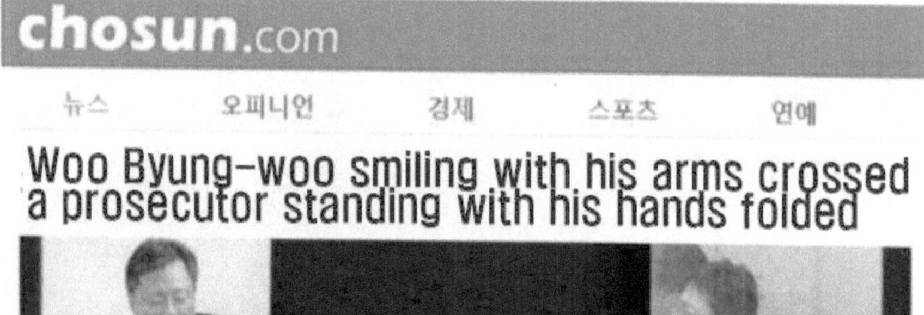

Woo Byung-woo (Left) treated like an emperor by prosecutors (Right)

handle the case in accordance with the law. Even during the investigation, the assigned investigator referred to me as a "dirty guy" who sued a colleague who had worked together and treated me in a disrespectful manner. After fully understanding all the facts, the prosecutor in charge called L and reprimanded him together with me.

"You will be subject to punishment if you do not reconcile with Mr Yoon Soo-yong. Since you used to work together, it would be better to resolve the issue amicably. Will you reconcile or not?"

"Yes, I will reconcile. We need to reconcile."

"After releasing your emotions and meeting as old friends, please have a drink together and reconcile. When you are done, go outside and write a reconciliation agreement and come back."

Feeling almost forced to reconcile, I was pushed out. L awkwardly smiled and said:

"Can we go over there and have a cup of tea?"

I followed him inside. He continued to mumble in a nonchalant manner.

"How did we end up in this situation..."

It made me angry because he said as if he knew nothing.

"Oh man! Didn't you, along with your wife, create this situation by filing complaints here and there, causing innocent person to be sued?"

As I raised my voice and expressed my anger, he lowered his head and apologized, admitting he was at fault.

"My wife is uncontrollable! Please understand and forgive her, thinking that it's something a naive woman would do."

He explained that his naive wife had submitted the complaint without his consent, hoping to gain some benefit. He asked me to understand and forgive her actions. In any case, he promised to take action to resolve all civil and criminal cases by the next day.

I reached an agreement with him to settle all civil and criminal cases between us, and I made sure he acknowledged that he had no rights to the copyrighted materials that we had jointly registered. I hoped this would bring an end to our disputes. We shared drinks and reminisced about old times, and I advised him to keep an eye on his wife. Together, we went to the prosecutor's office and declared that we had reconciled, submitting a withdrawal of the complaints I had filed. As a result, L was cleared of charges of copyright infringement, theft, and fraud. However, the charge of false accusation was still pending with the prosecutor in charge of L's case.

However, L did not honor our mutual agreement. When I informed the prosecutor in charge of L's case about the agreement we had reached, the prosecutor L stated that he could not acknowledge it because L's wife Y had not agreed to it yet in their own case.   As a result, L maintained his civil and criminal lawsuits against me through his wife, and thus did not uphold our previous agreement.

The prosecutor's office in charge of the case filed by L and his wife called me in for questioning almost daily and had me waiting around their office for hours on end, asking me the same questions over and over again. Unable to endure it any longer, I went to the prosecutor's office where I had previously filed a complaint and where I was forced to reconcile and withdraw my complaint, and informed them of the situation. When I requested that they handle the case I had filed in accordance with the law, they responded with the principle of *res judicata*[41], stating that a case that had already been processed could not be processed again.

When I told the prosecutor in charge of investigating my complaint

---

[41] a matter that has been adjudicated by a competent court and therefore may not be pursued further by the same parties

that the prosecutor L was harassing me by investigating a case that had already been concluded, they said they couldn't comment on another prosecutor's actions. The current prosecutor who was interrogating and harassing me was re-investigating a case that had already been concluded, but when I asked the prosecutor engaged for my complaint if they could do so, they responded with the arrogant statement that they cannot re-investigate, and that it is not their job to do the work of other prosecutors.

On the other hand, the civil lawsuit also harassed me constantly. Despite being a victim, I was in a hurry to defend myself as a suspect or defendant because they had filed the complaint first. I couldn't take it anymore, so I told my close friends about this unfair situation, and they introduced me to Lawyer K.

However, the lawyer they introduced to me was lazy and negligent, the same as the lawyer who had only taken the retainer fee from my father during our previous house fire case, and not actively defending me. In the reality where an individual's human rights are being destroyed by the tyranny of a single prosecutor, the lawyer K hesitated to intervene actively, maintaining a friendly relationship with the prosecutor.

His explanation was that if a lawyer who had to fight against the prosecutor created an unpleasant relationship with them, it would not help in handling other cases, which is absolutely wrong in Australia and the lawyer may be reprimanded if he or she explained as such.

Korean lawyers who fail to properly defend their clients in order to maintain a favorable relationship with prosecutors have been incomprehensible in the past and present, but given the historical corrupt practices of Korea's judiciary such as Privilege of Former

Post[42], it is easily understandable.

Last Defense

Ultimately, I found myself back where I started. I was left with no choice but to fight this battle alone, and I made a commitment to myself to seek justice for such unjust incidents in the future. I explored every possible avenue available to me, starting with sending letters of inquiry regarding the different provisions of the Copyright Law to entities such as the Legislation and Judiciary Committee of the National Assembly and the Supreme Court. After some time, I received relevant materials from them, which I presented as evidence of my compliance with the Copyright Law to the prosecutor's office investigating me. They were taken aback by the evidence and even inquired about its origin.

Their attitude towards me changed somewhat due to my proactive approach. Previously, they had unilaterally barked orders demanding that I reach an agreement by handing over the program. However, they now adopted a procedural and rational approach, attempting to persuade me in a more convincing manner. The prosecutor suggested to me:

"Mr Yoon, this is no more than wasting time. Let us instead determine the extent of the difference between your current program and the jointly copyrighted program, and make a decision based on that. If there is a substantial difference between the two, we will acknowledge them as separate programs and bring this case to a close. If we do not receive such a report, we will have no choice but to prosecute you for copyright infringement based on the assumption

---

[42] If a former judge or prosecutor works as a lawyer after retiring, the incumbent judge or prosecutor gives some kind of preferential treatment in the course of a trial or investigation.

that they are one and the same program."

"Are you suggesting that someone can compare the source code of such a vast program to make such a determination?"

"I will leave it to your discretion. Couldn't a university professor or another authoritative person compare the two programs and write a report?"

"Alright, then I will look into it and receive the report"

Despite both software programs being developed by me, I was surprised to learn that we needed a confirmation that they have different functions. Nevertheless, in order to bring this case to a close, I had no choice but to agree to it. If I didn't, I could have been presumed to have violated copyright law and faced prosecution.

I visited the head of the Computer Science Department at Busan University, despite having no prior acquaintance, and made a plea for help regarding the prosecutor's misconduct. The department head's sense of justice was stirred, and he resolved to assist me.

My strategy seemed to have paid off as the department head kindly agreed to write a report if I provide my source code to him and explained how much the two programs differed in terms of functionality.   At the time, software was still a valuable commodity, and my software was already somewhat known in the computer industry through newspapers and advertisement, so acquiring the source code for such software would be beneficial for the department head as well. Ultimately, the department head concluded that the two programs were functionally different after examining their source code.

The prosecutor L, who thought it was impossible to obtain such a report, was greatly surprised when he received the report from the head of the Computer Science Department at Busan University that I had submitted. After using all means and methods, but not coming up with any strong evidence, prosecutor L eventually gave up and found himself in a position where he had to punish the couple of L & Y for the offence of False Accusation[43] with his own hands, since he could no longer prosecute me for copyright infringement.

Unlawful Confinement

L's wife was inside the prosecutor's room, sobbing, and the prosecutor's comforting her was visible from outside. Although it had been suspected that the prosecutor's investigation was one-sided and biased towards me based on his previous actions, seeing their behavior confirmed that their relationship was indeed special. The investigator then told me to write a withdrawal statement for the offence of false accusation against L and his wife, in order to cleanly wrap up the case. I, who had suffered for over a year because of them, refused to do so, saying that I could not make a withdrawal statement.

The investigator and prosecutor proceeded to unlawfully confine me within the prosecutor's office by locking the door and coercively demanding the withdrawal of my complaint. Despite constituting the criminal offense of illegal confinement, such actions were unfortunately common within the South Korean prosecutor's office when dealing with individuals perceived as vulnerable. Moreover, they even threatened to investigate me on unrelated charges if I did not withdraw my complaint against L&Y. Ultimately, faced with such coercion, I had no choice but to acquiesce to their demands and sign and withdraw the complaint.

---

[43] *Article 156 (False Accusation) A person who reports false information to a public office or a public official for the purpose of having a criminal or disciplinary punishment imposed upon another, shall be punished by imprisonment with labor for not more than ten years, or a fine not exceeding 15 million won.*

And then, the prosecutor L and the investigator said together,

"Mr Yoon, we've actually grown fond of you through this case. If you need any help from us in the future, please don't hesitate to contact us. We'll be here to support you."

I was filled with frustration, injustice, and heartache to the point where I couldn't bear it.   I truly understood the meaning of the word 'unfair.'

That night, I went home and thought over the incident for hours on end. I felt upset about my helplessness in the face of the prosecutor's oppression, as well as the fact that I hadn't withdrawn the complaint in accordance with the Bible teaching – "Love one's enemies." I began to lose faith in the Korean government that governed this society. This was the society in which I was born, but it was not the society in which I could live without getting tangled up in money, power, and connections. As a result of this incident, I made up my mind to emigrate, and eventually, I moved to Australia.

Korea's First PC Cafe

The prosecutor's tyranny, which lasted for about a year, came to an end with my victory. However, the experience of being threatened by the prosecutor to the end and not punishing L remained my biggest trial in life, to the extent that I still remember the prosecutor's name to be "Lee 0". After becoming a lawyer in Australia, I tried to find the prosecutor's name on the list of Korean prosecutors but couldn't find it.   My intention in seeking the name of the prosecutor who had committed such egregious misconduct and yet continued to hold his position was to impress upon him the gravity of the harm caused by his actions. The prosecutor's name was also not found on the list of lawyers registered with the Korean Bar Association.

In any case, after sorting out my relationship with Mr L, I was finally able to focus on driving my software business forward. At that time, the software I had developed had received extensive promotion through newspapers.   Managing Director Lee ("Mr Lee"), of Korea Computerware Co., Ltd, who was a distributor in Seoul, offered to take charge as the national distributor so that I could focus solely on software development leaving business management to him.

In return, Mr Lee promised to pay me 5 million won per month, regardless of the software's income. At the time, this was a substantial sum of money, especially considering that the average monthly salary for a regular employee was less than 1 million won.

이달의 서적 & S/W BEST 10

'94년 4월

〈영풍 문고 제공〉			〈한국통신소프트웨어 프라자제공〉		
순위	도 서 명	출 판 사	순위	프 로 그 램 명	공 급 업 체
1	저는 컴퓨터를 하나도 모르겠어요.	키 출판사	1	아래아 한글 2.1 전문용	한글과 컴퓨터
2	HITEL길라잡이	한국 PC통신	2	FORNER (일반용)	코리아컴퓨터웨어
3	안녕하세요, 한글 2.1	정보문화사	3	FOXPRO25	트리움
4	메모리 관리	에스컴	4	이야기 6.0	온시스템
5	따라해보세요 한국 2.11 편집실무	한글과 컴퓨터	5	슈퍼토익 10 (고득점)	정보소프트
6	노턴유틸리티 7.0	에스컴	6	듀플래스 중학수학 영어	컴퓨터교재연구소
7	손노, 이현세 컴퓨터를 배우다.	동화 출판사	7	한글 윈도우 3.1	인포텍
8	C언어 기초 + 알파	교학사	8	슈퍼 캡스터디	삼성전자
9	3D studio R.3	한국 컴퓨터 매거진	9	VOCABULARY 77,000	정보소프트
10	PC사용자 가이드	프라운출판사	10	아래아 한글 2.1 전문 (RUP)	한글과 컴퓨터

Forner marked 2nd best in 1994

I willingly transferred the nationwide distribution rights to Mr Lee and decided to focus solely on software development. Occasionally, I would travel to the Seoul headquarters to conduct software seminar lectures, receive updates on business progress, and even train new employees. Mr Lee covered all expenses, including airfare and accommodation, so I didn't have to worry about any financial burdens.

However, Mr Lee had his own set of problems. He used to run a Daewoo Electronics dealership in Seoul, which was struggling with heavy debts when we first met. However, once he started selling my software for 600,000 won per set, he began to see significant profits. Mr Lee then saw it as an opportunity to pay off his debts and start earning money, which led to his request for nationwide distribution rights from me.   As he signed on dealerships throughout the country, he quickly made tens of millions of won, and Mr Lee was able to pay off some of his debts.

Then, when he brought in another person as an investor, they started to create a dissonance with each other. The new investor was a former gangster in Gangnam, and he asked for my acknowledgement to dispose of his room salon[44] business and invest in my software business.

When I went to the room salon in Gangnam, it was a pretty luxurious place. When they said they would dispose of all the high-end sofas and tables at a bargain price and use it as an office, I suggested using it as a "PC cafe," saying that the already installed interior could be utilized.

At the time, such a concept did not exist, so both employees and new investors readily agreed to my unique proposal. As a result, one section of the room salon was repurposed as an office for the employees, while the remaining space was converted into a "PC cafe" with the existing interior design. This marked the first-ever "PC cafe" in Korea.

Unfortunately, sales were dismal, and explaining the concept of a "PC cafe" to incoming visitors became a burden. Despite originally being intended for office use, the additional task of explaining the concept of a "PC cafe" without any resulting income ultimately led to the closure of the establishment after only a few months.

---

[44] A hostess bar where you can drink alcohol in a partitioned room

First Guarantee in My Life

Despite acquiring new investors, Mr Lee of Korea Computerware struggled with financial difficulties. Although substantial funds had come in from each regional distributor, I was unsure where the money had gone. According to his explanation, after paying me a monthly royalty fee of 5 million won and deducting operating expenses such as employee salaries and advertising costs, there was no money left.

At the same time, Mr Lee asked me to become a guarantor for a 100 million won loan application to the Korea Technology Finance Corporation(KTFC), using my software copyright as collateral. As it was a loan based on technology, they required a guarantee from the developer. I declined due to fear of the guarantee's obligation, but Mr Lee persisted in his request.

In November 1994, an Australian immigration visa became available, and I decided to return to Australia and to continue developing my software in Australia. Before leaving, Mr Lee guaranteed that if I left, he would pay me a monthly royalty of 5 million won. As a result, I decided to go with him to the KTFC to hear directly from the responsible person about the responsibilities and risks of becoming a guarantor.

"What happens if I become a guarantor but can't repay the loan later on?"

"Since this is secured by technology, the copyright for the software may be seized."

So, in other words, the explanation was that in the worst case scenario, the copyright for my software, "Forner," could be seized. So there was no reason not to provide the guarantee. Even if Mr Lee failed to repay the loan and "Forner" was seized, I could just develop another software.

In the end, I agreed to be a guarantee for the 100 million won technology loan for him before departing for Australia.

Later, I heard from him that they had already reached a prior agreement with KTFC employees to borrow 100 million won through me. And in exchange for that, Mr Lee had paid them millions of won as a bribe.

However, Mr Lee never sent the promised monthly royalty of 5 million won after my arrival in Australia, and instead sold the company to someone else without disclosing how the 100 million won was spent.

Story of Prosecutor's Dismissal

I am reminded of a case where a prosecutor and two police officers were dismissed in Western Australia long ago. Reflecting on my experience of human rights violations in the Korean prosecutor's office, I felt that the rule of law in Australia was certainly one step above Korea. Unlike Korea's prosecution monopoly, where only prosecutors can prosecute, each agency in Australia has its own prosecution authority.

Of course, unlike Korean police, Australian police have the power to prosecute and the prosecuting police officers play a role in court. However, in cases of serious criminal offenses such as murder, or criminal cases without a victim who can press charges, the Public Prosecutions office prosecutes on behalf of society for the sake of public order.

Andrew Mark Mallard, an Australian citizen born in Britain, was wrongly convicted of murder and spent 12 years in prison until the true culprit was identified in 2006. As a result, his conviction was overturned by the Federal Court of Australia. The two police officers and public prosecutor who investigated Andrew at the time had since been promoted to senior positions in Western Australia, but were dismissed due to their mistake 12 years earlier. Following an inquiry by the Western Australian Commission on Crime and Corruption, it was discovered that the two police officers and senior prosecutor had concealed crucial evidence that proved Andrew's innocence, and they were subsequently dismissed. Andrew received $3.25 million in compensation from the Western Australian government.

Police officers at the time coerced witnesses into making false statements in order to secure a murder conviction against the defendant. The public prosecutor, relying on those statements, did not disclose certain autopsy results to the defendant's legal team and argued in court that the wrench used by the defendant matched the victim's injuries, leading to an innocent person being imprisoned for 12 years. The prosecutor who handled the case was stripped of their position due to their responsibility for pursuing the case solely on the basis of information provided by the police, even though there was sufficient evidence to reveal the truth.

During the Park Chung-hee administration, loyalist judges who tailored their verdicts to fit the government's interests climbed the career ladder, and many of them now hold high positions in Korean society, such as members of the National Assembly or Supreme Court justices.

The case of Andrew Mallard in Australia is in stark contrast to the reality in Korea, where there is no way to hold these individuals accountable. In Korea, due to the customary Privilege of Former Position, it is not uncommon to see prosecutors or judges resign and start their career as an influential lawyer when their corrupt actions are exposed and become a social issue, but this is unheard of in Australia. In Australia, it is very difficult to be registered as a lawyer if you have ever received criminal or disciplinary action, especially related to past conscience issues, during the assessment process. Disciplinary actions may encompass a range of penalties and consequences, which may extend beyond the workplace or academic environment and could include punishments such as reprimands, suspension, or even termination from employment, as well as academic probation or expulsion from school.

Of course, the Korean Bar Association also considers past

disciplinary actions when registering lawyers, but in reality, this system is not effective. There was a case where the former head of the Jeju Prosecutor's Office, Kim Soo-chang, caused a stir in society by exposing himself and sexually assaulting a high school girl in a public place. During the police investigation, he even lied about his occupation and used his younger brother's name as an alias. He was dismissed from his post, but he did not receive any further disciplinary action and instead resigned and registered as a lawyer with the Korean Bar Association. It is reported that he now lives well and is even receiving special treatment at a famous law firm under a different name.

This is a similar case to the one published in the Seoul Shinmun newspaper on 28 November 2008.

In 1972, a murderer who had been sentenced to 15 years in prison for killing the daughter of a police officer in Jungcheon was acquitted after a retrial, 36 years after the incident. Jung Won-seop (74 years old at the time, 38 years old at the time of the crime) had been convicted of strangling a primary school student to death after sexually assaulting her and was sentenced to life imprisonment. However, he was found not guilty in a retrial by the Chuncheon District Court's Second Criminal Division (Chief Judge Jung Sung-tae) on the 28th of November.

In terms of politics, this is a 36-year wait to clear his name after being branded as a murderer following the incident. Especially since there have been several cases where those accused of espionage and other crimes related to the national situation have been acquitted in a retrial, but it is extremely rare for a retrial in an ordinary criminal case to result in an acquittal.

The trial concluded that "it is highly likely that there was a significant amount of assault, coercion, or cruel treatment of Mr Jung during the investigation process by the investigating police officers." The court also stated that "the evidence submitted by the investigative agency has significant defects that violate legal procedures, rendering the evidence unreliable or lacking in probative value, making it difficult to recognize the charges against Mr Jung."

The court then expressed its respect for Mr Jung, who had knocked on the door of the court with hope for a long time, saying that "there is no excuse for the fact that the law fell short of providing the minimum rights and legal procedures that the defendant should have rightfully enjoyed during the investigative process and suffered from the pain of being deprived of them. The law failed to listen to the defendant's appeal due to a lack of serious reflection and contemplation."

The case, known as the "Chuncheon Police Station Chief's Daughter Rape and Murder Case," involved the murder of a primary school student (a 9-year-old girl at the time) in Ududong Nonduk, Chuncheon, on September 27, 1972. Mr Jung was arrested on suspicion of killing the elementary school student and served 15 years of unjust imprisonment before being released on parole as a model prisoner in 1987. He then sought a retrial in Seoul High Court in November 1999 to prove his innocence, but it was dismissed in October 2001.

Unlike in Australia, there was no accountability for the police officers or prosecutors involved in the case at the time. Only Jung Won-seop, who had suffered human rights violations, was unjustly imprisoned. That's why in Korea, there's a saying, 'Don't get mad, get even!' Jung Won-seop was acquitted in a retrial in 2008, but because 10 years had passed since the statute of limitations for state compensation for human rights violations, he received no compensation and passed away on 18 March 2021 at the age of 87, feeling unjust. Jung had been imprisoned for 15 years for a crime he did not commit, and although he was released on parole in 1987 for good behaviour, his life and family were already destroyed. While he was in prison, Jung's father died of shock, and his family was scattered. His wife also suffered from misfortune, such as being in a car accident. Finally, in 2005, Jung appealed for his innocence to the Truth and Reconciliation Commission[45], and in December 2007, he received a recommendation

Jeong at a press conference in front of the courthouse

---

[45] The Truth and Reconciliation Commission was established in South

for retrial. Jung is now buried at Forest of Peace in Yongin.

Korea in 2005 to investigate human rights violations that occurred during the country's authoritarian period from 1948 to 1993.

Chapter 6 Migration & Life of Faith

After infant baptism at Korean Uniting Church

Migration to Australia

My home was destroyed in a fire caused by an unlicensed installer's illegal installation of a gas boiler, and despite my best efforts, I was unable to obtain any compensation or resolution for the damages incurred. Nevertheless, I ended up paying only lawyer's fees that drained my resources, and suffered human rights violations from the South Korean prosecutor's office due to a copyright case. Having experienced the fair society of Australia through studying in Australia, I concluded that I couldn't live a decent life in my home country of South Korea. Consequently, I promptly applied for immigration to Australia and composed an extensive letter to the Australian Embassy outlining my aspirations to live in their society and requesting their assistance, detailing the various challenges I had encountered in Korean society subsequent to completing my education in Australia.

After my compelling letter, I received notice that my immigration visa was approved within a short period of time. At the time, I had made some repairs to my fire-damaged home and resolved the copyright issue, so I was beginning to focus on launching my software business. Since it was a stable period for my business, I initially hesitated to move to Australia. However, I eventually decided to give up all of my business ventures and embark on a journey to Australia, considering the long-term benefits for both my life and my children's education.

From the nationwide distributor of the software I developed in Korea, I received copyright royalties of 5 million won per month, which allowed me to save some money. I believed that with this money, I could comfortably settle down in Australia.

Upon my return to Australia, my parents and in-laws saw us off much more warmly and comfortably than when we first departed to study in Australia.

Discord with an Aussie friend

Prior to my arrival in Australia, I reached out to my acquaintance Neville, a resident of Australia who lives independently. In response, Neville kindly offered me accommodation at his residence until I found permanent housing and even offered to meet us at the airport. During our student days, Neville served as the manager of the factory where my spouse was employed as a loom operator, and we enjoyed a close relationship with him.

On 22 December 1994, while awaiting a flight to Perth at Hong Kong International Airport, we encountered a former member of our church who was also returning to Perth following a visit to Korea. Upon our arrival at Perth Airport, the individual kindly extended an invitation for us to temporarily stay at his home if we had yet to secure lodging. However, as we had faith in our Australian friend Neville to pick us up, we graciously declined the offer.

However, Neville failed to meet us at the airport that night, and did not respond to our phone calls. Despite our excitement of arriving in Australia with our young son and daughter, we experienced an indescribable sense of desolation as we found ourselves stranded with no one to welcome us. Consequently, we were compelled to seek accommodation at a motel near the airport. The next morning, when I telephoned Neville again, he answered the phone. It turned out that he had mistakenly assumed our arrival on the night of December 23rd, instead of realizing that we were due to arrive at 12:05 am on December 22nd. Nonetheless, he promptly arrived at the motel to pick us up and brought us to his residence.

Neville was living in a three-bedroom house in Huntingdale, but upon arrival, we found that two of the bedrooms were already packed with his belongings, leaving no space for us. The kitchen and living room were also filled to the brim with various household items. Additionally, he was raising a puppy the size of a calf, which made it even more difficult for our family of four to find a place to live in his house. As we stood there in the living room, feeling bewildered, he suggested that he had already reserved a motel room close to his house where we could stay temporarily for a week.

We unpacked our luggage and rested at the motel, planning to have meals together at Neville's house. We had converted all the money we had brought from Korea, which amounted to around $100,000, and had already used some of it to buy a car, leaving us with about $90,000. With a small bank loan, we could have afforded to buy a house in a location like Wembley where average price of a 3 bedroom house in the area was about $100,000, but I was determined not to take on any debt. Instead, based on Neville's recommendation, we bought a reasonably-priced house for $68,000 in the Westfield area. We paid in cash and kept the remaining money as emergency funds and living expenses.

During that time, a disagreement arose between myself and Neville who was a shopaholic and despite living alone, kept several refrigerators running and filled each cooling unit to capacity with food. One day, due to an inadvertent mistake, the power of one freezer was cut off and all the food in it had to be discarded. Neville was convinced that our older child had unplugged the power cord by mistake, but I was not in agreement. Despite being an active child, our older child did not possess the recklessness required to tamper with the power without our consent, given his lack of knowledge about such matters.

Come to think of it, a few days ago, Neville had explained to us the layout of his house and had untangled a complicated mess of electrical wires while turning the lights on and off. At that time, it occurred to me that Neville might have accidentally disconnected the power, so I brought it up in conversation. However, this only caused him to become angry with us. Later, I saw him, who was physically imposing, sweating profusely while disposing of all the food in the refrigerator and cleaning up, shedding tears of frustration due to feeling wronged.

We were greatly taken aback by the sight of a physically imposing white man crying so inconsolably that we quietly left the house and returned to our motel, never to go back again.

During my time as an international student, I had lived with a white old landlord and experienced some minor conflicts, and it became apparent that there were cultural differences that we could not fully comprehend.

On the day we moved into the house we bought, we checked out of the motel and found out that Neville hadn't paid a single penny for the motel despite his statement that he had paid for one week for us. However, it turned out to be false.   As a result, we had to pay for the entire two weeks that we had stayed there.

And about a year later, I still had a lingering feeling about parting ways with Neville. So, I took the initiative to send a Christmas card as a gesture of reconciliation. Neville also responded with a Christmas card. With that, we were able to reconcile and meet again. We occasionally met until I moved back to Korea in 1998. After that, I completely lost touch with Neville, and I don't know if he is still alive or not, but based on his health condition at the time, I don't think he is still alive.

Prison Visit

Neville, in his younger years, worked as a manager in a factory and made a lot of money. He lived alone and spent his time as a hobby, almost every week, buying large amounts of food and items, and piling them up in his house without any room to walk around.

After reconciling with Neville, one day a call came from an unknown number. It was a call from Casuarina Prison, and the voice on the other end was none other than Neville's.

He asked me to meet him in person for a detailed explanation and requested that we visit him at the correctional facility where he was staying. Casuarina Prison, where he was being held, was a distant place about a 50-minute drive from our home. Although we didn't know why he made this request, we agreed to visit him for a reunion without hesitation. As we were also curious about Australian correctional facilities, one Sunday, I took my family to visit him at Casuarina Prison."

In my recollection, this was around 1995, and although I'm not sure what it looks like now, at the time, prison visits in Korea involved a plastic glass partition with intercoms for communication between visitors and inmates. However, Australian prisons allowed family members to freely mingle and interact with inmates in the same space, which was quite different and unique.

Some couples who appeared to be lovers engaged in sexual acts such as kissing, hugging, and petting without any hesitation, but the guards didn't seem to care. As we were having the visitation, a helicopter was flying above the prison. Some groups of visitors waved their hands at it. After inquiring about it, we found out that Alan Bond, the wealthiest man in Western Australia, had been imprisoned there, and it happened to be his birthday. While his family was visiting him, a helicopter with a banner wishing Alan a happy birthday was flying above the prison.

Anyway, according to my Australian friend Neville's explanation, he received a 10-month prison sentence for tax evasion when he worked as a manager at a factory several years ago and did not properly declare his taxes. Despite appealing to the court for leniency due to his advanced age and severe obesity at the time, his plea was not granted.   I heard that the Australian courts tend to impose prison sentences for cases of tax evasion whenever possible but I never thought something like this could happen to someone close to me.

Neville's request was nothing but asking me to put some money in the prison for him to use.   I wondered how someone who had to ask me for money to be kept in prison could go shopping every week and accumulate a pile of stuff at home.   However, without asking for a reason, I put the sum of $200 into his prison account.   At the time, the sum was equivalent to a week's salary for me.

After serving his sentence, Neville lived alone and maintained a relationship with my family until they immigrated back to Korea in 1998. However, contact was lost after I arrived in Korea, and it is currently unknown whether Neville is alive or deceased.

Theology and Pastoral Candidate

Upon arrival in Australia, it was discovered that the Korean Uniting Church where I had previously attended as a student had already splintered into several separate churches. The church members I knew during my time as a student, all urged me to attend their respective churches, leaving me in a quandary as to which church to attend. Ultimately, I came to an agreement with my wife to attend a nearby Australian Baptist church close to our home.

On the other hand, upon seeing a job advertisement for a programmer position at Speed Group, I applied and was employed immediately. Although the salary was not substantial, it was enough to sustain our lifestyle in Australia.

However, when many church members who were like family to me became estranged due to church issues, I became deeply immersed in thoughts of faith. Since I saw some pastors who had come to Australia on temporary visas to establish themselves and lure good-hearted believers, I resolved to become a pastor who would never seek personal gain, but only convey God's love to my neighbors. Eventually, I resigned from my job and enrolled in a theological college in Australia.

As I made up my mind to pursue theological studies in earnest, I recalled my brief stint studying at Busan Theological Seminary in the past, with the goal of obtaining the qualifications for studying in Australia. I also remembered how my father had made a vow to devote me to God through prayer when I was young. It felt like I had come full circle to fulfill God's will.

The Bachelor of Divinity course at Murdoch University in Perth is a joint education program entrusted by the Baptist Church and other denominations, and requires a bachelor's degree for admission even for those with different majors. I already had another bachelor's degree and was able to easily gain admission with a recommendation letter from the pastor of the Baptist Church I was serving under in Australia.

Even as a head of household with two children and a wife, I was able to focus solely on my studies as a full-time student thanks to the Australian government's welfare policies, which provided assistance with basic living expenses and tuition fees to at least maintain a minimum standard of living. Having experienced stopping my theological studies in the past in Korea, I was determined to complete my theological studies this time and become an excellent pastor.

At the point where I had four subjects left to graduate, I found out that the Australian Baptist Church was accepting applications for pastoral candidates and immediately applied. The candidate selection process involved document screening and interviews, which I attended with my wife and children. We had meals together from 10 a.m. to 4 p.m. as we were sometimes interviewed individually and sometimes as a group. Through various perspectives, they sought to confirm whether I was fit to become a pastor of the Australian Baptist Church.

At first, I thought the interview would be a casual conversation with fellow Christians, but as time passed, the questions shifted towards verifying my conviction in the Baptist doctrine rather than my personal calling. This shift left me feeling somewhat disappointed. I sensed that they were more interested in testing whether I was a good fit for their denomination, rather than assessing my calling and conviction to lead many people to God. As a result, I gave somewhat rebellious answers.

"What are your thoughts on baptism by immersion?"

I was aware of the answer they were expecting, but I did not say what they wanted to hear.

"I personally view both baptism and christening as symbolic acts."

"Do you then believe that one can be saved without receiving baptism?"

"I believe that salvation is a matter between God and the individual, so one cannot assess the existence or absence of salvation based on symbolic acts like baptism."

"Hmm... I understand."

My father was a Presbyterian pastor, and as a result of growing up in a Presbyterian church and practicing the faith from an early age, the Presbyterian doctrine held significant sway over my beliefs. Consequently, the doctrine of the Baptist faith, which required the rejection of Presbyterian baptism and the need for re-baptism, was difficult to accept. This conviction resulted in a great deal of hesitation even after receiving conditional approval to become a ministerial candidate, which mandated a one-year study of Baptist doctrine as a requirement.

"Am I a servant of God? Or am I a pioneer expanding the doctrines of the Baptist denomination?"

As these thoughts stirred in my mind, I came to the conclusion that I could not possibly become a pastor affiliated with a single denomination. At that time, President Park, an acquaintance who was conducting a significant business in Korea, reached out to me for help in leading a negotiating team for a merger and acquisition deal with a major American corporation. I saw this as a sign from God, and shortly after the IMF foreign exchange crisis [46] in early 1998, I submitted a leave of absence notice to the university and returned to Korea to assist with the M&A negotiations.

---

[46] A general term for the foreign exchange liquidity crisis that has occurred in Asia since 1997.

The Apostles' Creed

(Before immigrating back to Korea, I was a regular contributor to "Christian Review," a magazine published in Sydney, as an editorial board member. One of my articles was about the Apostles' Creed because at that time, there was a blind belief among churchgoers that not adhering to the Apostles' Creed was a sign of heresy, and I wrote the article to help guide them. However, a theology student sent me a rebuttal letter, and I was unable to respond properly because I was preparing to immigrate. Therefore, I am publishing this article here for the readers who might be interested.)

Can the Apostles' Creed be the standard for detecting heresy? We must seriously consider this issue. The attitudes of the ministers regarding the Apostles' Creed are generally as follows:

1. They are well aware of the non-biblical issues in the Apostles' Creed, but only avoid them on the pretext that they do not benefit the congregation's spiritual life.

2. Since the Apostles' Creed is regulated by the doctrine of the denomination, they are obedient to the denomination, believing that obedience is better than worship.

3. They are just rationalizing the original contents of the Apostles' Creed by almost changing the meaning.

4. They reject the Apostles' Creed and no longer use it in worship services.

The late Tak Myung-hwan[47], the former director of the Institute of Religious Studies, argues in his book "Research on Christian Heresy" that the first criterion for distinguishing heresy is whether or not the Apostles' Creed is professed as a statement of faith (Tak Myung-hwan, p. 75). This means that not reciting the Apostles' Creed during Sunday worship is considered heresy. What are the issues with this belief in the Apostles' Creed?

1) The Apostles' Creed is not the Creed of the Apostles

   It is widely known that the Apostles' Creed was not actually written by the apostles of Jesus' time. In fact, it was created by Roman Catholic priests as a means of denouncing heresy. Therefore, it seems inappropriate to refer to this creed, created by individuals other than the apostles, as "the Apostles' Creed" and use it as a standard for identifying heresy.

2) History of the Apostles' Creed

   The Apostles' Creed that we are memorizing today originated from the "Old Creed of the Roman Church," which was based on the Latin creed "Symbol of the Apostles" around AD 400. It spread through the Western Church and the Roman Catholic Church, but the Eastern Church never adopted it as an official confession of faith. Instead, they used a similar Nicene Creed[48]. In the early days, it was called a "symbol"

---

[47] Tak Myung-hwan was born in Buan, Jeollabuk-do in 1937. He began studying new religious movements in 1964 and had a particular interest in Christian heretical groups that deviated from traditional Christian teachings, which were classified as anti-social and criminal.

[48] The original Nicene Creed was first adopted at the First Council of Nicaea in 325.

because it was used as a standard to distinguish heresies and traditions.

3) Unknown Expression – From thence

Few people know what the phrase "From thence" of "From thence, He shall come to judge the quick and the dead" means. Reciting unknown words as an act of faith is influenced by the symbolic faith of Roman Catholicism. The phrase "From thence" is an old expression that means "from that place" with the corresponding preposition "from -." In other words, it means "from the place where Jesus ascended to heaven." It is incomprehensible that this archaic term, which has been used for over a century, is still being used without correction despite changes in Korean spelling for over half a century. Why is it that while everything else has been translated into modern language, only this part is kept in archaic language?

4) Incorrect expression - "...suffered under Pontius Pilate."

Jesus was condemned to the cross by none other than the chosen people of God, the Jews. The high priest, legal experts, and Pharisees made every effort to get rid of Jesus and finally succeeded through Pilate. Even from a modern legal perspective, Pilate is an accomplice, and the Jews are perpetrators of the crime. According to Article 31(1) of the Criminal Act of Korea, "Those who incite another to commit a crime shall be punished with the same penalty as the perpetrator," and Article 31(2) states that "The accomplice's penalty shall be reduced." Even from a simple secular perspective, we can see that inciting someone to commit a crime is a more heinous form of intellectual crime. However, why are the accomplices treated as perpetrators? The Bible clearly states that the perpetrators who executed Jesus were the ones who betrayed him in front of Pilate, "The God of Abraham, Isaac, and Jacob, the God of our fathers, has glorified his servant Jesus... You handed him over to be killed, and you disowned him before Pilate" (Acts 3:13). Therefore, the issue of Pilate raised by the apostles is giving the wrong impression by overselling only a part of the Bible, leading people astray from their faith. It is right to confess that Jesus suffered for "my sins," for He died for us to forgive our sins.

5) Deleted expression due to ambiguity – "He descended into hell"

The Apostle's Creed contains a passage that causes discomfort in its current form, namely "He descended into hell." This phrase was removed from the Korean version of the creed to alleviate unease, but it remains unchanged in the English version. Readers are encouraged to refer to both the Korean and English versions of the Apostle's Creed in the first chapter of the Bible. If taken literally, this expression implies that Jesus went to hell during the three days he was entombed. While this claim may be unfamiliar to Korean Christians who are only familiar with the Korean translation of the Apostle's Creed, it is not entirely unfounded. It is based on 1 Peter 3:19, which states that "he went and made proclamation to the imprisoned spirits."

6) Expression with a story – The Holy Catholic Church

Another issue with the translation is the phrase "Georughan Gonghoe" which is a translation of the English phrase "the Holy Catholic Church". The word "catholic" means "universal" or "worldwide" in English, and in some Korean translations of the Bible, it is translated as "Universal" to avoid using the word "Catholic". In general usage, there is no problem using the phrase "catholic church" to refer to the universal church. However, it is clear to anyone familiar with the background of the use of the term in the Bible that it was not intended in a universal sense.

At the time when the Catholic Church was hosting Peter as

its first pope, it claimed to be the only church representing all churches on earth. This was the time when the church condemned those who opposed it as heretics. While the Korean Church has translated it as "Georughan Gonghoe", many English hymns still use "the Holy Catholic Church". The phrase "Gonghoe" (Korean for "council" or "assembly") is vague and ambiguous because the term "council" in the Bible is always expressed as "the antichrist". Even the newly revised Korean Bible, which is adopted by many Korean churches, still uses the problematic term of "Gonghoe".

(a) "Take heed of men: for they will deliver you up to the councils, and they will scourge you in their synagogues." [Matthew 10:17, KJV]

(b) "Now the chief priests, and elders, and all the council, sought false witness against Jesus, to put him to death." [Matthew 26:59, KJV]

(c) "And as soon as it was day, the elders of the people and the chief priests and the scribes came together, and led him into their council." [Luke 22:66, KJV]

(d) "Then gathered the chief priests and the Pharisees a council, and said, What do we? for this man doeth many miracles." [John 11:47, KJV]

7) Doubtful expressions – The Communion of Saints

Many people mistakenly believe that "The Communion of Saints" in the Apostles' Creed refers to "believers having fellowship together." However, the meaning of the term in the time the Apostles' Creed was written is quite different from what we understand today. The Roman Catholic Church uses it as a doctrinal basis for the worship of saints and for the idea of communication between the living and the dead. Because of this belief, Catholic believers receive baptism on behalf of the dead, and they also serve and donate in their names. Of course, the term "saints" or "holy ones" in a biblical sense refers to all believers who have accepted Jesus Christ as their Savior (1 Corinthians 1:2), but the Catholic concept of saints refers to deceased individuals who have been canonized after a special deliberation, usually many years after their death. This Catholic concept has been adopted by some Protestant denominations today, and there are cases where ministers hesitate to call believers "saints." However, communicating with the dead is strictly forbidden in the Bible (Isaiah 8:20; Revelation 18:11).

8) Expressions omitted from the original text – "Curse be upon those who oppose this Confession of Faith"

Originally, the Apostles' Creed was used as a standard for discerning heresy. Therefore, it was a natural logic for them to have such expressions at the end of the creed. However, we cannot find such expressions in our current version of the Apostles' Creed.

Currently, if there is a church that protects the Apostles' Creed the most on Earth, it is the Catholic Church. They condemn those who oppose the creed as the greatest enemies of faith and heretics. Ultimately, the criteria for discerning heresy by Tak Myeong-hwan or the modern church's defense of the Apostles' Creed is nothing more than representing the medieval Catholic Church's stance. We know well the background of the birth of Protestantism caused by Luther and Calvin. The spirit of Protestantism that opposed the corrupted Roman Catholic Church is "Only the Bible, Only Faith". Anything else claimed beyond this is another gospel.

Reader's Letter

Hello, my name is Mancheol Kim (pseudonym) and I am from Brisbane. While reading the December issue, I came across an article by Soo Yong Yoon that left me with some questions. As Mr Yoon is identified as an editor of the magazine, I wanted to clarify a potential misunderstanding regarding the issue of the Apostles' Creed.

Firstly, it cannot be said that the Apostles' Creed was written by the apostles themselves, as Yoon stated. However, scholars argue that it was being used within the community of faith or the church before the Nicene Creed, and that its purpose was not to serve as a tool for Roman Catholic priests to enforce their dogmatic views. In fact, it was intended to help new believers in the early church understand the comprehensive summary of the Bible. On the other hand, it is known that the early Nicene Creed was also being used for similar reasons in the Eastern Church.

Secondly, it can be said that the assertion by the late Tak Myeong-hwan, that the confession of faith in the Apostles' Creed can be used to determine whether someone is a heretic or not, is a valuable testimony in today's world for similar reasons. His assertion can be seen as not just a simple logical conclusion, but rather as a result of clinical experience in the field. In fact, his death, which is known to us, can also be understood as a fight for truth against heresy, and therefore, his judgment can be considered correct. However, it seems that Yoon, without any experiments or logical pursuits, simply uses the title of " The attitudes of the ministers regarding the Apostles' Creed" as a pretext to cite four items that suggest the non-canonical nature of the Apostles' Creed. This highlights the narrowness and inaccuracy of his sources.

Thirdly, I would like to point out some problems in the analysis of

Yoon's understanding of the Apostles' Creed.

1) regarding the issue of Pilate's authority, it is a valid point that Yoon's interpretation of Jesus' suffering due to "my sin" is correct. However, the assertion that the phrase "who suffered under Pontius Pilate" is incorrect because it implies a logical argument of whether Pilate was a victim or an executioner is a questionable point. Of course, the Jews demanded that Jesus be crucified, and Pilate, who feared a riot, ordered the execution. It is clear that the legal authority for the execution was in the hands of Pilate, as we know that without his permission, everything related to the execution would have been impossible. Therefore, Yoon's judgment of whether Pilate was a victim or an executioner seems to be a matter of personal faith for Yoon or for the biblical reader of today, and the Apostles' Creed should be seen confessing this aspect not in a personal dimension but in a public dimension for all churches.

2) This is a discussion about the expression "holy catholic church." It seems that Mr Yoon is giving the impression that it is somehow connected to the Roman Catholic Church, and if this is a misunderstanding, I apologize. However, there may be a misunderstanding about the background of the phrase as I pointed out earlier. Also, Mr Yoon seems to be conflating the holy catholic church with the Jewish council that appears in the Gospels without distinguishing between them. This may be due to a textual misunderstanding. Clearly, Mr Yoon knows that "Catholic" means "universal" or "worldwide," but the word "church" in the Gospels is translated as "Council" (RSV). Therefore, it seems that all "councils" in the Bible, though it's unclear whether they are exclusively for anti-Christians, are referring to the church that Christ is the head of in the Apostles' Creed.

3) In both the "Doubtful expressions" and "Expressions omitted from the original text," it must be said that Yoon is continuously conscious of and using Roman Catholicism. And it is wrong to point out the concept of "saints" as an ordination of the dead in Roman Catholicism.

Even if Catholic believers use it in that way, it is not something that our Protestant faith uncritically accepted medieval content without criticism, as it is derived from the tradition of another church. Furthermore, it is incomprehensible and irresponsible for some pastors (although it is unknown which denomination they belong to) to be reluctant to refer to the brethren of the church "saints" without first acquiring knowledge and examining the implications of such language.

I apologize for any confusion that may have arisen from my statement about "expressions omitted from the original text". While I am unsure if such omissions exist in the Apostles' Creed, if they do, would they not be logically possible expressions? Let us examine the Apostles' Creed - is there any unnecessary content in our confession of faith? Based on this reasoning, it is reasonable to assume that such expressions existed until the time when Jesus could publicly be confessed as Christ in the early Christian society or in Rome. Furthermore, I would like to ask whether these "unknown" expressions are currently being used in our church, given that they are not known to us today.

Yoon mentioned clearly that we should return to the true gospel. That is absolutely true. However, what is the true gospel? Of course, we do not deny that there are misconceptions and rituals that have arisen from a fluctuating faith, as he pointed out. However, criticizing the beautiful tradition of faith in the Korean church and immigrant churches without prior in-depth study or discussion may be like trying to catch a grasshopper and ending up burning the field.

Especially, the Apostles' Creed has been treasured and passed down by our predecessors in faith from the early days of the Korean church to the present day. Isn't it clear that the true gospel is shining through our theological history like this? That's what I believe.

Kim Man-cheol (pseudonym)

Studies in Religion

The University of Queensland

My Reply to the Letter

Hello,

Your letter from the Christian Review has been received. Although it may seem like an excuse, my recent move from Perth, Australia to Korea has kept me extremely occupied. Now that I have settled in, I am finally able to respond to your message. However, I do realize that it has been a few years since you initially reached out, and if you have already graduated from Queensland University, it may be challenging to establish contact with you. For this reason, I am responding in this way. Please understand that I have opted not to use your real name to protect your privacy.

Upon reading your letter, I sensed a strong belief in the Apostles' Creed and detected anger towards my article that seemed to contradict your beliefs. However, one thing that struck me as puzzling was your admission at the outset that the Apostles' Creed was not written by the apostles themselves, yet you still argued for its veracity based on the idea that it had been treasured and passed down by our Christian forefathers. This presents a paradox. If what our Christian forefathers valued and conveyed is indeed the true gospel, then we must embrace medieval Catholicism, for Martin Luther's Reformation was essentially a rejection of the very gospel that our Christian forefathers treasured and transmitted.

Paul and Peter, who lived long before Martin Luther, vehemently criticized the Jewish tradition of not eating with Gentiles (Galatians 2:11-15). Jesus himself also received much criticism from the Pharisees and scribes for not adhering to the Jewish customs of his time (Mark 2:16, Luke 19:10). The reason I bring this up is because while you admit that the New Testament was not written by the apostles, you argue that since it was passed down by respected

Christian elders, it can be considered the true gospel. However, the Bible warns us not to nullify God's word by following our own traditions (Matthew 15:6) based on our heritage.

In this spirit, I would like to express my perspective as follows.

There is some discussion among scholars regarding the usage of the Apostles' Creed in the early Christian church. While some claim that it was utilized prior to the Nicene Creed, the specific source of this assertion remains unclear. It is possible that this claim stems from the preaching of certain pastors who hold a strong reverence for the Apostles' Creed. However, regardless of the opinions of scholars or pastors, the ultimate determination of the legitimacy of such claims must be based on the light of scripture.

When examining texts that document the history of Christianity, it becomes apparent that distortions can occur depending on the theological backgrounds of the authors. Proponents of the Apostles' Creed have been known to rationalize its use by appealing to sources outside of scripture. Such arguments hold little merit, as any tradition or practice that does not align with the teachings of scripture must be considered invalid.

You have claimed that the Apostles' Creed was utilized in the early Christian church as a means of instructing new converts and providing a comprehensive understanding of scripture. However, the basis for this claim is not readily apparent, and even those who lack formal theological training would be familiar with the persistent theological controversies and schisms that plagued the Catholic era. It is therefore important to rely on readily available theological resources to validate or invalidate such claims.

Secondly, it may be inferred that the proposition posited by the late Tak Myeong-hwan, which asserts that "the confession of faith in the Apostles' Creed can serve as a criterion to determine the orthodoxy of an individual, based on clinical observations," lacks biblical support. Paul's declaration of faith (Acts 24:13-16), despite being accused of heresy, provides an indication that heretics do not serve God, do not uphold the Scriptures, and do not possess hope in the resurrection. In 1 John 4:1-3, the spirit of antichrist is defined as denying the divinity of Christ or refusing to acknowledge His incarnation. Nowhere in the Bible is there a statement that enables the determination of a heretic based on clinical outcomes. Moreover, the contention that "simply without any experiments or logical pursuit" suffices in determining the standard of faith is misconceived, as faith cannot be determined through empirical or rational means. As beings devoid of power before God, we are akin to the dead, absent the shed blood of Christ. A humanistic faith is erroneous.

Thirdly, while claiming that the suffering mentioned in the Apostles' Creed is a matter of personal faith for individual readers of the Bible to discern, it was argued that we should view the Creed as a public confession of the Church, rather than a personal matter. However, there is a contradiction in your statement. The idea of personal faith and the public confession of the Church are not compatible. You may think that the Church is formed when many individuals come together, but the Church mentioned in the Bible refers to the body of Christ (Ephesians 1:23), which is not something we create ourselves, but something that the Holy Spirit works in us. Therefore, each individual who is born again by the Spirit of God can also be considered part of the Church. Furthermore, as I mentioned before, the Bible clearly states who inflicted suffering on Jesus (Acts 4:10). If what the Bible says is true, then we must realize that those who put Jesus to death are none other than ourselves.

Fourthly, my focus in this article is not on comparing the Holy Catholic Church and the Jewish council. I want to clearly state that the main focus of my article is on the origin of the term "Gonghoe" in the Apostles' Creed, which comes from the Korean word "Gonggyohoe", meaning Catholic Church.   When "catholic" is used in a lowercase form, it means universal or general. However, when the first letter is capitalized as in "Catholic Church," it refers to the Catholic Church in Rome. In an attempt to remove the Catholic

Church's connotation, "Gonghoe" was poorly translated as "council," leading to confusion with the Jewish council mentioned in the Bible. When conveying any message or writing, is there a need to use terms such as "enemies of Christ" or "monsters of heresy," even if it is not intended to harm? Is there any need to cause confusion by claiming that these terms are different from those in the Bible, such as "enemies of Christ" or "monsters of heresy"?

Fifthly, you are absolutely right to claim that the use of "Doubtful expressions" and "Expressions omitted from the original text" is something that I was conscious of the Roman Catholic. This is because the Apostles' Creed itself cannot be understood without taking into account the Roman Catholic tradition.

Furthermore, you mentioned that the concept of "saints" being identified by Roman Catholics as the "ordination of the dead" is a mistake. However, it seems that you may have misread my article. What I was trying to convey is that some pastors object to the use of the term "saints" because they believe that it is misunderstood as referring to the dead as revered by Roman Catholics, rather than the true meaning of the term.

In the end, the essence of your letter can only be understood as accepting the Apostle's Creed as true gospel not because it is deemed fit by the standards of the Bible, but rather because famous people in his surroundings have believed it for a long time.

Faith is an issue between God and each individual. It is already evident from the history of medieval Catholicism how wrong it is for the Church to represent and determine individual faith. I earnestly hope that you will meditate on the word of God daily and listen carefully to the words spoken by the Holy Spirit.

Sincerely,

Soo Yong Yoon.

The Reason I Left the Church

As the firstborn son of a household with a father serving as a pastor, there is widespread curiosity as to how an individual who previously pursued theological education could depart from his religious institution.

Have you heard the expression, **'one's hands bend inward** [49] '? During my father's lifetime, I refrained from speaking out about the corrupt practices of fallen pastors as it would have felt like dishonoring my parents.   However, it should be noted that witnessing the malfeasance of some pastors was not the sole factor contributing to my decision to leave the church.

Rather, I arrived at my conclusions after studying theology and engaging in biblical exploration to discern God's will.   The act of departing from a religion, particularly a church, in contemporary society requires considerable fortitude, given that most individuals within the social circle hold religious convictions.

In my view, the crux of Christian faith is its conviction regarding the afterlife. Regrettably, in recent times, an increasing number of individuals have been inclined to perceive faith as a philosophical pursuit. Although this perspective may not be religiously untenable, it does represent a significant departure from the biblical tradition.

As attested by the words in Revelation 3:16, "So because you are lukewarm, and neither hot nor cold, I will spit you out of My mouth."

---

[49] 'one's hands bend inward' is the Korean proverb for 'men are blind in their own causes'

Pastors who know the secret

There is not a single successful pastor in Korea who has remained untainted by corruption. Major incidents reported in the news include the personal misconduct and embezzlement committed by Pastor Cho Yong-gi of the Yoido Full Gospel Church and his family, the allegations of adultery with a girl in her 20s and financial wrongdoing by Pastor Kim Ki-dong of the Sungnak Church, the nepotism and corruption by wealthy pastors Kim Sam-hwan and Kim Ha-na of the Myungsung Church, and the inappropriate comments and real estate speculation by Pastor Jun Kwang-hoon of the Taegeukgi Army[50].

While it is difficult to find individuals with proper moral discernment who can view these incidents objectively, it is concerning that many congregants have adopted a servitude mentality, rendering them unable to judge these pastors accurately. The words,

"He who has ears, let him hear" (Matthew 4:23)

serve as a call to all individuals to listen carefully and discern the truth.

My recollection is stirred by a remark made by my spouse after observing such corrupt pastors. She posited,

"The fact that these well-known pastors can abandon a lifetime of faith for temporary wealth and sexual temptation suggests they have realized that the Christian faith is a fallacy. Otherwise, how could they engage in such behavior?"

Upon reflection, it seems that many pastors in our surroundings are striving to learn from the successful businesses of these corrupt

---

[50] The Taegeukgi Army is a term used to describe those who organized counter-demonstrations against the candlelight vigils calling for the impeachment of former President Park Geun-hye.

pastors, and perhaps those who have already succeeded are revealing their true colors.

Through this criticism, we should not forget about other pure pastors like my friend, an evangelist Lee Jong-bae, who silently practice their faith and resist the temptations of the world. While we cannot judge them, if they truly have a heart to carry the cross and follow Jesus, they will not view my criticism merely as criticism.

Pastors, My father's Friend

On August 27th, 2019, my father passed away suddenly from a heart attack at the age of 85. I had always disliked my father while he was alive while he was alive. This was because I thought he had made my mother suffer.

After retiring as a pastor at Gohwa Church in Hadong, Gyeongsangnam-do, a church that was struggling financially, my parents were unable to support themselves. As a result, my younger sister and I sent them money every month for their living expenses. However, seeing how they relied on each other and lived together after retiring made me soften towards my father a little.

Even though golf is a sport that many people enjoy for exercise these days, my parents couldn't afford it. Instead, they became monthly members at a nearby billiard hall and spent most of their time there to stay healthy.

Nevertheless, my father passed away on 23 September 2019, due to a heart attack. When he was alive, he used to say,

"I will live until the age of 87 and then go to God."

Every time he said that, I would think to myself,

'I wish he wouldn't say things like that, as he is not a superstitious person.'

My Father's Funeral Conducted by His Friends

However, my father passed away at the age of 85, before he could fulfill his self-promised lifespan.

During my father's funeral, several of my father's friends who were also retired pastors visited the hospital daily to conduct worship services, and a few close acquaintances even remained with our family until the cremation ceremony. Their support was deeply appreciated, and I am grateful for their kindness during this difficult time.

At the end of the funeral service, I was asked to speak as the representative of the family, and I spoke the words that were on my mind without giving much thought.

"I would like to express my sincere gratitude to all those in attendance today on behalf of our family. Our late father was a man of unwavering conviction, which he demonstrated throughout his lifetime. Had our father held communist beliefs, our family would have experienced significant hardship as we would have been unable to align ourselves with his convictions. . . ."

The somber atmosphere of the funeral seemed to deepen even more with my somewhat meaningful words. Afterward, at the crematorium, I and our family hosted a meal for two pastors who had accompanied them and afterwards, sent them on their way with an envelope containing roughly 100,000-200,000 won as a gesture of gratitude.

And just as we were about to leave the crematorium to dispose of my father's ashes, the pastor who had received the envelope earlier came back and asked to speak with me.

"What can I help you?"

"I wanted to let you know that although they couldn't attend the crematorium here, there are in fact four pastors who have been helping your father's funeral. However, since the money you gave me is not sufficient to share among four of us."

My mind went blank.   Were they not my father's friends who selflessly volunteered to lead the service, without any solicitation from my family? Furthermore, I had already engaged a funeral director and paid a substantial sum of money, thus the involvement of these individuals was not a prerequisite to fulfilling the funeral rites. Additionally, at the time, my mother was still alive and had a broad network of acquaintances who could have also lent their assistance.

However, the pastor explained that the money I had provided was insufficient to divide amongst themselves who conducted the service. It was an indescribable situation, but I responded without showing any signs of dismay.

"Is that so?" I asked. "How much more would be required?"

The pastor replied,

"We're not entirely sure. Whatever you can manage would be appreciated..."

Since we were having our conversation in front of the crematorium restaurant, there were many people passing by. I said

"Okay, I understand"

and pulled out my wallet to count some cash right then and there. The pastor who saw me was probably conscious of the people around us, so he was taken aback and just waved his hand to indicate that it was okay before quickly leaving.

Several years later when my mother passed away, I didn't inform any of my parents' pastor friends.

Heaven and Hell

On 17 July 2022, my mother passed away. She was the same mother who, when I was 10, lying in bed sick, left me with the words,

"Take care of your younger siblings when I'm gone."

It was that same mother who had now passed away. Due to her last words to me as a child, I have lived my life preparing for death, and continue to do so to this day.

When embarking on a long journey or facing a critical surgical procedure, I always make preparations for the possibility of my death. Some years ago, prior to undergoing a colonoscopy and fearing that I may not emerge from general anesthesia, I gave my wife money that I had set aside for emergency, which caused her to be taken aback.

Nevertheless, my longstanding habit of being mindful of my mortality has been rekindled by my mother's passing, prompting me to contemplate my own death once again. Though my mother had a firm belief in entering paradise after death, I do not view it as a matter of faith but rather as a matter of hope.

Many church members claim that God created both heaven and hell, but then why is there no reference to either in the Old Testament? Instead, the Old Testament refers to the afterlife as a state of sleep in Sheol. Sheol, which is also known as "the pit" or "the grave," is described in the Old Testament as "the underworld," "the unseen world," or "a dark land covered by deep darkness."

The word Sheol is expressed in the New Testament as the word Hades, and it is believed that everyone sleeps after death. "After saying this, He went on to say,

'Our friend Lazarus has fallen asleep, but I am going there to awaken him'" (John 11:11).

However, modern church members unanimously believe that they go directly to heaven or hell immediately after death.

The acquaintances around who learned of the mother's passing all offered words of comfort to me, saying things like,

"Your mother has gone to heaven,"

or

"I hope your mother finds rest in a better place."

The description of heaven and hell in the Bible is truly problematic. The detailed depiction of heaven and hell is found in the famous **"parable of the rich man and Lazarus"** in Luke 16. Many Christians use this passage as evidence for the existence of heaven and hell, but I see it as evidence for their non-existence due to the following reasons.

1. The rich man looked up and saw Lazarus in heaven, nestled in the arms of "Abraham." But how could Lazarus, who had died, be held in the arms of "Abraham," a creature made by God?

2. The rich man in hell and Lazarus in heaven were aware of each other's existence. If so, wouldn't the people in heaven be more agonized? How can good people who love their neighbors as themselves, be living happily in heaven while their family members or neighbors are suffering in the burning hell?

In Genesis, God who created humans said to Adam,

"You shall surely die on the day that you eat of it" (Genesis 2:17).

However, the serpent said to Adam and Eve,

"You will not surely die" (Genesis 3:4).

In Ecclesiastes 12:7, it says,

"The dust returns to the earth as it was, and the spirit returns to God who gave it."

But in the New Testament, it is widely believed without a doubt that when a person dies, they immediately go to either heaven or hell.

Christian believers who believe in Jesus as God believe that, just as Jesus was resurrected from the dead on the cross, we will also be resurrected after death and go straight to heaven or hell. But if we immediately go to heaven or hell after death, what is the meaning of resurrection?

Religious reformer Martin Luther said,

"The doctrine of the immortality of the soul, along with other absurd views, is found in the rubbish of the Roman Catholic catechism" (The Problem of Immortality, p256, by Petavel).

Theologian Tindale also said,

"Forsake the idea that put them [the departed souls] into heaven, hell, purgatory, and that Christ and Paul are arguing to prove the resurrection. . .if the soul is in heaven. . .Why Resurrection?" (Reprint by the Parker Society in 1850).

There is no doubt that this proposition is practically impossible to accept.

Despite this, it can be argued that the contemporary Church's belief in heaven and hell owes a great deal to the influence of Paul. His preaching has become so highly esteemed that, in some respects, it would not be remiss to refer to the faith as Paulism rather than Christianity, with his teachings holding greater weight than even those of Jesus.

In the face of the frailty of human mortality, no one can confidently speak of the world after death. Instead, I will personally endeavor not to be swayed by the greedy ambitions of corrupt religious leaders on this earth who seek to expand their influence.

My Talents

The parable of the talents is found in Matthew 25:14-30. In it, a wealthy man entrusts different amounts of money (talents) to his servants before going on a journey. Upon his return, he finds that most of the servants have used the money to earn more profits, but one servant, out of fear of losing the money, simply kept it and returned the original amount to the owner. The wealthy man criticizes the servant who returned only the original amount.

This parable is generally interpreted to mean that a life attitude of making the most of the opportunities given to us as humans is more righteous. As for me, I find it difficult to accept the life after death described in the Bible by interpreting and understanding the teachings of the Bible to the fullest using my talents and abilities.

The existence of the soul is also skeptical. If the universe moves according to God's plan, then the principle of the universe is God's will. From the point of view of the problem of the soul, if there is input, there must be output. In that sense, it is difficult to accept the church's teaching that there is no annihilation but birth. How can the soul continue to be created while someone who did not believe in Jesus for a short time on earth can be punished forever without dying? It is not at all rational.

Someone once told me that it is safer to bet on faith, assuming that there might be heaven and hell after death. However, God sees our hearts.

"The Lord does not look at the things people look at. People look at the outward appearance, but the Lord looks at the heart." (1 Samuel 16:7b)

"Lord, you have searched me and you know me. You know when I sit and when I rise; you perceive my thoughts from afar." (Psalm 139:1-2)

In other words, it means not to be deceived by faith that believes in the theory of gambling.   I think that utilizing one's own talents to understand the principle of the universe, that is, God, is like being a good servant who has gained profit by using their talents, just like me.

Chapter 7 Troubled Society

My family in 1999

Reverse Immigration to Korea

In 1998, immediately after receiving a notification of approval as a conditional pastor candidate from the Australian Baptist Union, I received a call from President Park in Korea. He requested assistance during the negotiation process for a potential merger with an American company.   He was involved in the supply of semiconductor parts.

When I left for study in Australia, President Park generously provided me with a computer called the "Famicom," which can be considered the first personal computer, recognizing my need for a computer during my computer studies in Australia.

Although I felt a sense of obligation to honor President Park's request due to my gratitude towards him, I also realized during my time as a police officer that I as a police officer did not have the financial capability of treating others to meals like many entrepreneurs who hosted and treated police officers. This realization made me consider starting a business that would allow me to host and treat others.

Reasons for Reverse Immigration

While studying theology, I received financial assistance for living expenses from the Australian church I attended, as well as Austudy and tuition assistance from Centrelink[51].   However, I realized that it would be difficult to live comfortably financially if I became a pastor in the future. At that time, a friend whom I often discussed things with

---

[51] Centrelink is a Government service which provides support to Australians who face financial hardship.

asked me a question:

"You say that you have been called by God to be a pastor, but why should your family have to sacrifice for your calling?"

This question remained deeply engraved in me.

Furthermore, the biggest reason why I decided to return to Korea was to naturally foster bilingualism in our children. At the time, our first child was in fourth grade and our youngest daughter was not yet of school age. Even though we spoke Korean at home, our first child had already developed a heavy accent when he spoke Korean due to speaking English with Australian children all day at school.

It wasn't easy to go back to Korea, as it required the cost of flights and moving expenses for our family of four, as well as the cost of renting a place to live in Korea. Despite this, it became possible because President Park, who had risked everything during the company merger, helped us a lot. This was right after the IMF crisis, so President Park was in a desperate situation where he had to quickly finalize the company merger.

Although I did not have prior experience in corporate mergers, President Park believed that I have a superior knowledge of the world's affairs due to my experiences as a police officer and a student studying in Australia. He trusted that I would negotiate well on his behalf. Prior to my involvement, President Park had hired well-known interpreters and lawyers to conduct negotiations, but this may have caused more expenses and did not seem to be to his liking.

First Stock Investment

I decided to return to Korea and pursue more active economic endeavors, putting my theological studies on hold. Initially, I sold most of our household contents in Australia at greatly reduced prices through local garage sales, and only sent over the essential items to

Korea.

Upon my arrival in Korea, I initiated the search for a suitable apartment for my family's residence. However, as my house in Australia was still unsold, I secured a loan from a Korean acquaintance with the mutual understanding that I would reimburse the amount once the house was sold.

After the sale of the Australian property, the funds were transferred to Korea, whereupon a relative advised me and my younger sister to invest our funds in Hansol M.com[52], which was planning to merge at the time.

Heedless of the urgency to repay the loan with the sale proceeds, I rashly invested all my funds in Hansol M.com, with the intention of repaying the loan once the investment had accrued sufficient profit.

However, the stock price of Hansol M.com began to decline even before the merger announcement. When questioned about this, my relative assured me not to worry, explaining that large investors were shaking the stock price to secure shares, and that it should not be sold under any circumstances. Due to this advice, I held onto the falling knife. Eventually the merger announcement came but the stock price briefly soared after the announcement. It could not recover from the previous decline and soon began to fall again.

This was the first time in my life that I had invested in stocks, and unfortunately, it ended up costing me my house. However, thanks to President Park who had invited me to Korea, who paid off my loan as a token of appreciation for my contribution to the negotiations, I was able to avoid the worst-case scenario of being in heavy debt.

---

[52] Korea's former KT-affiliated CDMA mobile communication company that started as Hansol PCS

Invisible Force

When I immigrated back to Korea in 1999, one of my biggest concerns was my children's adjustment to school. I took my older child to H school near our home, worrying that he wouldn't adapt well to Korean school life since he was not familiar with it. At the time, school bullying was a social issue, and I had heard about the problem of corporal punishment in Korean schools through the news before coming to Korea.

Moreover, there were times when my son was teased by white children in his Australian school, calling him "ching chong[53]". When my child, who had poor English skills at the time, asked us what it meant, we were at a loss for an answer. I immediately went to the school and reported the incident to the principal, requesting that all the students be warned to prevent the problem of bullying against our child from escalating any further.

Given the concerns expressed by those around us regarding our children's education when we informed them of our relocation to Korea, I became even more apprehensive about how well my children would adapt to their new school environment.

When we arrived at the school, the principal greeted us warmly at the entrance. I was so relieved and thought to myself,

'Wow, Korean schools have really changed a lot. I should proudly tell the people in Australia how great Korean schools are.'

When I took my child to the school, we both had different concerns.

---

[53] A derogatory term used to mock and stereotype people of East Asian descent.

I was worried that my child might experience exclusion due to bullying, while my older child was concerned about the issue of corporal punishment at school. However, with the warm consideration of the principal, all of our worries were completely alleviated.

My child was assigned to a class with a competent teacher who was expected to consider my child's situation carefully. We went to class 2 of 4th grade, and introduced ourselves to the teacher, explaining that we had just moved from Australia. The homeroom teacher also showed a great interest in my child, which made me feel relieved.

'I think it was a really good decision to have our child educated in Korea,'

I murmured to myself as I walked home leaving my child. Suddenly, someone rushed out of the school office and told me that the principal was looking for me. I thought to myself,

'Maybe they want to know more about the education system in Australia.'

I walked into the principal's office with that thought in mind.

The principal kindly welcomed me and gestured for me to sit on the sofa, asking,

"Do you smoke?"

I replied,

"No, I'm sorry. I don't drink or smoke."

The reason I don't drink or smoke isn't so much due to my devout Christian beliefs, but rather because it doesn't agree with my physical constitution. If alcohol tasted sweet or cigarettes had a pleasing flavor, I probably wouldn't have declined the principal's offer.

"What did you do in Australia?"

The principal asked me personal questions and I casually explained why I came to Korea and what I was doing here. However, the principal's questions didn't continue any further. There was a moment of silence and the principal called someone to the office to bring documents for his signature.

After asking me a few formal questions and having me sit down, the principal's behavior of rummaging through documents was quite quite odd to me.

'There must be some urgent approval documents to go through,'

As I gazed out at the empty field of the school, memories of my elementary school days flooded back suddenly.

I vividly remember the faces of teachers in the past who sent me home for not paying the School Membership Fee (later followed by the Nurturing Membership Fee), and their biased treatment towards wealthy students. I wonder what those narrow-minded teachers are doing now. I also recall being punished for not bringing the required materials to art class, such as pastels, due to my family's financial situation.

Although there may not be poverty like in the past, I hope that schoolteachers do not treat disadvantaged students with such insensitivity these days.'

"You may go now,"

A chilly voice broke me out of my reverie of old memories. It seemed like the principal had finished all of his paperwork and was waiting for me to leave. My expectation of being asked about the education system or life in Australia was shattered, and I couldn't help but wonder why he had called me in the first place. As I slowly stood up, I tried to piece together what had happened and came to the conclusion that the principal was probably expecting some sort of material benefit from me.

The awkward atmosphere in the principal's office was indescribable. I felt an invisible force suppressing me, demanding that I quickly hand over the prepared envelope and leave. I couldn't just leave the office once this thought occurred to me.

"Principal, may I ask you something?" I asked.

"Yes," he replied.

"I saw a news story once when I was in Australia that in Korea, parents are supposed to give envelopes to schools to help take care of their children. I was wondering if this school also practices this custom?"

I had expressed my concerns quite directly. The principal replied,

"Our school would never do such a thing."

But when I returned home that day, my heart was heavy. The principal's behavior had given me a bad feeling, and I couldn't shake off the anxiety I had about my child's education. What if the homeroom teacher makes a demand? How should I respond? My worries about the school weighed heavily on my mind.

My son's Graduation from Hwajeong Elementary School Korea

The Purpose of Traffic Enforcement

Traffic enforcement is carried out according to the Road Traffic Act. Article 1 of the Road Traffic Act states that "this Act aims to prevent and eliminate all dangers and obstacles in traffic on roads, and to ensure safe and smooth traffic." Therefore, the legislative purpose of the Road Traffic Act is to promote smooth traffic flow, and the objective of traffic enforcement should be to achieve this purpose. However, in some cases, there have been doubts about the fairness of traffic enforcement in Korea, as it appears to prioritize revenue collection over the principle of equal enforcement.

Dotted and Solid Line

Previously, I had to go to Jangsa-dong in Jongno 3-ga by car. At that time, the bus-only lanes were drawn on both sides of the road, whereas now they are marked in the center line in Seoul. Upon receiving a green light to proceed straight at the intersection of Jongno 3-ga, I started to cross the road. However, as soon as I got onto the road, the car in front of me was stuck in traffic, making it impossible for me to move forward, and cars behind me quickly piled up, one after another. The alleyway I intended to turn right into, leading to Jangsa-dong, was fairly empty. At the dashed line of the bus-only lane, I turned on the right turn signal and entered the bus-only lane.

Surrounded by traffic congestion in front and behind, I thought that 'if just one car could get out of the way, it would help traffic flow much better.' I attempted to turn right into the alley on my right-hand side, but it was also congested. Now, I was blocking the bus-only lane, and the bus behind me was honking impatiently, displaying the typical impatience of Koreans. To let the bus through, I had to go back to the left lane and join the straight traffic lane. However, the left lane was already packed with other cars, making it impossible for me to get in. The only way I could let the bus through was to continue driving on the bus-only lane a little further, then make a right turn at the next alley. In order to clear the way for the bus, I drove up the bus-only lane for about 2-3 meters and turned right into the alley.

Afterwards, upon receiving a notice of violating the bus-only lane a few days later, I realized how foolish my behavior had been. The reason was that between the entrance to the Jangsa-dong alleyway and the next shopping alleyway, the dotted line indicating the bus-only lane was interrupted by a solid line indicating a bus-only area of about 1-2 meters. Therefore, in principle, I should have continued to block the bus-only lane until the left lane was available, briefly entered the left lane to exit this 1-2 meter section, and then re-entered the bus-only lane marked by the dotted line to make a turn. However, at the time, the reality was that both sides of the road were blocked by cars, making it impossible to follow the rule. Therefore, clearing the way for the car by quickly driving along the bus-only lane to the next alleyway was the best option for traffic flow.

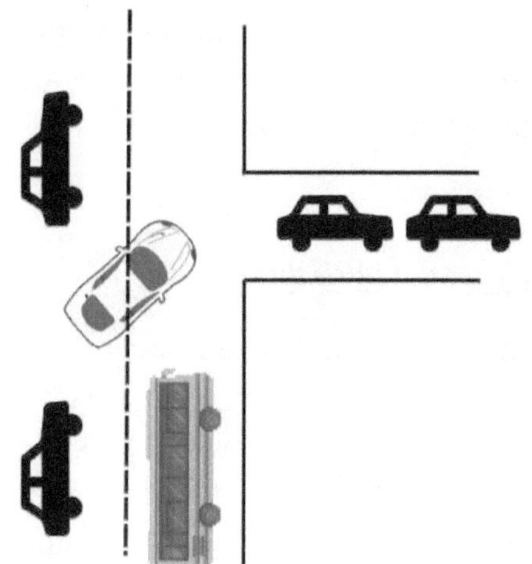

I explained the situation to the responsible person at the

municipal office over the phone, but it was of no use because my situation did not fall under the exceptions specified by law. The exceptions refer to transporting emergency patients or situations requiring urgent evacuation, which did not apply to my case, and that is why even passing the solid line by just one meter constitutes a violation of the bus-only lane. Moreover, if I were to contest the violation, the penalty would likely be even more severe, as there is almost no record of such objections being accepted, with a success rate of less than 1%.

The feeling of being blocked or stuck in something, I developed a habit of carefully observing exclusive lanes in Seoul. When I observed the bus-only lanes in Seoul at that time, I noticed that there were not just one or two places where the dotted lines suddenly changed to solid lines for about 2-3 meters and then changed back to dotted lines. I could also see that all the cameras and enforcement officers for bus-only lane violations were concentrated in these areas.

Enforcement agents or traffic police officers are placed in places where drivers tend to make mistakes for crackdowns, rather than maintaining order to alleviate chronic traffic congestion. In other words, traffic police are deployed to the general public for the purpose of cracking down on traffic violations. Where police or enforcement agents are stationed for the purpose of pure traffic order, they are not functioning except for the President or a high government official or on special occasions.

Crackdown like theft

In 1992, I had urgent business to attend to at my job in Busan. However, the reality of the roads made it challenging to park my car. Despite my reluctance, I parked my car illegally and rushed to the third floor of the building to obtain the necessary documents. It took about ten minutes for me to go up to the third floor and get a document envelope. Hurriedly running out to avoid getting a parking sticker, I couldn't help but feel frustrated. My car had disappeared in just ten minutes. The car was definitely locked, but it seemed like, by any stretch, a car thief had intentionally targeted my car.

I immediately contacted the police station to file a report. During the call, the officer advised me to inspect the area where my car was parked to see if it had been towed by a parking enforcement vehicle. After thoroughly examining the location, I noticed a yellow sticker on the ground indicating that my car had been towed to a Haeundae-gu towing company.

I was astounded by the swift response time of the towing company. The distance between Dong-gu and Haeundae-gu typically takes about an hour by taxi, yet my car had been relocated in a mere ten minutes. The efficiency of the towing process was a remarkable feat of enforcement.

I took a taxi to the towing location in search of my car, but it was not visible there either. I presented the yellow sticker I had found earlier to the individual in charge and explained my intention to retrieve my vehicle. However, the attendant informed me that my car had yet to arrive at the storage facility.

As a result, I had to wait for the tow truck to arrive at the storage area, which seemed to take an unnecessarily long time compared to the speedy crackdown on my car's illegal parking. After waiting for approximately thirty minutes, a blue tow truck finally arrived, transporting my car to the storage facility.

I had to pay a total of approximately 100,000 won, which included fees for illegal parking and towing, to recover my car. Despite finally being reunited with my vehicle, the entire experience left me feeling uneasy and dissatisfied.

Later on, I found out that private towing companies team up with parking enforcement agents to tow as many vehicles as possible, as their revenue depends on it. Even if the parked cars do not significantly disrupt traffic flow, these towing operations are conducted opportunistically, and tow trucks quickly snatch the cars as soon as before drivers show up.

Parking on verge

As an individual residing in Australia, I have experienced receiving parking fines on numerous occasions, possibly due to my inadequate parking habits. On 26 January 2004, a significant public holiday commemorating Australia Day, I drove to Cottesloe Beach with my family. As Australia's weather is the opposite of Korea's, I distinctly recall that the weather in January of that year was exceptionally hot. As it was a public holiday, all official parking lots in the vicinity of the beach were full to capacity with parked vehicles. While searching for an alternative parking spot, I noticed several cars parked with one wheel on the road and the other on the grass verge in front of a nearby house. I proceeded to park my car adjacent to these vehicles. However, after parking, I noticed a sign which read "No Parking on verge." This indicated that parking was not permitted on the edge of the road. Therefore, I carefully maneuvered my vehicle deeper into the grass and parked it there.

When I returned to my car later, I found a $100 parking ticket stuck to it. At the time, I was a law student and didn't have much extra money, so the fine was a significant amount for me. It was particularly frustrating to receive the ticket on an Australian national holiday.

I decided to write a letter of appeal to the issuing authority, highlighting the literal meaning of "No Parking on the verge," my current status as a student with no income and a parent of a boy and a girl, and the fact that many cars had illegally parked on the road during the Australian national holiday event.

Upon receiving my letter, the responsible person at the authority deemed it reasonable and notified me that the parking ticket they had issued would be invalidated. As a result, I was able to save $100. Would this have been possible if it had been in Korea?

According to an article in the Hankyoreh newspaper on December 15, 2009, some district councilors in Seoul were exempted from illegal parking fines up to a maximum of 22 times a year under the guise of legislative activities. Similar to myself, councilors who were fined also submitted statements expressing their opinions, but ironically, their statements were accepted 100% of the time for all 22 cases, while my statement, submitted to the same district office in Korea, was never accepted because it did not meet the legal definition of an emergency situation. Could it be said that the words "if you feel unjust, strive for success[54]" originates from here?

There are many stories about my experiences related to parking stickers. One memorable experience happened on the campus of Curtin University in 1990. I received a parking violation sticker for parking a student car in a visitor parking lot. It was shocking to receive a $30 violation ticket, a significant amount of money for a foreign student who was already struggling financially. I was certain that the car was not parked intentionally in the visitor parking lot but mistakenly, as the sign indicating visitor parking was not visible due to overgrown leaves. I went back to the parking area and drew a map showing that the sign was not visible from the direction the car had entered. I explained that there were no other signs indicating visitor parking and that there was no time to look for one as there was an urgent matter to attend to at the university administration office. Fortunately, the university accepted my explanation and withdrew the parking sticker issued. If this had happened in Korea, I would have had to pay a fine without any leniency, as strict enforcement of the law is customary in such cases.

---

[54] A Korean idiomatic expression equivalent to "Don't get mad, get even!"

Honesty = loss?

While Korea presents itself as a country that upholds the law and principles, in reality, there are many instances of illegal activity taking place. Customs law violations are one such example. When I worked as a detective at an airport in the past, working at the airport was known among police officers as a highly lucrative position, and jokes were made that if someone couldn't buy a house after a few years, they were considered incompetent. Of course, this was a corrupt situation of the past, and it's likely that many improvements have been made since then. However, I wish to look back on these old stories.

People who purchase a lot of goods overseas and enter the country contact the relevant official before entering the country to inform them of their date and time of entry. The official then volunteers to work at the customs entry checkpoint at that day and time. When the person enters the country, they find the official they know working at the checkpoint from afar and receive customs inspection. Since they already have an agreement with each other, the official just do a superficial check on the top of the luggage, without bothering to check the lower layers, assuming that there is nothing much to be concerned about, and quickly finish the inspection.

Afterward, there is a second transaction between these two individuals. The official convinces the person who passed customs duty-free, saying,

"You will actually have to pay this much in taxes, so you should give me half of it."

The person who passed customs duty-free then negotiates with the logic,

"Isn't this the government's money?"

Although there are now many efforts to prevent corruption, such as designating inspection booths at the customs checkpoint, when I recall the past era, it seems like a truly lawless place. One of the reasons I decided to study in Australia was that I was disgusted by such a situation that I could not help but witness.

When traveling between Korea and Australia, I mainly bring Korean cuisine when going from Korea to Australia. Australia is a country with very strict regulations on food imports, and heavy fines are imposed if violated. However, if a person declares the food honestly, they may be allowed to bring in a small amount for family consumption if it is not a strictly prohibited food item. I always declare the Korean food I bring to Australia honestly and humbly, and sometimes receives compliments from the Australian officials for doing so.

Many Korean expatriates visiting Korea from Australia often bring with them Australia's specialty, royal jelly honey, and even things like dried abalone, beef, and oranges to Korea. At that time, Korean oranges were considered to be rare and expensive, so I bought about $10 worth of Australian oranges to introduce the taste of them to my parents. I arrived at Gimpo Airport with a bag of about ten oranges, when the quarantine announcement was broadcasting that those who brought in agricultural products should report to the quarantine office. Following the announcement I went to the quarantine office with the orange bag to report it. I thought that the oranges would pass through because they were fresh and in good condition and a small amount, but the officer in charge told me to leave the oranges behind.

"My oranges are not in large quantity and we will eat them with family immediately"

"Oranges are not allowed to be imported."

"But I have seen many other Korean expatriates bringing oranges and beef to Korea?"

"They probably didn't declare them at the quarantine office. Since you have already declared them, there's nothing we can do. If we let them pass, we would be derelict in our duties."

The words of the official in charge were, in essence, that once something has been declared, even if they wanted to turn a blind eye, they couldn't. It was a logical conclusion that it would have been better not to declare anything at all. It was a feeling of frustration.

My acquaintance also honestly declared various items on the customs declaration form, even including chocolates and snacks. However, the customs officer returned the form and asked them to exclude chocolates and snacks from the list. The customs officer's words were that, according to regulations, declared food items should be confiscated, so it would be more convenient for both parties if minor food items such as snacks were not declared on the form. This was a measure taken by Korean customs officers who work under inflexible rules and regulations that require declared items to be processed, to ensure flexible handling of their duties.

In Korea, there are too many cases where following the law results in losses, while ignoring it leads to gains. I believe that those who honestly declare the contents should receive significant benefits and those who enter without reporting should be subjected to heavy tariffs or penalties. Therefore, it is necessary to create "a society where honest people can live well[55]", not just in words but also through institutional measures.

---

[55] This is the propaganda that the Korean government historically convinced the people

Australian and Korean Doctors

Until a few decades ago, I thought that Australian doctors were the kindest in the world. That was because every time I went to an Australian doctor, they would kindly explain medical knowledge and I could always learn something new. When I asked about the contents of the prescription or questions about pharmacological effects or related medical knowledge, Australian doctors were pleased that the patient showed an interest and kindly explained it.

However, it seems that there has been a shortage of Australian doctors in recent years, as many doctors from Africa, Bangladesh, India, Bhutan, Sri Lanka, Burma, and other countries are now seen practicing in Australia. Of course, I do not want to discriminate based on race, but I want to share an anecdote with a young African doctor who replaced the Chinese home doctor that I often visited, and I will now share that story.

African Doctor

If you take a comprehensive blood test, they usually print out the results for you.   However, on this day, the African doctor said that due to recent change of the government policy, if I want my blood test results printed, I have to pay $20 (approximately 16,000 won).   So, I had no choice but to take a picture of the results on my phone screen. Even though $20 might not seem like a lot, I felt like it was a waste to spend money on something like this.

When I got home, I called the Department of Health to ask if there was a policy to charge patients $20 for printed blood test results. They told me there was no such policy and that there are regulations in place to prevent doctors from charging excessive fees for printing test results. They said that if a doctor wants to charge for printing the results, they can only charge for the cost of the paper and ink, which would be around 10 or 20 cents per A4 sheet.

So when I met with this doctor next time and told him about the result of my inquiry to the Department of Health, he denied ever saying that and claimed that it was their hospital's policy to charge $20, which was an excessive fee, for printing the test results. I told him that charging 10 or 20 cents per page would be a reasonable cost, but he responded by saying,

"I don't want to see you from next time."

So I said "OK" and switched to a home doctor to Cannington Medical Center, where I currently go, who is a Sri Lankan doctor. I hoped that my medical records from the hospital I used to go to would be transferred to Cannington Medical Center by signing a request form to claim the transfer of my medical records. However, the African doctor reported to Cannington Medical Center that there were no medical records left.

Upon hearing this, I contacted the Department of Health again to explain the situation. The doctor said that they have a legal obligation to keep my medical records and asked if I wanted to file a formal complaint. I answered "Yes" and filed a formal complaint.

About two weeks later, they sent me a meager two-page medical record, which only included recent blood test results. Just then, an officer from the Department of Health called me and asked if I had received all my medical records. I replied that I had only received recent two-page blood test results and had not received any medical records for the past ten years.

The officer said she would check again, and when she did, the African doctor explained that he had recently acquired the hospital from the Chinese doctor and that my medical records were only what he had. She also said that in such cases, the African doctor could not be held responsible.

I decided to put an end to this matter and not waste any more time on it. However, it seems that finding the kind and compassionate 면 Australian doctors I once praised has become challenging. Nowadays, when scheduling an appointment with a doctor, I have to specify the consultation length in advance - either a standard consultation of 15 minutes or a special consultation of 30 minutes. As a result, it has become increasingly difficult to have the same level of lengthy and meaningful conversations with doctors like I used to in the past.

Authoritative Korean Doctor

Although it may not be entirely fair to compare the attitudes of Korean doctors from several decades ago to those of Australian doctors today, my experience when I was in Korea led me to believe that Korean doctors were the most unfriendly in the world at that time. After having arrived in Korea for only a short time, I sought medical treatment for his persistent pollen allergy. Similar to when receiving medical treatment from Australian doctors, I asked the Korean doctor about the names and quantities of the medicines written on the prescription they were writing. Unfortunately, the doctor did not respond at all. I asked again, raising their voice slightly, to clarify what the medication was for.

"The medicine is to stop coughing, as you said you are coughing."

"What is the name of the medicine?"

"Well, just take it once and come back in three days if the symptoms persist. Next patient please!"

The doctor completely disregarded me, responding in a tone that suggested, 'How dare you have the audacity to ask for the name of the medication if you already know so much about it?' It was due to the attitude of Korean doctors like this that I tried to avoid going to hospitals in Korea as much as possible.

Nowadays, Korean prescriptions are cleanly printed, and if you search for the medicine name on the internet, you can easily find out what it is. However, at that time, Korean doctors wrote prescriptions in a cryptic handwriting that was impossible to decipher, and they would give the prescription to the nurse to pass on to the patient. So, patients would unknowingly take the medication they were given at the counter without knowing what it was.

A while ago, while visiting and staying in Korea, I felt very heavy and tired, so I visited an internal medicine clinic in Gangnam. Due to a negative preconception I had about Korean doctors, I approached the doctor with a very formal and distant attitude, but the doctor showed me a very friendly and kind demeanor.

The doctor's kindness led me to receive a shot he recommended called 'Beolteog-Injection[56]'. I looked it up on the internet and found that it has a great effect in instantly rejuvenating one's energy when feeling tired. However, after receiving the injection, my heart was pounding all night, and I thought I was going to die.

While my mother was in a Korean nursing hospital, I was saddened to witness the medical staff treating patients as mere revenue generators. However, having experienced the healthcare system myself, I now believe that Korean doctors have become much more empathetic compared to the past. Nevertheless, I can't help but wonder if their kinder demeanor is driven by commercial motives.

Experience at the Emergency Room

This is a personal account from a time when my mother was alive.

---

[56] It is a Korean nickname for the Myers' cocktail, a popular formula among complementary and alternative medicine providers for IV vitamin therapy.

One day, while my brother-in-law was driving and bringing my mother home, because of my brother-in-law's sudden braking, my mother who was sitting in the front passenger seat hit her head severely on the front windshield of the car. Despite feeling dizzy, my mother insisted that she didn't need to go to the hospital and asked me not to worry, taking into consideration her relationship with her in-laws. I felt that it was my responsibility as her child to have my mother see a doctor, even just once. So, as soon as my brother-in-law left, I took her to the emergency room of a major hospital in Busan.

Upon arrival at the hospital, I explained that my mother had hit her head severely on the front windshield while riding in a car. The place of admission then categorized it as a car accident. I thought that perhaps the hospital had classified it as such due to issues with processing medical insurance payments and other related matters.

A young on-duty doctor arrived and examined my mother. The doctor said,

"Since there are no signs of trauma, we need to take a brain scan, so please go to the emergency room and follow the procedure for getting a brain scan done."

When I asked about the cost of the scan, the doctor informed me that it would amount to 500,000 won, equivalent to $600AUD. At that time, this represented two-thirds of my monthly salary, which was a significant sum for me, as I had just returned from living in Australia.

"Is my mother's condition concerning enough to require a brain scan?"

"We cannot know until we take the brain scan."

I felt frustrated. In my opinion, there didn't seem to be much of a problem, and given the recent economic difficulties my family faced due to a fire, I didn't see the need to spend 500,000 won on a brain scan. My mother also agreed that we should just go home. I asked the question again.

"Doctor! The cost of a brain scan of 500,000 won is too much for us to afford right now, so we can't take the scan, but we plan to have the money ready in a few days to take the scan. If we don't take the scan now and there is a problem with my mother's brain, what kind of symptoms can occur? And what is the likelihood of her being in a traumatic state as you see it now?"

"We can't know anything until we take the brain scan."

"If we must take the brain scan, wouldn't it be possible for you to take the scan now and we will bring the money as soon as we have it?"

"I cannot do that. Please try going to another hospital."

"Doctor, if your mother were in this situation, what would you do?"

"..."

In that moment, I became extremely disgusted with the heartless attitude of the doctor.

"Excuse me, isn't this too much? Can't you at least say something before taking a brain scan? Isn't it the doctor's duty to save lives, not to increase hospital revenue by taking brain scans?"

As I shouted, the doctor went inside and the emergency room security stopped me. Still angry, I went to the emergency room reception and demanded a refund, saying that it was unreasonable to pay a registration fee of 5,000 won, equivalent to $6AUD, for just one sentence saying that my mother needed to take a brain scan. Pressured by my insistence, the hospital administration returned the 5,000 won to me without saying a word.

I later found out that getting admitted to a Korean hospital after a traffic accident can result in numerous costly medical tests due to customary procedures. Apparently, for Korean hospitals, traffic accident patients are considered the most likely to pay.

I was worried about my mother's brain being affected by the shock, so I asked a doctor I knew personally if there were any symptoms of brain damage in such cases. He reassured me that unless she had vomited after the shock, I didn't have to worry. The next day, my mother spent the night without any issues and there were no abnormalities in her brain until she passed away. In my opinion, the young doctor was incompetent and lacked the basic spirit of Hippocrates[57]. He should have provided some medical explanation for what to do in such cases when a patient cannot have a brain scan.

Furthermore, one of the advantages of the Australian healthcare system is that once a patient is admitted to the emergency room, doctors carry out all the necessary tests and treatment before asking for payment. Unlike in Korea, there's no need to pay first before undergoing tests or surgery. Also, since most medical expenses are covered by health insurance, patients don't have to bear any costs.

––––––––––

[57] Hippocrates was an ancient Greek physician who is often referred to as the "Father of Western Medicine." He lived in the 5th century BCE and is credited with establishing medicine as a profession distinct from other fields such as philosophy and religion. He is also known for his contributions to medical ethics and his famous oath, the Hippocratic Oath, which is still used today to guide medical professionals in their practice.

A Kind of Social Distrust

A day in 2001, while returning to the parking lot after seeing off an acquaintance at Incheon International Airport, I was approached by a young man in his early thirties. He explained that he was a disabled person residing in Gangwon-do who had lost his wallet on the way to the airport due to his work obligations. He requested my assistance with some cash, assuring me that he would repay me as soon as he returned home.

The young man was neatly dressed and did not appear to be a professional beggar. He walked upright and spoke fluently, which led me to believe that he was not physically handicapped. I therefore inquired further before providing any financial assistance.

"You don't look like a disabled person at first glance."

"Yes, I am a disabled person with slightly lower grades."

He pointed to his car's handicapped symbol sticker on the window. I immediately thought that maybe he was truly a disabled person. I once saw an acquaintance of mine who appeared perfectly healthy but was using a disabled sticker on his car due to sexual impotence.

'I too may lose my wallet and be stranded with nowhere to go...'

I calculated the lowest possible cost for him to get back to Gangwon-do, factoring in the cost of gas and tolls, and gave him 50,000 won, equivalent to $60AUD, in cash from my wallet, along with my business card, asking him to repay me as soon as he arrived home. He expressed his gratitude multiple times, promising to contact me as soon as he arrived in Gangwon-do to repay the loan.

However, there was no contact from the allegedly disabled person that evening. Of course, I had no intention of requesting reimbursement.

In the event that he called me that night and requested my bank account details for a transfer, I had planned to decline and respond with,

"Just forget it. Help others in need when they face similar difficulties."

However, as a day or two passed without any contact, I initially thought,

'Perhaps he is just busy with other matters,'

but later I began to feel uneasy. Although I didn't expect anything in return, when my wife mocked me for lending 50,000 won, NOT 1,000 won, to a complete stranger on the street without any contact information, while I assured her that he was not that kind of person, my once confident demeanor was slowly shattered.

When I shared my experience with the boss in the adjacent office, I was infuriated to hear that in Korea, such fraudulent behavior disguised as begging is rampant, and he advised me to just ignore it and give them a thousand won (equivalent to $1AUD). I thought,

'It's because of people like them that society is full of distrust and those who are really in need cannot receive proper help. If we leave that person as they are, they will commit the same fraud to others, and then they will become even more scammers and victims will increase, further fueling society's distrust,'

I couldn't just sit still after reaching this conclusion, so I immediately filed a criminal complaint, recalling the license plate number of the sedan that the person with a disability sign had pointed to.

About a week after submitting the criminal complaint, I received a call from the police station asking me to come in and give a detailed statement about the incident. Towards the end of my statement, I added a plea to punish such individuals who undermine society's trust.

About a month later, I received a call from a detective at a police station in Gangwon Province.   Despite the suspect's attempt to return the money that day, he claimed to have forgotten my contact information and thus could not contact me. Even though I anticipated such an excuse given his situation at the time, I could not bring myself to trust him.   The reason being, the help he needed was because he had lost his entire wallet and was in a difficult situation. It was hard to accept that he also managed to lose the contact information of the person who helped him. Moreover, if he really did forget my contact information, shouldn't it have been his responsibility to call me directly and apologize instead of the police officer handling the case providing an explanation?

Anyway, the detective in charge of the Gangwon province police station told me that if I gave him my bank account details, he would make him immediately deposit the money. He said as if the suspect was his own relative. I initially didn't intend to receive the money, so I told him that he didn't need to repay me. However, the detective explained to me that if I wanted to avoid punishing the suspect and giving him a chance to avoid it, I had to be compensated for the damages. Reluctantly, I had to give him my bank account details.

The next day, the detective called me to confirm if I received the deposit made by him.

"Have you confirmed that the money has been deposited?"

"I haven't had time to check yet."

"Can you let me know as soon as you confirm the deposit?"

"Yes, I understand."

At the time, I was too busy to even step into the bank and confirm the deposit, and a day had passed without doing so. The next day, the responsible detective called again.

"Have you confirmed the deposit?"

"I'm sorry. I haven't had a chance to check yet, but if he said he made the deposit himself, the money should have been transferred, right?"

"Then, could you give me your fax number so I can send you the deposit receipt to confirm?"

"But wait, why is the other party not contacting me, and why are you being so proactive, Detective?"

The detective seemed taken aback by the question.

"Oh, yes, I'll tell him to call you back," the detective said.

Shortly after, the allegedly disabled person called.

"This is Kim Kisul (pseudonym)," he said.

"Oh, Mr Kim, why didn't you contact me? I was disappointed," I said.

"I'm sorry. Actually, I lost your business card."

"On that day, you lost your wallet, your notebook containing various contact information, and you had difficulties. I can't understand how you lost my business card, too."

". . ."

I wanted to vent my frustration, but if it was true that he lost my business card, I felt like I was being too harsh. So I didn't say anything further and hung up the phone.

Difficulties in Transferring a Car

There have been several changes of government in Korea to date, each one of which has called for streamlining administrative procedures. However, in my experience, there seems to be little difference between the method for transferring vehicle ownership a decade ago and the current system.

I would like to share my experience on this matter. I intended to give my car, which I had been driving in Seoul to my younger brother in Busan. In order to transfer the ownership of the car, I inquired about the process at the vehicle registration office. They informed me that I needed a certificate of transfer of ownership, a certificate of the car owner's seal, a copy of the owner's resident registration, and a recent receipt of the vehicle tax payment.

"How should I fill in the vehicle sales price section since I am giving the car to my younger brother as a gift? Can I just write 0 KRW?"

"Since you cannot prove that it is a gift transfer, please enter the minimum price of 100,000 KRW."

"But we are siblings, and it should be considered a gift transfer."

"Still, since it is difficult to prove, just write 100,000 KRW."

To be truthful, I invested more than 200,000 won from my own pocket to extensively fix up the car, as I intended to gift it to my younger brother. In addition, I also provided him with funds for gasoline and other expenditures at the time of handover. Nevertheless, on the official transfer document, it was inaccurately indicated that I sold the car for a mere 100,000 won and transferred its ownership.

My brother in Busan, who went to the district office to apply for a transfer of ownership with the various documents I provided, called me on my cell phone and said,

"Brother! They said I need a certificate of full payment of automobile tax. They won't accept the car tax payment receipt you gave me."

At that moment, I felt extremely frustrated. I had followed all the guidelines provided by the vehicle registration office, yet the government representative in Busan was making irrational requests. Obtaining the certificate of full payment of automobile tax again would necessitate a visit to the corresponding office in Seoul, and the amount of time and effort I had already expended in sending it to my brother in Busan was indescribable.

"Sangyong! Explain the geographical situation of Seoul and Busan to the person in charge, and tell them that the staff at the vehicle registration office in Seoul said that a receipt of automobile tax payment is sufficient. If they insist on a certificate of full payment for the vehicle, make them understand that it would cause significant delays."

From the lack of any news after that point, it appears that the government official in charge of my younger sibling's situation may have understood our circumstances. If that is the case, then it can be considered a matter that the official could have accepted at their discretion.

even if there isn't a specific incident, we as ordinary citizens in Korea who feel powerless, can't help but think that we're very pitiful. Perhaps we're living with a false sense of pride, based on an education that simply tells us to be proud Koreans without truly understanding the concept of warm national welfare, convenient administration, or protecting citizens' rights. Sometimes I feel that there is not much difference between the blind faith of North Korean residents in the leadership of Kim Il-sung as the source of their well-being, and the national pride of South Korean citizens who believe that "South Korea is the most livable country in the world."

Of course, I love South Korea as my motherland. However, I don't really agree with the statement that it is the most livable country. There are often cases where people who have nothing, no power, and no close relatives around them suffer from injustice. Of course, there are many government officials who exercise their discretion conscientiously, but it does not seem like they are exercising that discretion for the powerless and those who have nothing.

By the way, in the World Happiness Report 2022, Australia ranks 12th as the most livable country, while South Korea ranks 51st.   In the 2023 World Happiness Report, it was noted that while Australia maintained its position, South Korea's ranking dropped significantly from 51st to 57th place.   This report evaluates the quality of life by considering various factors such as economy, social support, health, freedom, and generosity. Australia received high scores in various fields such as natural environment, education, health, and social support, while South Korea received high scores in social support, health, and freedom, but relatively low scores in terms of economic factors and satisfaction with quality of life.

To transfer ownership of a car in Western Australia where I live, each person fills out a Notification of Change of Ownership form, which includes the name, address, license number, and previous date and amount of the buyer and seller. They confirm each other's identity with their driver's licenses. Prior to purchasing a vehicle, an internet-based lookup system is available for anyone to easily check whether it's a stolen vehicle or not.   The transfer fee is calculated based on a predetermined rate chart according to the selling price of the car, making it a very straightforward process.   There is no need to provide a certificate of full payment of automobile tax. If vehicle tax is not paid, anyone can know whether it has been paid or not because they cannot receive the vehicle registration certificate, which must be given to the buyer when selling the vehicle. After each person sends their copy of the form to the licensing authority by mail, the transfer process is complete. Unlike in Korea, there is no need to attend a government office and worry about document issues.

Chapter 8 From Entrepreneur to Law Student

Avnet Merger Celebration (Author is at top left)

Founding Director of Avnet Korea Co., Ltd.

President Park, who had invited me to Korea while I was studying theology in Australia, owned businesses in Busan, Seoul, Hong Kong, and the United States. However, the multinational corporation, Avnet Group, informed us that they were only interested in acquiring the businesses located in Seoul and Busan, citing their existing presence in Hong Kong and the United States as a factor in their decision.

The negotiating team from Avnet Group included a lawyer from England, a representative from their Singapore branch, and an accountant and lawyer from their head office in the US. They employed logical reasoning to try and bring down the price, and ultimately, we reached an agreement for a reasonable sum.

This experience afforded me the opportunity to travel to various

With Korean executives after merger (author:far right)

locations, including the United States, Singapore, England, and Hong Kong. After being confined to Australia for several years studying theology, I relished the chance to explore new places while working. I even entertained the idea of pursuing a career that would allow me to earn a living while traveling, but a harrowing plane turbulence accident later caused me to reassess my priorities.

In order to create a company that would be attractive for acquisition by Avnet, President Park enlisted the former president of Motorola Korea, who was well-known in the semiconductor industry, to become the inaugural president of Avnet Korea. This introduction facilitated a positive atmosphere among the negotiating teams.

During the negotiation process, President Park's employees decided to join Avnet Korea, resulting in my natural assumption of the role of the inaugural director of Avnet Korea. Our office was strategically located in close proximity to Exit 4 of Seolleung Station, in a building that provided convenient access to transportation and various amenities.

As commuting proved challenging due to heavy traffic, I devised a solution to arrive at work promptly by waking up early around 6 am, parking my car in the underground parking lot of the company building, and visiting a nearby sauna to bathe and rejuvenate before beginning my workday.

My daily operations consisted of morning meetings with employees to discuss strategic initiatives, followed by meetings with key stakeholders and communication with Avnet's headquarters located in Singapore and the United States. As my workload became more manageable, I embarked on the project of converting software that I had previously developed into a Windows-compatible version, which proved to be a worthwhile endeavor.

At the time, the venture boom was taking off in Korea, and starting a venture business had become a kind of trend that everyone was jumping on. It was during this time that President Park suggested that I try my hand at a venture business.

"You need to try running a business in order to have a vision in life. That's where opportunities lie," said President Park.

I found his words to be reasonable. I had failed to properly blossom a business in the past due to unreliable partners, and I felt that this was a chance to do it right.

"How much funding would we need?" President Park asked.

"Well, it's a software business, so if we consider the cost of office space, package creation, advertising, personnel expenses, etc., I think we could start with around 300 million won (equivalent to $380,000AUD)," I replied.

"I'll provide that kind of money. Go ahead and dream big," he added.

The investment of 300 million won received from President Park was a way to receive it legally without tax as compensation for the successful merger.

With that, I resigned from my position at Avnet Korea and began my venture journey.

Origin of the Double Ledger

In 2000, with a capital of 300 million won, I started a venture business. First, I obtained an office and registered my business before starting to develop the necessary products at home. I wanted to save expenses as much as possible. So, I purchased equipment such as computers for product development with the expected capital, and spent about 20 million won from the capital on necessary expenses. For me, this expenditure was the actual cost spent on preparing for the business.

Now that the product development was complete, I needed to establish a corporation with the office's capital.   However, to do so, I was told that I had to deposit the actual 300 million won capital in the bank. Since I had already spent about 20 million won (equivalent to $25,000AUD), I decided to deposit only 280 million won and treat the 20 million won as start-up preparation costs. But it was not easy to do so under the current registration law.

Therefore, rather than going through difficult and complicated procedures, it was suggested that a reasonable loophole should be used. In other words, even though I had already spent 20 million won, in order to match the 300 million won capital, I had to create false accounting records as if expenses were incurred from the moment the corporate registration was established. This is how the practice of double ledger in Korea began, and it was strictly required that it be done in a legal and legitimate manner. However, the experts around me didn't seem to understand my explanation that we needed to establish the corporation based on reality, and they seemed to brush off my concerns by saying that there had been no issues so far and I was being overly sensitive. It felt like I was seeing the reality full of contradictions where people argue for doing things legally and by the rules, while in reality, things don't always work that way.

It may be difficult to do things legally and properly, but the commercial law offers a loophole that allows for false representation. Let's take a closer look at the issue of establishing a corporation. Even for someone who doesn't have actual capital, establishing a corporation with several hundred million won of capital is a piece of cake. That is, by paying only the interest on the amount deposited in the bank as capital for a few days, through a lawyer, it is possible to establish a fraudulent corporation with thousands of millions of won in capital without actual capital.

In an effort to obtain more detailed information on incorporating a corporation, I made several phone calls to government agencies such as the Seodaemun District Office or the Jungu District Office, but the lines were always busy or no one picked up even when the call went through.

After many twists and turns, I finally managed to establish the corporation, but I couldn't find any government agency that could provide me with detailed information on business registration or corporate accounting. When I called the local government or tax office, they just told me to ask an accountant or a lawyer.

The system itself is also problematic. I was told that expenses can only be recognized if paid by credit card, so I tried to pay for expenses with my personal credit card. However, my accountant advised me that since July 2000, only corporate credit cards are accepted. I went to several banks to apply for a corporate credit card, but it was not easy to obtain one for a newly established corporation. In most cases, a corporation must be in operation for at least six months before being eligible for a credit card. It's a paradox. The bank refused to issue a credit card, while the tax office only recognized payments made with a corporate credit card.

I contacted the responsible tax office to inquire about obtaining a corporate credit card, explaining that I had not been able to get one. I asked if they could accept personal credit card usage or guide me on getting a corporate credit card from a bank. The person in charge said they would respond promptly after I provided my phone number, but even after two days had passed, they didn't contact me. So, I called the tax office again and spoke to another person as the first one was unavailable. He informed me that until the end of 2000, even corporations were allowed to use personal credit card receipts as tax-deductible expenses.

Publicly, from July 2000, corporate usage of personal credit cards was announced to be not allowed. However, individual exceptions were made until the end of the year, making the situation ambiguous. This is typical of Korean bureaucracy, which often leads to a legal grey area.

Returning to the topic of double ledger, a senior executive from a well-established company who had been in charge for a long time gave me some advice. He said that when operating a corporation in Korea, it's crucial to avoid a deficit at all costs. Reporting a deficit or a significant decrease in sales compared to the previous year will inevitably lead to a tax audit, with no way to escape unscathed. Therefore, companies must report that their sales are increasing every year. To achieve this, they should not report their actual sales at the outset but slightly overestimate them. This way, even if sales do decrease slightly in the following year, the tax office report will always show a slight increase.

Double ledger is an essential aspect of this system, but strictly adhering to this principle often leads to various inconveniences. Unfortunately, in Korean society, people who endure these inconveniences to maintain their integrity are not respected but often treated as troublemakers.

If one company reports its purchases and sales accurately, other related companies are also obligated to do so. However, in a kind and loyal Korean society, a company that is the only one being honest about its purchases and sales might be ostracized and face difficulties. If a company becomes ostracized in business transactions, it becomes challenging for it to survive.

Therefore, the importance of double ledger is becoming increasingly apparent.

Real Estate Bubble

I searched around everywhere to find an office. The buildings that were clean and appealing were too expensive, and the ones that were affordable were dirty and unappealing.

"Do you know of any office spaces available for rent?" I asked.

"Yes, how many pyeong[58] are you looking for?" the person on the other end of the line asked.

"I'm not sure, but I think around 30 pyeong would be good."

"We don't have any spaces that size available."

As he was about to hang up, I urgently asked,

"Excuse me, can you hear me?"

"Yes, I can hear you."

"Then, what sizes are available for rent?"

"We have spaces that are 22 and 25 pyeong."

I was frustrated that I didn't know the exact size of the office space available for rent on the other side.   From then on, I had to change the way I asked for information.

"Is there any office space available for rent there?"

"Yes, how many pyeong are you looking for?"

"Somewhere between 20 and 40 pyeong would be great."

---

[58] 1 pyeong (one pyeong) is 3.3 square meters

"Oh, really? We have a 33 pyeong space."

"What's the net size of the space?"

"It's probably around 28 pyeong."

In Korea, it's important to confirm the net size of the space because there can be a significant difference between the net size and the advertised size. Since the net size of the 33 pyeong space was close to 28 pyeong, I visited the building management office to make a contract after putting down a deposit and preparing the money for the contract fee, which was due within two or three days.

The day before signing the contract, I brought a tape measure to the office to measure the space for placing my desk and bookshelf. However, when I measured the net size of the office, it was only 22 pyeong instead of the advertised 28 pyeong. It was a big mistake, too big to ignore.

"Excuse me, the net size of the office seems to be very different from the stated size."

"I don't know. Please inquire with the building management office tomorrow."

I left because the security guard stated that it was not his concern.

The next day, the manager of the building called.

"Are you Mr Yoon?"

"Yes, who is this?"

"This is Y Building."

"Yes, go on?"

"I heard that you came to measure the office yesterday?"

"Yes"

"How was it?"

"You said it was around 28 pyeong, but when I checked it myself, it was much smaller than 28 pyeong."

"How much was it?"

"It was about 22 pyeong. This is too big of a difference, so there is a problem."

"On the day of the contract, did you personally visit the office to check it out?"

"Yes, I estimated the size with my eyes. But when we actually measured it, we found out that it was only 28 pyeong, which is a big difference. With such a difference, we could enter a much better building for the same rent. The building next door, Building K, has an elevator and a parking lot, yet the price is the same as here."

"What's the size of the other place?"

"They said it's 30 pyeong, but the net size is only 21 pyeong."

"I see. We will measure the net size and call you back."

Do they lease the property without knowing the net size of the office? That was really a situation where one could click their tongue. A little later, the phone rang again.

"Mr Yoon!", it was the landlord.

"Yes, what's up?"

"We measured and found out it's only 24 pyeong. You said Building K was 21 pyeong? We have three more pyeong here."

I wanted to argue about how the K Building could be compared to their building, but decided to hold back and said,

"We can't just compare the two buildings based on square footage alone. The K Building has elevators and parking spaces, and the surrounding environment is also better. Anyway, it's not true that it is more than 28 pyeong there."

The landlord replied,

"No, I never said that the size is more than 28 pyeong."

I argued back,

"What are you talking about?   My wife also heard you say it."

"Do you have evidence?"

". . ."

There was nothing to say. It was like someone telling lies to lease an office space, but when it came time to actually sign the contract, they asked for proof.   In the end, I was not able to rent the office, and only wasted 400,000 won (equivalent to $500AUD) for registering the corporation at the address.

If a property owner in Australia makes false claims in their advertisements, it can lead to serious consequences. Violating the country's leasing contract law can result in significant penalties for the owner. This is because, prior to leasing the property, owners are required to disclose essential details regarding the lease agreement to tenants in writing, such as the total area and monthly management fees.

When a newly built venture building in Mapo-gu was completed and put up for sale, I thought it might be better to buy one with a loan for the office, rather than leasing it. The building was very well built and looked very attractive to anyone who saw it. The construction was done by a well-known Korean company, S Construction, so everything seemed perfect.

There was a brochure promoting the building in the sales office, and the staff provided helpful guidance. They provided me with a thorough explanation of the building's interior, leaving me with the impression that it was certainly on par with a large corporation. I had a bitter memory of the actual area of a previous office I leased, so I asked about the actual pyeong first.

"It comes out to be about 52%. For a total area of 35 pyeong, the net area becomes about 18 pyeong."

"Is there an exact measurement?"

"Yes, just a moment. For 35 pyeong, it's 17.88 pyeong."

The responsible staff proudly showed their list of actual area by pyeong and compared their price to similar buildings in the area, stating that their building had a much higher efficiency rate than others. Everything seemed well-planned and trustworthy.

"Um, could you lower the price a bit?"

"Are you short on money?"

"Yes."

"I'll check for you."

The staff made several calls to inquire about the price.

"You can get DC for about 100,000 won per pyeong."

"Can't you go any lower?"

"This is already a big discount."

"Okay, I'll think about it and get back to you."

I spent the whole day thinking about how to manage my future finances, and the next day I decided to purchase the office space through pre-sale. When I went to the pre-sale office to sign the contract, the responsible staff introduced me to another staff member with a worried face.

"This is Kim Hyung-wook (alias)."

"Nice to meet you. I'm Soo Yong Yoon."

"You're here to sign the contract, right?"

"Yes."

"To be honest, we haven't received approval yet from the higher-ups to offer you the DC option you requested, so it may take a few more days. I'm sorry."

"Oh no, that's not good. I need the office space urgently."

"We're just employees of the company and don't have any real power. Please wait until this Wednesday, and we will definitely get in touch with you."

"Okay, please make sure to contact me by Wednesday."

However, I waited until Wednesday evening, but there was no news. Since I was in a hurry, I made the first phone call.

"We agreed that you would contact me by Wednesday, but..."

"I'm sorry. We haven't received the payment yet, so we... will definitely contact you by Thursday."

Helpless, I waited until Thursday evening, but there was still no news, and now I became curious about what the other person's intentions were. I even started imagining various possibilities, like whether they were engaged in double dealing. When I called again on Thursday evening, they asked me to wait until Friday. But when Friday came and went without any contact, I called again, and they told me that the DC didn't go through this time. Since it had been two weeks since I started looking for an office space, I had no choice but to purchase it through a pre-sale contract without negotiating the price.

After stamping the pre-sale contract, I left the office and looked at the contract again. It said the office space was 34.39 pyeong, and below it, in parentheses, it said (54.35m2 of exclusive area). It was awkward that some parts were measured in pyeong and others in square meters. I asked the staff member if 54.35 m2 was equivalent to about 18 pyeong. The staff member replied yes and offered to calculate it accurately using a calculator.

The staff member looked bewildered as he examined the calculator's display, and then said in a slightly alarmed tone that it was 16.44 pyeong.   I pointed out that the initial consultation staff had introduced the office as having a usable area of 52% and a net floor area of 17.88 pyeong.   He then said that there was only a difference of 1.44 pyeong and suggested that it was probably just a mistake on the part of the consultation staff member.

It was simply unbelievable that there could be such a discrepancy in the net floor area when the office was worth tens of millions of won. It had previously caused a contract to be cancelled when the net floor area was reduced from 28 pyeong to 22 pyeong. However, I couldn't afford to waste any more time on this office issue, so I calmly communicated my concerns.

After all, it's certain that there's a difference of 1.44 pyeong, so DC should cover the amount equivalent to 1.44 pyeong."

The responsible staff member said with a stern expression, "Didn't we apologize for our mistake? If you're going to say it like that, cancel the contract."

I was stunned. They were so shameless and unscrupulous. It felt like they were saying,

"Why are you making such a big deal out of this small difference?"

To me, it seemed like something much more fundamentally flawed with Korea's real estate system that divides the sale area and net area. This may be the beginning of a real estate bubble. The construction company could inflate the sale area to make more money, even if the net area was just a small percentage of it. It's only people like me, ordinary citizens, who shed tears over the bloated sale area. This, to me, is the real estate bubble.

I hope that we can reform our system to eliminate confusion between sale area and net area, and only use net area. Additionally, the unit of measurement should be mandatory to use both square meters and pyeong. Currently, we are using square meters instead of pyeong, but for those who are used to using pyeong, they still have to convert back to pyeong, which is inconvenient and leaves consumers at a disadvantage.

Claim Against Guarantor

While preparing for the business, the head office of the Small and Medium Enterprise Bank(SME Bank)[59] in Seoul contacted me. They notified me that I was the guarantor for a loan of 100 million won that Mr Lee, the previous business partner, had received from the Korea Technology Finance Corporation before 1994, and I was responsible for repaying that money instead.

If I had to repay 100 million won from the initial capital of 300 million won, I would face a shortage of planned funds, which would lead to disruptions in my business.   So, I visited the SME Bank to find out more about the situation. They argued that since I was the technical guarantor, I had an obligation to repay the money if the previous partner, Mr Lee, did not.

When I asked to meet with the responsible persons who initially explained to me about my obligation, they told me that they had all retired or quit and were no longer there. When Mr Lee, the previous partner, had applied for the loan of 100 million won and asked them about the obligations and responsibilities of a technical guarantor, they had advised me that the worst-case scenario was that only my software could be taken away, which was incorrect.

Eventually, I had no choice but to repay the entire 100 million won by myself. They told me that if I couldn't repay the money in a lump sum, I could repay it in installments every month, and we reached an agreement on that.

---

[59] SME Bank was the original lender for the Korea Technology Finance Corporation

I faithfully paid the agreed installments every month. Then one day in 2003, I received a lawsuit for debt confirmation from the Seoul Central District Court. The SME bank told me not to attend the court hearing since they were just confirming the deadline for the debt, which was ten years and that they were extending the deadline. However, I could no longer trust their words, so I decided to attend the hearing on the day of the trial. The judge was surprised to see me standing up when he called out the case number and spoke to me in bewilderment.

"What is your name?", the judge asked.

"I am Soo Yong Yoon, the technical guarantor for that case."

"Oh, I see. You guaranteed it, right?"

"Yes, but there is a dispute because the guarantee conditions explained by the bank officials at the time were incorrect."

"What is the problem?"

"At the time, the officials said that the technical guarantor would only be liable for the worst-case scenario of losing software copyright, but it is unfair that they now want all guarantors to pay. Additionally, those officials also received a significant amount of money from the applicant, the former CEO, under the condition of a 100 million won loan. I was just a software developer who was used by them."

"I understand."

When I refuted in court like this, the SME Bank voluntarily withdrew their application from the debt confirmation lawsuit, omitting the my name. As a result, I was able to legally escape from the bank's debt.

Venture Registration and Startup

As the need to begin my business as soon as possible was paramount, I ultimately decided to proceed with the contract, despite a discrepancy of 1.44 pyeong in the net floor area. This decision was made to provide peace of mind to President Park, who had invested in our venture. Failing to do so may have resulted in wasted time and resources spent searching for an alternative office space.

To secure early occupancy, the sellers required an upfront payment of 50% of the purchase price. In order to expedite the move-in process, I agreed to this condition and made the payment accordingly.

"Regarding the VAT receipts, can we issue them all at once upon settling the remaining balance?"

"Indeed, as I was in the process of obtaining venture approval, it would be more convenient for me to receive the receipts in that manner."

Upon moving in, I was faced with numerous tasks, including the procurement of desks and chairs that would fit the office space, as well as conducting thorough resume reviews and interviews to facilitate the recruitment of new employees.

To obtain venture approval, I had to register the software I developed. During the upgrade from a DOS[60]-based "Forner" program to a Windows-based software of which all functionalities were improved.

---

[60] A DOS, or disk operating system, is an operating system that runs from a disk drive

The program's name was changed to "EBED" meaning "servant" in Hebrew, symbolizing my software's faithfulness to serve humanity.

After acquiring the software registration certificate, I applied for venture company approval. Attempting to accomplish all of these tasks within a brief period was overwhelming for me. Finally, the day came when the venture assessment team arrived at my office. By that time, the office desk, sofa, and furniture had all been purchased, and several employees had been recruited, giving the company a professional appearance.

The assessment team consisted of professors from a prestigious university and government officials. I demonstrated the program I had developed and presented my business plan. One of the professors, impressed by the idea of a "software that makes software," gave me a business card and expressed his desire for my success.

Venture Business Certificate

And some time later, my company, ASoTech Co., Ltd., was registered as a venture business and became eligible for various tax deductions and benefits. With the completion of the venture registration, the company designed various materials such as boxes, leaflets, and advertisements to showcase their software products.

In the midst of this, Mr Lee, the former distributor of my previous software product, "Forner," visited me. He said that he's been in hiding since he couldn't pay back the 100 million won he borrowed from SME Bank, and he wanted to use the nationwide distribution rights of the new "EBED" software that I recently launched as an opportunity to start over if I would give it to him. While I sympathized with his situation, I did not want to get entangled in debt and credit relationships once again, so I firmly refused his request.

"Mr Lee, I understand your circumstances, but it doesn't make sense to give you nationwide distribution rights after I have already prepared everything. If you want to do business again, I can give you the distribution rights for a single region, and you can try managing it."

Mr Lee was angered by my words. He had given me 5 million won per month as software royalties in the past, albeit for a short period of time, and therefore he thought that he was entitled to the nationwide distribution rights for my new software. However, I had also suffered as Mr Lee's guarantor and had paid off a significant portion of his loan of 100 million won, so I didn't feel like I owed him anything. I couldn't understand why he was getting angry with me.

A leaflet for EBED

Later, when I became a lawyer and met Mr Lee again in Seoul, I found that Mr Lee was still living in hiding as an air conditioner installer. It was a sad sight to see the once-successful businessman, who had fallen so quickly and couldn't make a comeback.

Issue of VAT Refund

I bought an officetel in Gongdeok-dong, Mapo-gu, which was constructed by S Group, to start a venture business. Although the construction company was S Group, another company was in charge of management. As my company was a venture company, I could receive a 100% refund of the value-added tax, so I paid the down payment and requested a VAT receipt.

"Shouldn't the VAT receipt be issued after paying the balance? We are currently receiving the down payment directly from you because we have not received the remaining construction cost from the contractor, so we will have the contractor issue the VAT receipt when you pay the full amount."

As it was not urgent and there were still a few months left until the balance was due, I agreed without much hesitation.

After a few months, I paid the balance and moved in, but even after the VAT reporting period had passed, I did not receive the VAT receipt. I went to the management office of the contractor because the builder had received all the remaining payments from the contractor and already withdrawn their office. The person in charge said that they had already issued the VAT receipt. When I asked when it was issued, they replied that when the down payment was made several months ago, they had sent the receipt to the address indicated on the sales contract, and that they had already completed the VAT reporting for the previous quarter.

During signing the contract, the contracting officer requested that I provide the address of the corporation for them to issue a receipt. In response, I explained that the corporation was a new entity and had not yet established a corporate address. The contracting officer suggested that any address could be used for the receipt, as it was not the actual address to be utilized.

Consequently, I provided the address that had previously been associated with a failed contract due to an issue with the floor area when I assumed that the address would be used as the registered address of the corporation, in case a lease contract was signed in the future.

While providing the address, I also requested that any future correspondence be sent to the unit I had purchased since no one was able to receive the correspondence at the address written on the receipt. Regrettably, the contract manager failed to notify their colleague in charge of the agreement and issued the value-added tax invoice with the address provided on the receipt.

I immediately contacted my tax accountant and asked him to notify the tax office about the issue so that I could receive a refund of the value-added tax. As my business was registered as a venture enterprise, I was eligible for a 100% refund of the VAT, which amounted to a significant sum of approximately ten million won (equivalent to $12,000AUD"). The tax accountant said that he knew someone at the tax office and would try to negotiate with him directly.

After attending the tax office, the tax accountant returned and said that it would be difficult to receive a VAT refund unless the construction company issues a new tax invoice as the construction company had already processed the VAT in accordance with the regulations. Even if I were to obtain a new VAT receipt, there would still be a fine due to the late declaration of the VAT, and this fine would be almost equivalent to the amount of the VAT refund.

At that time, the only option for my company was to sue the construction company for breach of contract and seek damages. However, the construction company representative was dismissive and asked when they had made such a promise and this made it uncertain that there would be any guarantee of success in a lawsuit without any evidence.

At the time, I did not want to be overly rigid and stick to the law in order to adapt to the flexible Korean society. I had believed the verbal promise that I would receive a VAT receipt after paying the balance. It was the worst experience that could happen in Korea's tax system, where VAT receipts must match the sales exactly. Due to this experience, I did not receive any benefit from the VAT refund for real estate acquisition that venture companies are entitled to, and I am still curious as to where the VAT discrepancy went.

Australia also has a value-added tax system called GST (Goods and Services Tax) like Korea, but unlike Korea, it does not require a unique identifier for purchase and sales transactions to match precisely in terms of date and amount. In Australia, businesses with an annual turnover of less than AUD 2 million (equivalent to KRW 16 billion won) are classified as small businesses and can choose to report their GST statements, called Business Activity Statements (BAS), monthly, quarterly, or annually. Even if purchase and sales records do not match, most businesses still conscientiously report their taxes.

Tax evasion is one of the biggest crimes in Australia, so if one is caught evading taxes, regardless of age or gender, they will face harsh penalties. If I had been in Australia, the tax authority would have been required to refund the GST. Since I did not receive a GST receipt and the issuing company has already issued a tax invoice, which has not been used for the GST refund application, it would not be a significant problem for them to simply reissue the tax invoice.

Masters Tower in Dohwa-dong, Mapo-gu

It appears that content is more important than form in Australia whereas form is more important than content in Korea.

In this regard, while Koreans are personally warm and friendly, they have a much colder and more impersonal system than Australia. Many Korean systems are designed to be as meticulous and error-free as possible, for fear of abuse, but as the tax filing deadline approaches, many businesses resort to buying and selling fake GST receipts to fill in gaps in their purchase and sales records, which is a problem. As the saying goes, "there is no limit to those above us"

Hospital Abuse

As an individual, I hold a less favorable view of medical practitioners in Korea. While I apologize to the majority of ethical and conscientious doctors, I have had unpleasant encounters with a significant portion of physicians in Korea, who have been unethical and discourteous.

During my tenure in the software industry in Korea, I developed an itchy rash on my knee and visited a nearby hospital, H Hospital. When I stated my reason for the visit, the hospital strangely directed me to the Department of Family Medicine. With my outpatient registration card in hand, I proceeded to the designated department, where I found a small box at the entrance with a sign that read, "Please insert your registration card here and wait to be called for your appointment."

After waiting for over 30 minutes, I heard a voice call out my name, "Mr Soo Yong YOON, please come in." I entered the examination room and was greeted by a middle-aged doctor who stood tall and was in good physical shape. He had a slim physique and appeared to take good care of his body. He asked me,

"What seems to be the problem today?"

to which I replied,

"I have developed a rash on my knee, which is quite itchy."

"Could you tell me how long it has been bothering you?"

"It's been about a week, but I've had a similar rash before. I have a strong allergy tendency, so I'm not sure if it's an allergic reaction."

"Okay, I understand. Please wait outside for a moment."

After waiting outside for a little while, a nurse called out to me again.

"Mr Yoon, please take this and go to the billing department to pay and get tested. Please come back tomorrow."

"What kind of test am I getting?"

"We're going to do a simple blood test."

Without being provided with detailed information in English, the nurse at the clinic presented the patient with a document. I was asked to pay a personal contribution of 28,000 won (equivalent to $35AUD) which was said to be the amount after applying the medical insurance. Upon payment, the nurse gave me several pieces of what appeared to be Test Request Forms and instructed me to go to the clinical pathology department. Once there, I was asked to extend my arm, and the nurse used a syringe to collect a blood sample. After the blood was collected, as I was about to leave, the nurse suggested that since the blood sample had been taken incorrectly, she might have to take another sample, which made me feel very uncomfortable as I hated receiving injections.

"I've already had a significant amount of blood drawn. Can't we divide the sample and test it separately?"

"I'm sorry, but there is a specific amount of sample required for the test..."

Reluctantly, I received another injection and went to the next room. When asked to pull down my pants all of a sudden, I asked what kind of injection it was for. The nurse only said it was an antibiotic injection. I came to the hospital due to a skin rash that resembled eczema and itchy symptoms, so I didn't understand why I had to receive an antibiotic injection. When I asked about it, the nurse told me to ask the doctor and that they would only administer injections according to the prescription. I ended up receiving a total of four injections, including a muscle injection. When I left, they told me to come back the next morning after fasting, without giving me any detailed explanation. I had no choice but to pay the amount requested, receive the injections as instructed, and leave without knowing much about what was happening.

In the afternoon at around 3 o'clock, I went to the hospital and was given a test result sheet filled with various test values and was told to go to the Family Medicine department on the third floor. After waiting for about 40 minutes at the Family Medicine department, my name was finally called and I was taken inside.

"Mr Soo Yong Yoon, there is no problem with your liver function and everything looks normal. Your blood sugar is slightly high, but it seems normal as it hasn't been long since you ate."

I came to the hospital because of the itching on my knee, but I don't know what liver function and blood sugar have to do with it. Despite not knowing anything, I paid for various injections and tests for two days. I understand that I don't have medical expertise, but I think it's only right for the doctor to at least explain the rationale behind the tests to the patient.

I could have put up with that much. If there are tests necessary for the doctor to accurately diagnose the patient's condition, then they must be conducted. What really angered me, however, was something else entirely.

I endured the two-day ordeal and the inexplicable expenses just to hear the words "there's nothing wrong with the test results." In order to avoid repeating these unexplained tests at another hospital, I requested a copy of the test results to be kept on file, from the hospital's administrative department. But they told me that the test results cannot be disclosed to the public. They insisted that the results are always kept in their own hospital, and if necessary, I should come back to their hospital to access them. They added that hospital records cannot be disclosed to third parties. I was dumbfounded. These were my own medical records and test results, but I couldn't get access to them? Since it was a test result, and not hospital records, it was natural for me to assume that the results should be made known to the person being tested.

When I insisted on getting the test results, they told me to get approval from the doctor in charge. Since I couldn't wait for my turn again for a long time, I went back inside immediately and opened the door. A nurse asked me,

"What's going on?"

"I want the results of the test I just took." I replied,

then she told me to go down to the administrative department, saying that she would contact them for me.

And after waiting for about ten minutes in front of the administrative department, they asked me to pay 9,600 won and gave me a bill. I had already paid 28,000 won for the medical examination fee yesterday, so I wondered what this bill was for. Upon examining the invoice, I found that the patient's co-payment for medical expenses was around 5,600 won (equivalent to $7AUD), and there was a photocopying fee of 4,000 won (equivalent to $5AUD). When I asked what the photocopying fee was for, they said it was for copying the results of the examination. I was filled with anger that I had been tolerating until then.

"Excuse me, isn't it outrageous for doctors to unilaterally perform tests that patients did not request and then charge the patients for the cost of those tests? And is it reasonable to charge patients for photocopying the results of those tests under the guise of a photocopying fee? The government is currently advocating for administrative convenience to be improved in all social organizations, but isn't it wrong for hospitals to charge patients at will without considering their position? I cannot pay the photocopying fee. Although it is not a large sum of money, the amount of 2,000 won charged for a single copy is ridiculous, and charging an additional 4,000 won for photocopying the results of a test for which I have already paid 28,000 won is wrong."

"Our hospital regulations allow for this."

"I am not an employee of this hospital, so I have no reason to follow such regulations, and moreover, such regulations are wrong and should be corrected."

As I was waiting in front of the administrative department, the person in charge of the department appeared and asked,

"What's the matter?"

"I went through all this trouble, but it seems excessive to charge for copying fees." I replied.

"Actually, it includes not only copying fees, but also the cost of the hospital's official seal. Because the hospital is responsible for the documents that leave the hospital, a fee is charged to cover that responsibility."

"I don't need the hospital's official seal, and if copying costs extra, I don't mind writing it by hand. All I need is the test results that I paid for at this hospital."

In reality, even if I have test results with the hospital's official seal and I go to another hospital, in Korea, medical records are not recognized between hospitals, so I would have to undergo all the tests again from the beginning. Therefore, the idea of the hospital taking responsibility for the documents is practically meaningless.

Anyway, after my strong objection, the administrative officer at the hospital refunded the 4,000 won copying fee and provided me with copies of the test results without the hospital's stamp.

Other patients who were watching this scene approached me and said,

"You did well. There are too many things that need to be fixed in this hospital."

Some readers may say, "You could have just paid the small amount of 4,000 won instead of going through all this trouble." I have heard such comments before, but I have my own conviction that 'the more people like me there are, the society will gradually improve,' so occasionally I stick to my stubbornness like this.

The Unfairness of Banking System

In contemporary United States, individuals who infrequently engage in bank transactions may not receive high credit scores. The measure of good credit centers on how much money one has borrowed, and then repaid on time without defaulting. Consequently, some people who do not require banking services will borrow and repay money repeatedly to maintain a high credit score. In other words, to obtain a high credit score and borrow money from a bank, one must first borrow a small amount of money, repay it, and then borrow again while increasing one's credit score.

In contrast, the credit rating system in Korea differs from the aforementioned. According to a bank employee with whom I spoke, while there are various criteria for credit evaluation, one significant factor is the average balance rate, which reveals how much money one has saved in the bank. The assessment does not consider creditworthiness in terms of borrowing and repaying funds, but rather the financial ability to always maintain funds within a bank.

Due to these requirements, obtaining a loan from a bank in Korea can be an absurd experience that requires one to have money to borrow money. In other words, the relationship between having money and being able to borrow money is an illogical paradox when it comes to banks. Of course, I know that nowadays there are systems such as credit loans for employees, but I understand that the amount of money provided is minimal. The concept of a bank is to provide a safe place to store money, but it also serves as a mediator for those in need of financial resources to utilize through borrowing in accordance with their credit rating. However, this function is only applicable to those who are financially capable.

Many people praise Korea as a great place to live, but there is always a caveat that follows: "if you have money...". It seems that having money is a prerequisite to enjoying life in Korea.

Even opening a corporate bank account is not an easy task. Each bank requires different documents, such as a corporate seal certificate, making it necessary to have dozens of these documents if one wants to open multiple bank accounts. When I explained the convenient system in Australia, where one copy of the certificate of incorporation can be enough for the bank to confirm and copy as many as necessary, the bank representative explained that their request for original certificate was not at the discretion of the responsible person but a legal requirement that must be adhered to.

The unreasonable practices of commercial banks do not end here. Once, when my PC banking password did not work, I called the bank and asked for a new password or to be informed of the forgotten password. However, the bank call centre told me to apply for a new PC banking service instead. In Australia, it is possible to find a password over the phone. For example, the bank receptionist can reset the password and inform the customer of the initial password. The customer can then log in using the provided password and change it immediately.

The following episode involves a password.

An elderly lady presented her bankbook to a female teller and requested a withdrawal at a bank counter. When the bank teller asked for the password, the grandmother whispered

"pigeon."

"No, please tell me your password, grandma."

Reluctantly, the grandmother said,

"Coo coo coo coo[61]."

Currently, Korean banks have improved in this area by providing a password input keypad at each teller desk, allowing customers to enter their password without bank tellers knowing. This system is adopted about 10 years later in Korea, an IT advanced country, than Australia. It is regrettable that Korea is imitating other country's systems rather than trying to be ahead of them with their own innovative systems.

---

[61] "Coo" is the same as the pronunciation of the numeric number 9 in Korean.

Bank's Discretion

While running a business as a venture company called ASoTech in Korea, I received a Hong Kong dollar equivalent to KRW 100,000 issued by National Bank in Hong Kong. The top of the check indicated that payment could be claimed from Y Bank in Korea. As the recipient of the check was addressed to me personally, and knowing the principle of "Participantism[62]" in Korea, I took time out of my busy schedule to visit Y Bank with my check, stamp, and ID.

As I arrived at the bank counter, I noticed there were already many people waiting in line. Looking at my ticket number, I saw that there were about thirty people ahead of me. I pulled a magazine from the rack and sat down in a corner, waiting for my turn to be called. After what seemed like a while, I heard my number being announced, and I quickly made my way to the designated counter, presenting my check and requesting to exchange it for Korean won. The bank teller scrutinized the check and then said,

"Foreign currency checks need to be processed by the foreign exchange department."

The bank teller informed me that foreign currency checks require processing by the foreign exchange counter. Despite feeling frustrated and unfairly inconvenienced after waiting for my turn for so long, I understood that the unique nature of foreign exchange operations necessitated a different counter.

Accordingly, I proceeded to the designated counter and resumed waiting for my turn. Once it arrived, I handed over the foreign

---

[62] Participantism here means that the person himself/herself must be present.

currency check to the teller, who proceeded to verify various details through computer and phone systems before requesting that I complete some necessary forms. I provided my personal details, such as my name, address, phone number, and Y Bank account number, along with my identification for verification purposes. The teller copied and attached my ID to the required documents, confirming my identity.

"Sir, you're all set now. Please leave the check with us and return in approximately five days to collect your cash."

"Is it not possible to receive the cash immediately?"

To which the teller replied,

"Due to the foreign nature of the currency, we must request the issuing bank to provide us with cash, which we can then distribute to the customer. It is the issuing bank's responsibility to authenticate the validity of the check and ensure its legitimacy."

"But the check amount is not that significant. Can't you pay me now?"

The teller responded,

"I regret to inform you that such an action would be in violation of banking regulations, and is therefore not permissible."

I found the situation to be incredibly frustrating. When converting the value of the check to Korean won, it amounted to approximately 100,000 won, and even after deducting a commission fee of approximately 5,000 won, the bank's potential loss was not significant. Additionally, I provided my resident registration card for identification purposes, and most importantly, there was more money in my account at Y Bank than the value of the check. Therefore, even in the event that the check bounced, the bank did not have any reason to be concerned about recovering the funds.

Furthermore, what is the function of a bank? Is it not to provide a solution to the temporal and spatial inconvenience of depositing and withdrawing money through the guarantee between banks, even though they are far apart from each other, and to receive a commission in return? Moreover, if a bank in Hong Kong designates Y Bank in Korea as the payee, should not Y Bank in Korea assume the role of the bank in Hong Kong in Korea? Upon considering these points, I came to the conclusion that such inconvenient practices need to be improved.

"Sir, if the regulations are like that, I think the regulations should be improved."

"I don't have the authority to change the regulations."

"Who has the authority?"

"The bank manager has all the authority."

"Then please let me meet the bank manager."

While I was having this kind of conversation, a senior staff member sitting behind the bank counter came out.

"What can I do for you? Oh, aren't you the CEO of ASoTech?"

"Yes, you visited our office a while ago with the branch manager."

"What's going on? This person is the CEO of ASoTech in our jurisdiction."

"..."

"I came all the way here to exchange my Hong Kong check, but despite the fact that it was for a small amount, I was told to come back in five days to receive the money. I have an account with this bank, and the balance is more than enough to cover the amount of the check. Moreover, I presented a valid identification to take full responsibility in case there was an issue with the check. However, I was told that I must come back next time according to the regulations, which was frustrating, so I decided to speak to the bank manager."

I talked about the role of a bank and the practical steps that could be taken to improve customer convenience through the revision of bank regulations.

"You're absolutely right. However, we tend to be a bit conservative, so there are still many areas where we fall short. But what power do we have? In any case, Mr Kim, please pay the money now. I will take responsibility for any issues that arise."

I'm not sure whether the bank processed the check at a higher level for the sake of customer convenience, or whether the bank clerk used an illegal means to cater to the needs of an individual, but both of them seemed to be some problems. I wondered if I would have been able to exchange the check immediately if I hadn't been the CEO of Asoteck. Instead of feeling the joy of being able to exchange the check instantly, I felt only a bitter sense that our society wasn't one where people with power, ability, voice, or status were treated well.

Nevertheless, I would like to express my gratitude to the Y Bank employee who recognized me at the time and provided me with the necessary convenience.

Refusal of Investment and Termination of Merger Agreements

In order to promote my software "EBED", I decided to advertise on the Seoul subway system. I applied for an advertisement on Line 2, which is said to have the highest advertising effect among the circular subways, but there were too many applicants and I had to wait for more than six months.

I therefore decided to advertise on the subway line 3 as there was no other option. In addition, advertisements were also placed in electronic newspapers and other media. Despite spending approximately 10 million won per month on aggressive advertising costs, sales always fell short of the advertising expenses.

At the time, it was said that my software had a great idea that was well

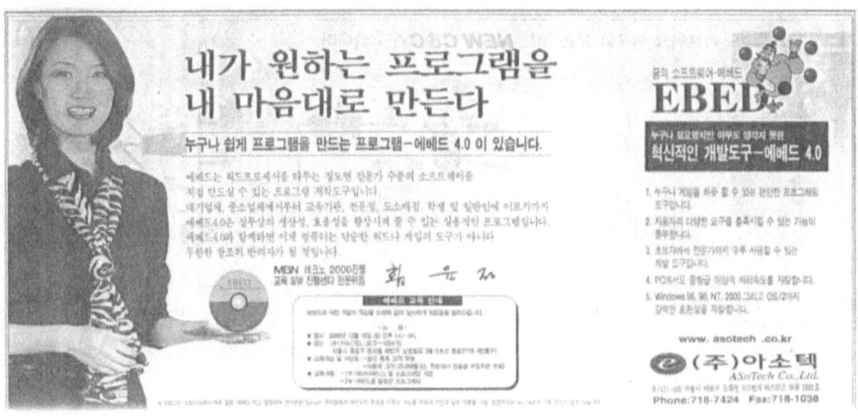

Advertisement on Subway Line 3 in Seoul

recognized externally in terms of functionality, but in terms of design, my design ideas were lacking as they had developed it alone. As all four to five employees were in charge of sales and promotion, the design had to be outsourced.

As things were unfolding, a fund manager from Choheung Securities took note of my business acumen and showed a genuine desire to get involved. To get the business listed on South Korea's KOSDAQ, it was crucial to meet the basic capital requirements and fulfill essential criteria such as technological expertise. The fund manager from Choheung Securities offered to take charge of all these aspects and lend a helping hand.

On the day designated for institutional investors to come in via Choheung Securities, the fund manager requested the company's bank account information. Once the investment funds were received, the plan was to utilize them to recruit more personnel, develop software, and manage the company without any further financial worries, as the Choheung Securities fund manager had agreed to oversee all other relevant matters.

I promptly shared the great news with President Park, who had invested 300 million won in the company.

"President Park, we finally have institutional investors who are willing to invest in our company,"

I reported to him. However, to my surprise, CEO Park declined the offer, stating,

"Upon further consideration, I don't think we need to accept any investment. If we need more funds, I can contribute more myself. I don't want outside investors interfering with our company management for no good reason."

I acknowledged his reasoning and replied,

"I understand. Then I will decline the investment offer and trust only in your support."

Subsequently, I rejected Choheung Securities' investment proposal. Unfortunately, when I later required additional funds, President Park was unable to invest due to unforeseen circumstances, leaving our company in a precarious situation.

In order to run a business, it was necessary to find an investor with strong financial resources, so I searched various places and finally had the opportunity to demonstrate my software in front of the Chairman of the H Group. Filled with high expectations, I spent the night preparing an impressive presentation about my business plan. Finally, on the day of the presentation, I arrived at the H Group's meeting room where the Chairman, executives, and other key members of the group were gathered.

I planned to first explain the future vision of my software business and my company's plans, and then demonstrate the software. However, during the presentation, the Chairman interrupted and expressed that he only wanted to see the software and nothing else, as if saying "Don't waste our time with unnecessary talk, just show us the software!"

Despite feeling disappointed, I had no choice but to comply with the Chairman's request and immediately moved on to the software demonstration.

As I was explaining the software, the Chairman of H Group interrupted and asked,

"Did you develop it?"

Already feeling disheartened, this single question completely crushed my remaining enthusiasm.   Thinking,

'I'm going to be humiliated and probably won't receive any investment after wasting my time explaining. I should at least protect my pride,'.

"Yes, I developed it, and I'm demonstrating it to find investors. If someone else is demonstrating software to receive investment, it's a fraudulent act. How can an investor invest without having faith in the developer? I'll stop here,"

I said before packing up and leaving.

The researchers who attended the event held onto me, expressing their apologies and regret numerous times. Even the Chairman of H Group seemed perplexed by the situation and there were murmurs among them.

Subsequently, while searching for alternative investors, I was able to make contact with Mr Kim, who used to be a distributer in Mokpo area for my old software. He was running a machine control research institute in Mokpo and was keen on expanding to Seoul. Given our company's financial challenges, we agreed to merge the two companies, wherein Mr Kim would operate in Seoul through our company and conduct business there. Meanwhile, I would only have to manage the Mokpo research institute once a week.

As such, the two companies unexpectedly merged, and Mr Kim came to Seoul with some of his employees to work with my team, while I went to the Mokpo research institute to manage his employees.

After several months had passed, one of my employees quietly told me that there was something he needed to say. He said that he found out that Mr Kim, the CEO of the other company, was using my Seoul office to do something else with his own employees, without my knowledge.

I realized that after the merger, Mr Kim had taken the original copy of the merger agreement and said he would give me one copy after having it notarized, but I had not yet received it. So I asked Mr Kim for a copy of the notarized merger agreement. He sent me the original copy of the merger agreement, which had not been notarized and had the part with his company's seal torn off. I immediately called Mr Kim and asked him what was going on.

"I am sorry, big brother!"

He apologized and said that he could not fulfill the merger agreement. Later, I found out that Mr Kim had been using my office as a base to carry out his company's project, and after several months of doing business in Seoul, he had decided that he could do it on his own without the merger.

However, even if that were true, he had used my office and employees, and I had been going to his company's research center in Mokpo once a week, incurring considerable expenses. The damage I suffered was immeasurable. It was also a mistake to trust him and leave my business entirely in his hands.

He was a devout Christian from Mokpo, and at least in terms of his religious conscience, I never thought he could betray me like that. Despite the advice of my acquaintances around me who said, "Don't trust people from Jeolla Province," it was a bitter experience to proceed with the merger.

However, I do not believe that this is a characteristic of people from Jeolla Province. This is because I know many other good people from Jeolla Province who are much better than Mr Kim. Although I returned to his Seoul office and tried to revive his business, the already declined business was in an irreparable state.

Memories With Staff

Many business owners may view their employees as a transactional relationship based solely on financial exchange, where money (in the form of salaries) is exchanged for services rendered. However, my perspective differs significantly. I believe that business management and employees should strive to become a unified family. Adopting a familial approach to employee relations differs substantially from a purely transactional mindset of providing employees with sufficient remuneration.

Unfortunately, I have heard some business owners express frustration when employees leave work before them, feeling as though the money invested in the employees has been wasted. These owners may view their employees as commodities, something that can be bought and sold in a purely economic sense. While it is theoretically correct that one can purchase an employee's services with money, human relationships are far more complex and require a more nuanced approach than simple monetary transactions.

Eccentric Programmer

Following my return to Korea from studying in Australia, I developed and independently marketed software titled "Forner" after parting ways with my previous business partner. During this time, I collaborated with a former employee named Choi Jae-ho, who was an atheist. Our interactions included multiple discussions concerning theism.

I asked him,

"Atheists try to live well in this life because death is the end, right?"

To which he responded,

"Yes, isn't it the same with theists trying to live well in this life?"

I continued,

"You are right, but don't those who say there is no God have no ethical standards?"

He answered,

"Since there is no God and there is no afterlife, I am trying to live a more upright life in order to make this one life worthwhile."

Despite the difficulty I encountered in grasping Choi Jae-ho's argument, his conduct evinced the credibility of his assertions. He had a particular characteristic of "drunken master" drinking alcohol and doing martial arts, claiming that he needed to have a few drinks of soju to get his head clear to write programs. In response, I decided to purchase a significant amount of soju and keep it stocked in the company refrigerator, just for him. This was to ensure that he could drink it whenever he came to work.

In reality, Choi Jae-ho's programming skills were exceptional. At that time, he handled programming languages such as Fortran and Assembly, which were considered difficult, and gave me much assistance.

Of course, I believe that the reason why I was able to make the most of the talent of an eccentric programmer like Choi Jae-ho was because I treated him with a familial mindset and that heart was reciprocated. If I had subscribed to the notion of simply purchasing the services of my employees, I would not have been able to uncover the hidden talents possessed by individuals such as Choi Jae-ho.

Welfare to the Employees

The conversation took a brief detour to the past, but let us now return to the present situation at AsoTech, despite the limited initial capital of the company and the inability to offer high salaries, efforts were made to provide welfare benefits that were on par with those offered by more affluent organizations. As a consequence, the implementation of a five-day workweek, a benefit that was then exclusive to employees of foreign companies, was realized alongside the provision of daily lunches at the workplace.

At the time, Korean society lacked a culture of splitting the bill when dining out, which frequently led to concerns about the appropriate party to bear the cost of group meals. However, by my company assuming responsibility for providing lunch, employees were relieved of such anxieties. It was widely assumed that this practice fostered amicable relationships among colleagues by emphasizing the communal act of sharing meals, irrespective of the quality or expense of the food consumed.

However, it seems that it is difficult for all employees to become close with each other due to the complexity of human relationships. One female employee asked me to pay for her lunch separately. I asked her what was going on because her request sounded like she didn't want to socialize with the other employees. However, her answer was that she was on a diet, and if she didn't eat lunch, she would feel like she was losing out and would be forced to break her diet. Since there were only four or five employees at the time, if one person couldn't fit in with the group, it would ruin the atmosphere of the small company. Therefore, I refused her request for separate payment for lunch, and in a spirit of working together, she ultimately quit the company. I suspect that if my company had more employees, it would have been easier to deal with this situation.

I recollect a time when I had made plans to go to a nightclub with my employees. After a dinner gathering, we were all in high spirits, and I suggested going to a nightclub. This kind of spontaneity, where a boss would suggest buying dinner for their employees and then suggest going to a nightclub, is rare in Australia. However, in Korean culture, it's not uncommon for bosses to take their employees out for entertainment late into the night according to their mood. At least, that's how it was at the time.

One of the employees led us to a nightclub that was reputedly popular. My employees went inside and I followed them, but suddenly a security guard at the entrance stopped me at the last.

"The seats are full, so you can't enter," he said.

"But my group has already gone inside," I replied.

"I'm sorry, but you can't enter," he said.

"If I don't go in, who will pay for the drinks?" I protested.

"Sorry, but you still can't enter," he said.

Later, I learned that this establishment only allowed young people to enter, and individuals who looked older like me were not permitted to enter for 'quality control[63]' purposes. Although such an action would be deemed illegal under anti-discrimination laws in Australia, it was permitted in Korea under the guise of 'full seats.'

Our proposal to have an enjoyable night at the nightclub fell apart.

---

[63] In Korea, the term "quality control" in entertainment venues refers to the restriction of entry for customers who appear to be of a certain age. Although such actions are considered discriminatory and inappropriate, some entertainment venues tend to maintain their customer base and image by restricting entry for those who appear to be of a certain age.

Lead Woo

When ASoTech, a software venture company, was facing financial difficulties, I had one employee who I saw as my last hope. Lead Woo, having spent a lot of time abroad due to his diplomat father, shared my vision, spoke English fluently, and possessed extensive software knowledge, making him a mentally determined employee.

To take my software business to the next level, I made the decision to translate all of our software user manuals into English, with the goal of exporting them overseas or collaborating with foreign investors. Initially, Lead Woo entrusted the translation to an external company, but when we received the draft, it did not meet our expectations. Both Lead Woo and I agreed that the quality of the translation was unsatisfactory. As a result, we made the decision to translate the manuals ourselves, despite the additional time it would take.

Since then, Lead Woo dedicated himself to the translation work, and with my supervision, completed the user manual one by one. As the translation was nearing completion, I planned to introduce my software to the overseas market through Lead Woo's efforts.

However, to my surprise, Lead Woo submitted his resignation. Despite feeling exhausted from the translation work, he committed to finishing the job before leaving. At this point, the typical approach would have been to offer a salary increase or reward him for his hard work. However, Lead Woo denied the fact that his resignation was to seek further amount of incentive from me. Therefore, there was no way for me to change his mind.

After Lead Woo left, there was a sense of emptiness, as if a molar was missing. After that, while trying to merge with a company in Mokpo, my company was closed.

Reunion with Staff

In order to avoid the worst-case scenario of not being able to pay employees' salaries and having to close the company, I gave the employees a three-month notice and informed them that if the company was unable to secure funds by then, it would close down.

However, I also assured them that if the company was able to recover, they would be able to continue working. Throughout this time, I kept my employees informed of the company's financial situation and any updates. Despite these circumstances, my employees continued to help and support me, even assisting with the final company cleanup before leaving.

The damage caused by the failure of the venture company has affected not only our family but also the diligent employees who believed in

Meeting with the Employees of AsoTech in 20 years

and followed me, for which I always feel sorry. Then, a few years ago, which was about 20 years after closure of the company, I received a message through SNS from Lead Woo.

"Hello, sir? We would meet ourselves to date.   If you have a chance to come to Korea, we all want to see you."

I was pleasantly surprised and deeply proud to learn that even after leaving ASoTech, the employees have maintained contact and connections with each other.

Years ago, while visiting Korea, I reunited with my former employees at the Choedaepo restaurant where we used to have company dinners. It was truly after more than 20 years. They had all gotten married and had children, becoming reliable middle-aged individuals. Meeting them again felt like a joyful rejuvenation for me.

Since then, whenever I have the chance to visit Korea, I continue to enjoy pleasant gatherings with them. Building such precious relationships has brought me another source of happiness in life.

Addition of New Business Type

In February 2002, I had to close the doors of the corporation I had been running. Due to various reasons such as lack of operating funds and poor management, I simply didn't have the strength to sustain the corporation. I made every effort to return even a portion of the investment funds by distributing or disposing of the remaining furniture and household items to the shareholders who had recently participated, even though it was a small amount.

The remaining debt was 100 million won in bank loans and 100 million won in private loans. In addition, the monthly office management expenses of 500-600,000 won were a burden to me, as there was almost no income. The private loan of 100 million won was personally lent to me by President Park, who had supported all the funds since the early days of the startup, and he demanded that it be repaid with interest. Therefore, I felt that simply closing down the company would be disrespectful to President Park and decided to transfer the ownership of the corporation's office, worth 150 million won at that time, to him.

While organizing the office and preparing to dispose of the last corporate-owned office space, an important fact came to light.

My corporation, designated as a venture enterprise in August 1999, purchased an office-tel. At the time of acquisition, the corporation received a tax exemption for the real estate acquisition tax as a benefit of being a venture enterprise. However, as the corporation now attempts to dispose of the property, it has been revealed that it will be required to pay a tax three times the amount that was originally exempted, which was not previously considered. While explaining the situation, I conveyed to the relevant authorities that the underperformance of our company's sales and the lack of operational capacity necessitated the closure of our business. However, I was informed that such a penalty was unavoidable under the current regulations. One possible solution is that the corporation must own the office space until the expiration of the venture designation in August 2002, and continued operation at the same address. It is noteworthy that mere ownership of the real estate without the continuation of business operations at the same address is not permissible.

I had no choice but to keep the company until August 2002. At that time, the current law was not practical, and it always assumed the worst-case scenario of abusing the law, making it difficult for honest people to live while complying with the law. Therefore, for about six months until August 2002, I had to pay monthly bank interest of about 800,000 won and office building management fees of about 500,000 won every month without fail.

On the 5th of September 2002, an interested party expressed their desire to lease my office space. Subsequently, we executed a lease agreement and they began occupying the premises. However, as the lessee was also a corporation, they were obliged to designate my office address as their primary place of business. Regrettably, this posed a challenge as the regulations stipulated that two corporations could not operate at the same address. Furthermore, since my own corporation was not actively engaged in any business pursuits, I was compelled to submit an application for temporary closure. Nonetheless, this proved untenable due to my company's rental income, which necessitated the issuance of tax invoices for the rent. In other words, if the company proceeded with temporary closure, it would be precluded from issuing tax invoices for rental income.

Furthermore, it is notable that the receipt of rental income from real estate, even in the absence of temporary closure, was deemed impermissible. This was due to the fact that the real estate business was not registered as an authorized business type in my corporation's articles of incorporation. If a business type is not registered in the articles of incorporation, it cannot be added to the business registration certificate. Moreover, in cases where a tax invoice is issued without the business type being registered, a surtax is liable to be imposed. Furthermore, there is a potential surcharge for failure to issue a value-added tax receipt in an attempt to circumvent the aforementioned surtax.

To add real estate leasing to the business type of the corporation, a shareholder meeting must be held to amend the articles of incorporation, and it takes considerable time and cost to complete the registration process, including legal fees and registration fees. Only when the business type has been officially added can the corporation lease out its real estate. Despite explaining the situation to the tax office representative, who acknowledged the current legal restrictions, there was little that could be done. This has placed a significant burden on individuals like me who need to sort out their business affairs.

In 2002, Busan hosted the Asian Games amidst an atmosphere of reconciliation between North and South Korea. As a result, there were significant changes, such as North Korea sending athletes and cheering squads to South Korea. When the North Korean team participated, their national flag was displayed as a national symbol. However, the current National Security Law prohibits the display of the North Korean flag in the country, and South Korean citizens are required to obtain approval from the Ministry of Unification to communicate with North Korean residents.

Despite the strict regulations, some individuals have opted to take extra-legal measures to communicate with North Korean residents or cover events related to North Korea without obtaining prior approval. Many people have talked with North Korean residents, and numerous media outlets have covered North Korean cheering squads and athletes without obtaining the necessary approval for contact with North Korean residents.

This raises the question of whether it is possible to live in South Korea while strictly adhering to regulations. If the regulations are to be strict, they should be enforced stringently, or if not, they should be based on common sense and have some flexibility. However, the current situation is such that it can be challenging to live within the bounds of the law.

Iran like North Korea

Following my immigration back to Korea in 1998, I was involved in a venture business that ultimately failed, leading to my return to Australia in December 2003 at the age of mid-forties with depleted financial resources. As a result of this experience, I suffered a severe loss of confidence. I began to feel socially rejected and started having delusional thoughts that people I knew were avoiding me because of my business failures. This realization prompted me to take action, and drawing from my previous experience in the biotechnology industry, which I briefly worked in before returning to Australia, I initiated negotiations with a state-owned enterprise in Iran.

As a result, they offered me a contract with a $200,000 deposit, an annual salary of $70,000, and 30% ownership of the company's shares in exchange for my software technology and biological reactor control technology. The company provided living expenses for my house and car in Iran, allowing me to send the entire $70,000 salary

Seminar for bio-reactor in India (Author at front left most)

to my family in Australia. This opportunity gave me a new sense of purpose and a chance to rebuild my life.

The Iranian individual who entered into the contract with me was introduced as a highly competent figure within the Iranian government, possibly at the ministerial level. Despite this, they seemed unfamiliar with international transactions and suggested that the $200,000 down payment be divided into three installments and paid upon my arrival in Iran. However, I held a firm position that I couldn't travel to Iran unless some of the down payment was paid in advance for my family in Australia, resulting in a tense standoff between us.

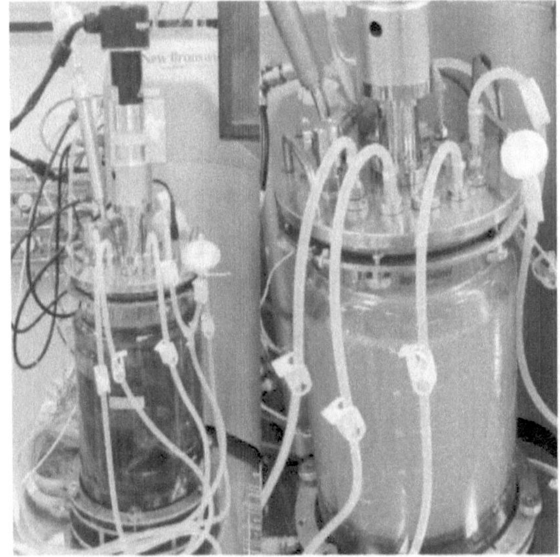

Lab Bioreactor

Eventually, they agreed to make the down payment through the Iranian embassy in South Korea, so I made preparations to travel to Iran to receive the payment and hire a Korean engineer to work with me in Iran. When I arrived at the Iranian embassy in Korea, they promptly paid the down payment with a Korean check, as if they were expecting me. I was pleasantly surprised by the efficient and courteous service, which far exceeded my expectations based on my experience with other foreign embassies. With the Korean engineer, whom I had hired, I headed to Iran, feeling a mix of excitement and nervousness about the business venture ahead.

When I embarked on my trip to Iran, I had grand aspirations. Upon receiving my Iranian visa, which was issued through an officer of the

Iranian Presidential Secretary's Office, I observed the process with optimism, thinking to myself, 'Surely, Iranian state-owned enterprises must possess abundant resources.' It was then that I began to dream of building a successful business through an Iranian company.

Although I had high hopes for my new venture in Iran, living there was far from convenient. The internet was so slow that even accessing basic websites became a frustrating task. To make matters worse, calling my family in Australia required several complicated steps using a phone card and the poor call quality frequently caused disconnections. Eventually, I resorted to using email as a more reliable method of communication.

Iranian TV had only three channels, but they were all catered to Muslim audiences, leaving me with no options for entertainment. Watching foreign broadcasts was illegal, as satellite reception was prohibited. Sometimes, cheerful music played, but I was informed that it was illegal to even tap my fingers or feet to the rhythm. To my surprise, a women's underwear section at the department store in Tehran was concealed with black cloth, fueling my curiosity even more. Although I found a foreign movie CD, all the scenes that prominently featured women's breasts were either censored or distorted, making it impossible to comprehend the full plot.

The value of Iranian currency was too low, and I couldn't use my overseas credit card to buy plane tickets, so I had to bring an attache briefcase full of Iranian currency with me to pay for the tickets. There were not many legal ways to exchange Iranian currency and send money abroad, so in order to send money to my family in Australia, I had to first give the Iranian currency to a black-market money changer and then through several other exchange shops connected to overseas exchange shops, I was able to deposit the money into my bank account in Australia. Therefore, it was very difficult to actually receive money from my business partner.

Although I was willing to tolerate the inconvenience of such a lifestyle, I couldn't bear the lies of the Iranian officials who were my contract partners. They said they would deposit the second installment through a foreign exchange dealer, but even after 3-4 days, it had not been deposited into my Australian bank account. They constantly asked various technical questions, insisting that since the money would be eventually deposited and therefore we should start work first. They showed me documents claiming that I owned a 30% stake in the newly established company, but they were all in Persian script, and I had no way to confirm their contents. The deposit confirmation never arrived in my Australian bank account, and the Australian family members who were supposed to receive monthly salaries were also not paid, which was extremely frustrating.

Following a period of one month, during which there was no deposit of the salary and second installment into my Australian account, I expressed my dissatisfaction with the Iranian employee appointed as my contact person. Subsequently, I demanded a meeting with the individual responsible for overseeing the contract in question. As per our agreement, a meeting was scheduled to take place the following morning at 10:00 am in our apartment. I waited until 10:30 am, but received no communication from the other party. Upon reaching out to them, I was informed that they were en route to the apartment but delayed by traffic, resulting in a slight delay. I continued to wait until noon.　Following my subsequent call, I was informed that unforeseen work-related matters might further delay their arrival and was advised to have lunch in the interim while they made their way to the apartment. Regrettably, no apology was extended for the inconvenience caused. The meeting, originally scheduled for the morning, was subsequently rescheduled for the next day at 10:00 am.

My spouse and I are inclined towards being meticulous and exacting when it comes to fulfilling commitments. While we may be accommodating in other aspects, we exhibit a low tolerance towards individuals who fail to uphold their promises.

After the Iranian partner postponed the appointment for not just 10-20 minutes or 1-2 hours, but for a whole day, I was extremely angry.

I unilaterally notified them that if they didn't show up at the apartment by 10am the next day and the payment was not confirmed, the contract would be canceled. The Iranian partner was well aware of our financial situation as they had previously agreed to cover our accommodation expenses, consequently requiring us to bring minimal funds. Despite the ultimatum that I had communicated to them, they failed to respond to our calls and ultimately failed to attend the scheduled appointment.

I called the Korean embassy to inquire about legal recourse against this state-owned Iranian company that violated the contract in this manner. According to the Korean embassy staff,

"Iran has a similar regime to North Korea, making it very difficult to respond legally, and many Korean companies have left Iran, applying the law as they wish to foreigners."

In my case, if I make a mistake, there is a possibility that the responsibility for the contract breach will be placed on our side, and I may be permanently detained in Iran.

It was only then that I regained my senses and could think of nothing but escaping from Iran. Receipt of the second installment was not important. Subsequently, I approached the embassy staff seeking assistance in purchasing a plane ticket, however, they informed me that they were unable to provide such assistance. As a result, I proposed the idea of depositing funds into the account of the Korean Ministry of Foreign Affairs, given our current financial constraints, and subsequently applying for a loan of Iranian currency to facilitate the purchase of a plane ticket. However, the embassy staff declined to provide assistance, stating that it was beyond the scope of their responsibilities. The proud Korean diplomatic mission seemed to be of no help to citizens in distress abroad, at least without attracting media attention...

In the end, I resorted to seeking assistance from another Korean individual who was operating a small business in Tehran. I proposed to transfer the required funds to his specified account in Seoul at an exchange rate favorable to him, and he agreed to provide us with the necessary Iranian rials to purchase plane tickets.

As there were no direct flights available to Seoul, we had to take a circuitous route by traveling first to Dubai and then to Seoul via Iran on the following day. With a sense of urgency, we hastily packed our belongings and left Iran, experiencing a feeling of escape from the situation.

The day after our arrival in Dubai, I checked my email at an internet cafe in the city and discovered a message from the Iranian partner indicating that we had left Iran and warning that legal action would be taken against us for contract violation if we did not return immediately. In response, I sent an email to all parties involved in the contract in Iran, proposing that if the money was transferred first, we would return to Iran immediately. However, they rejected my proposal, insisting that we had to return to Iran first to receive the payment.

The Korean engineer I brought from Seoul suggested that we just go back to Iran and demand our money, but I had already experienced their irrational behavior and did not want to be dragged around by them anymore. So, the next day, we boarded a flight to Seoul with a stopover in Iran. The waiting time at the Tehran airport for the connecting flight was about three hours, and we were on edge as if someone was coming to arrest us. After narrowly escaping Iran, I returned to Australia. Shortly after my return, my wife heard on the news that a Korean missionary named Kim Sun-il [64] had been abducted by armed militants in Iraq. She applauded my decision to

---

[64] A South Korean interpreter and Christian missionary who was kidnapped and murdered in Iraq in 2004

give up the contract and return home decisively, saying that if I had stayed in Iran at that time, she would have feared for my life.

Betrayal of Samsung Card

Following the closure of my software venture, I experienced a sense of regret that precluded an immediate return to Australia. As a temporary measure, I opted to shift my professional focus to the biotechnology industry while concurrently embarking on extensive overseas travel.

Together with my Korean business partner, I traveled to New Hampshire in the United States to visit a globally renowned bioreactor company. As I had previously initiated discussions with the head of the company during a solo visit, I brought along the manufacturing plant manager of a bioreactor company based in Daejeon to engage in supplementary negotiations.

In order to reduce costs, we opted to share a single hotel room instead of reserving two separate rooms at a higher expense. To this end, I remitted 50% of the room fee in cash to the other partner who subsequently provided his credit card to settle the hotel bill for us.

Subsequent to my return from a business trip to the United States, I perused my Samsung card statement and noted a charge of KRW 600,000 attributed to the New Hampshire hotel stay. Upon contacting Samsung card customer service, I was advised to direct my inquiry to the hotel as the transaction in question had been initiated by the hotel.

I communicated with the receptionist at a hotel located in a different time zone in the United States and eventually managed to ascertain that the charge in question pertained to the accommodation expenses incurred during our previous stay at the hotel. The hotel manager explained:-

"As your companion's card was declined for payment, we charged the lodging expenses to your card, given that you shared the room."

I had already paid my partner in cash an amount equivalent to 50% of the accommodation fee, and I never provided my credit card to the hotel. Thus, I questioned how it was possible to charge my card. The hotel receptionist explained that they had charged the credit card I had used during my previous stay at the hotel, as they had a record of it.

However, I couldn't understand how the payment was processed with the card that was already expired, which I used during my stay back then.

I contacted Samsung Card to inform them of this and stated that the amount could not be recognized as the overseas hotel had used an expired credit card. In response, Samsung Card informed me that they could not refuse the amount charged overseas and that I, as the cardholder, needed to request a refund from the hotel. The hotel and Samsung Card were passing the responsibility back and forth.

Logically, upon careful consideration, I realized that while the hotel that used the expired card without my authorization is also at fault, the greater responsibility lies with Samsung Card, which approved the payment request made with an expired card at its root.

I eventually filed a lawsuit against Samsung Card for a refund. However, when I was about to file the lawsuit, I realized that Samsung Card had a branch in every province in the country, which made it difficult for me to determine where my card was issued from.

I initiated legal proceedings against Samsung Card seeking a refund, and owing to the unambiguous nature of the case, Samsung Card did not mount a defense, resulting in a swift and favorable outcome for me. It is conceivable that their legal counsel had advised them against pursuing the matter, in light of the apparent lack of legal merit.

Subsequent to my successful litigation against Samsung Card, they sent me a single check to settle the refund claim without providing any explanation. No apologies or expressions of regret for any inconvenience caused to me were made by them. Nonetheless, at a later date, when I attempted to pay for a meal using the Samsung Card, the transaction was declined. Upon contacting the card company for clarification, I discovered that the card had been suspended as a retaliatory measure in response to the litigation against them.

This unscrupulous and clumsy conduct by Samsung Card left me with a negative impression and resulted in a decision to dispose of the Samsung Card.

Last Resort

After terminating my contract with Iran, I returned to Australia and applied for jobs in several places to start over. In my younger years, I had a successful career and would receive offers whenever I sent out my resume. However, now that I am in my mid-40s, I have sent out many resumes to Australian companies, but have not received any responses. This made me feel deeply depressed, as if I had failed in life.

I had lost the confidence to continue submitting my resume. However, due to the support of Australia's social security system, I was able to sustain a modest lifestyle with the weekly child support and living expenses for my two children, despite being unemployed. As a result, I found myself questioning my prospects at this stage of life, having depleted all of my assets. This led to a state of distress and melancholy, with daily reflections on my life choices.

Previously, I had achieved great success in my career, leading the merger of Korean and American companies and serving as the invited director of a Korean subsidiary of a major American corporation. However, my subsequent venture business venture resulted in the loss of my entire capital of 300 million won. In combination with the failure of my contract with Iran, I was unable to perceive any hope in my life. At times, I even contemplated taking drastic measures, such as the news reports of middle-aged suicides.

However, during negotiations with numerous American and British lawyers during the merger process, I became acutely aware of the importance of legal knowledge. This realization rekindled a lifelong dream of mine, namely to become a lawyer, which I have yet to pursue.

My wife readily agreed to my plan. She has always been like that, never opposing anything I wanted to do. I am always grateful to her for believing in me and standing by my side.

Initially, I was apprehensive about studying alongside young students at my mid-40s age. However, my concerns were allayed when I came across a newspaper advertisement by Charles Darwin University, which was recruiting law students for their distance learning program. I promptly applied and was admitted, which allowed me to save a year of the four-year law program due to my prior studies in Australia.

The online format of the program made no significant difference from attending classes on campus, as I could attend real-time lectures and participate in individual tutorial sessions, where discussions and submission of assignments were mandatory. The only difference was that I could not see my classmates' faces. In fact, it was a suitable method for someone with a personality similar to mine, like lynx, given that the only thing missing was seeing each other's faces

From that moment on, my daily routine consisted of waking up at around 6-7 in the morning, studying before breakfast, attending lectures right after breakfast, and then searching and studying various legal precedents. My wife would call me for lunch, which I would quickly finish and then rush back to my room to either attend lectures, prepare homework, or participate in individual instruction sessions and discussions. After dinner, I would continue studying until around 11-12 at night. Despite not being a young individual with boundless energy, I still had a certain level of self-assurance in criminal law and criminal procedure due to my prior work experience as a police officer during my youth. The acquisition of knowledge in copyright law, following the experience of being subjected to human rights violations by Korean prosecutor L, and the engagement in business contract negotiations with American lawyers in the context of a merger, have proven to be invaluable experiences.

During that time, there was one neighbor who made things difficult for me. He used to visit me without any prior notice and would start talking for a long time, even when I told him that I had important things to do, like studying for exams or preparing for lectures. Despite my protests, he persisted in his behavior.

This acquaintance often made comments such as,

"I know how difficult it is to study at an older age. But I have known many people who started studying late in life and it never helped them in the end."

Such remarks were not helpful and only added to the burden I was already carrying.

This person's advice, when taken to heart, boils down to

'Studying at an older age is not only difficult for oneself, but also for one's family, so it's better to quickly get a job that makes money.'

While it is unclear whether this advice was given out of genuine concern for me, who is desperately studying as a last resort, it was nonetheless a difficult message to hear given my prevailing circumstances. Nevertheless, I had no choice but to take it to heart and say,

"I will remember your words."

The acquaintance who used to visit my home unannounced stopped coming around after I obtained his legal practicing certificate, and didn't even offer congratulations.   Having encountered many strange people in various environments, I know that there are many peculiar individuals in the world, but this acquaintance was particularly incomprehensible to me.

Chapter 9 Life as Australian Lawyer

At the office room of the author

Too Strict Conflict of Interest

Although law school graduates in Australia are required to undergo judicial training and complete their studies, obtaining a Legal Practicing Certificate is not possible unless they secure employment at a lawyer's office. This rigorous requirement forces many law graduates to abandon their dream of practicing law and opt for regular jobs instead. In contrast, the legal profession in Korea operates differently, as passing the exam enables law school graduates to obtain a Legal Practicing Certificate.

Despite the strict requirements for obtaining a Legal Practicing Certificate in Australia, the country boasts a much higher ratio of lawyers to the population compared to many other countries, including Korea. As of 2019, the number of lawyers in Korea per 10,000 population is only 5.8, which is significantly lower than countries such as the US (38), UK (22.7), Germany (19.9), and France (10.3). In contrast, Australia has a ratio of 38 lawyers per 10,000 population as of 2020, similar to that of the United States. However, if there is an attempt to increase the number of students admitted to law schools, the bar association is typically the first to oppose it.

After completing the three-year law school program, I received a $200 prize for achieving the highest grade in the corporate law course. I decided to attend the Judicial Training program at the ANU university in Canberra. In Australia, the Judicial Training program is a six-month course and can also be completed through correspondence. However, the final week of the program involves a mock trial and attendance is mandatory.

Fortunately, I was able to get in touch with my old friend, Mr. Lee Yang-won, who was living in Canberra, and decided to stay at his place during the training. Mr. Lee Yang-won is someone I can consider as a fellow international student whom I first met around 1987 when I came to Australia to study. We were two pairs of married individuals who developed an intense bond with each other within a brief span of time. However, after a few months, they moved to Sydney, and our relationship ended regretfully. Despite the common situation as international students, they were very

In front of the Canberra Supreme Court
after completing the judicial training.

impressive to me because as soon as they arrived in Sydney, they sent me a box of Korean shrimp snacks knowing that I liked shrimp snacks. I was very grateful and happy to have such a friend who had a special place in my heart and once again to be in debt to them.

Upon completion of the judicial training program, in order to be admitted as a lawyer in Australia, one must either be employed by a law firm or have an offer of employment for a minimum of 6 months from a law firm, which must be provided as proof. Thus, even after completing the training program, if one does not have a job at a law firm, they cannot be admitted as a lawyer. Therefore, it is not uncommon in Australia for many law graduates to be unable to become lawyers even after completing the judicial training program.

During my period of judicial training, I asked a female professor who had served as my mentor to introduce me to a law firm in Canberra in order to help me become a lawyer. As she had been kind to me throughout the training period, I thought that she would be willing to assist me with this simple request. If I were employed at a law firm in Canberra, I would be admitted as a lawyer by the Canberra Supreme Court, and once that happened, I would submit my resignation to the Canberra firm and transfer my qualifications to Western Australia, where my family lived.

However, after giving it some thought, I realized that I didn't really need to ask the professor for help. If she introduced me to the law firm in Canberra and I broke the employment contract with them after being admitted as a lawyer and achieving my goal, it would be a selfish act and would damage the professor's reputation. Being separated from my family for an extended period of time was also terrible for me. So, I sent another email stating that I would look for a law firm on my own and asked her to disregard my previous request.

Shortly after, the professor contacted me and suggested having a conference call on Friday at 3 PM. I mistakenly thought that the call was about my potential employment, so I readily agreed to the proposal.

At precisely 3 PM, upon entering the teleconference room, I observed the presence of the professor and the personnel in charge from the Judicial Training Institute. The professor inquired as to the veracity of the email that I had previously dispatched, to which I responded affirmatively. I politely conveyed my desire to avoid imposing any undue burden upon her by making such a request. However, to my surprise, the professor claimed that my earlier email showed a lack of ethical consciousness and constituted a ground for disqualification from being admitted as an Australian lawyer. Even though I had withdrawn my earlier request in the second email, she suspected that I had briefly entertained the idea of submitting a false certificate of employment for a period of more than six months, with the intention of deceiving the bar association. She informed me that he was considering submitting an opposition to my admission as a lawyer.

The situation felt absurd to me. I couldn't tell if the professor had an exceptionally high level of ethical awareness, or if there was a genuine issue with my own ethical awareness.

Even if I could prove that I would be employed at the law firm for more than six months, it is entirely possible and realistic to leave the firm and move to another state due to personal circumstances. And besides, suppose I never mention that I would transfer my qualification to Western Australia before the six-month period and pretend that I intend to work in Canberra for life. Then, if I were to resign later, citing my family's presence in Western Australia as an excuse and transfer my qualification to that state, it will be difficult to determine which one is more honest and ethical. Furthermore, wasn't that professor supposed to be my mentor?

Even though three weeks had passed since I first sought the help of the professor, the issue remained unresolved. When I reached out to her again, she informed me in a cold tone that she no longer had the authority to make any decisions regarding my case. Apparently, she had referred the matter to the Ethics Committee of the Judicial Training Department. Upon hearing this news, my heart sank and I was overwhelmed with a sense of indescribable pain and disappointment.

I remained unable to discern the specific mistakes I had committed. Consequently, I found myself increasingly exasperated and opted to draft a comprehensive letter explicating my circumstances, which I subsequently submitted twice to the Ethics Committee. However, the director of the Judicial Training Department dissuaded me from dispatching further correspondence, deeming my intentions to have been sufficiently expressed. He warned that sending additional letters might even prove to be counterproductive and recommended that I maintain silence until the day of my ultimate admission to the legal profession.

Subsequently, a mere seven days prior to the scheduled admission date to the legal profession, I received the ultimate verdict from the Ethics Committee. Upon perusing the contents of the decision, I ascertained that it had concluded that I had solicited the assistance of the female professor in securing an introduction to a law firm and had subsequently clandestinely arranged to relocate to Western Australia. The committee had deemed such behavior to be equivalent to an endeavor to deceive the Bar Association. However, considering that I had retracted the request soon after, they decided not to submit an opposing opinion to my admission as a lawyer.

Despite my vehement disagreement with the Ethics Committee's evaluation that my intended relocation to Western Australia constituted a deliberate attempt to deceive the Bar Association, I recognized that contesting their decision had the potential to engender a postponement of my admission to the legal profession and an unfavorable outcome for myself. As a result, I ultimately communicated my acceptance of the Ethics Committee's decision.

Perhaps that female professor seems to demand ethical standards of lawyers that require adherence to the moral level of the Bible, which states that those who harbor lust in their hearts are no different from adulterers.

But I tell you that anyone who looks at a woman lustfully has already committed adultery with her in his heart." (Matthew 5:28, NIV)

I cannot ascertain whether the Judicial Research and Training Institute in Korea emphasizes such a high sense of ethics as described. However, upon becoming a practicing lawyer, it became apparent to me that conflicts of interest were among the most frequent and sensitive issues that required careful consideration when interacting with Australian lawyers.

In the case of the current President of Korea, Yoon Seok-yeol, while he was serving as the Prosecutor General, he was suspended for 2 months for various illegal activities such as illegal surveillance of judges by his subordinates, obstruction of investigations related to the Channel A case, protection of aides and obstruction of investigations. The district court found the disciplinary action against Yoon Seok-yeol to be justified, and even suggested that a more severe punishment, such as dismissal, could have been imposed. Yoon Seok-yeol later became the President of South Korea and appointed one of his close aides as the Minister of Justice, replacing everyone involved in his disciplinary case as his subordinates and currently undergoing an appeals trial against the decision.

Korea has also enacted a conflict of interest prevention law similar to Australia, and it has been in effect since 19 May 2022. However, such conflicts of interest, which is unimaginable in Australia, as being committed by the president and the Minister of Justice are not being properly filtered out.

Anyway, for me, it feels like the brakes are always on, with nothing ever going to be easy. I have a visible scar between my eyebrows from a fall I took while playing blind as a child. Additionally, due to inadequate acne management during my time in the military, my facial skin has a rough, pitted texture similar to that of an orange peel. While this may not create the best first impression when meeting new people, I've learned to accept my imperfections and focus on the things that matter most.

Someone who saw my appearance suggested that "the scar between my eyebrows causes me to face obstacles with every task I undertake" and recommended undergoing plastic surgery to remove the scar. Even my spouse has encouraged me to consider surgery, but I have chosen to embrace the scar and reject the notion of physiognomy as mere superstition. Instead, I am determined to overcome any obstacles that come my way through my own efforts.

One of the reasons why I completely ignore superstitions is because of my personal experience. Before getting married, my wife and I checked our compatibility using a computer program. The program predicted that we would not be compatible and would eventually end up in a failed marriage. It even went as far as to say that "if we were to get married, we would ultimately end up in ruin." Despite this warning, I paid no attention to it, and we have been living together without getting divorced, even though we have had our share of ups and downs.

K Group Litigation and Investigation

In 2012, I worked as an advisory lawyer for K Group in Korea. During that time, the Chairman of K Group, J, was having an affair with the female Vice Chairman. However, their relationship became strained due to J's eye contact with another young woman, Choi.

Meanwhile, the Vice Chairman of K Group established a new corporation with key employees within the group and exchanged necessary documents via fax. However, this was discovered by the employees who were loyal to the Chairman.

At the time, in order to completely break away from the Vice Chairman due to this issue, Chairman J of K Group called a shareholders' meeting and dismissed the Vice Chairman from the position of representative director of K Co., Ltd., which can be considered the holding company of K Group, on the grounds that the establishment of a new corporation by the Vice Chairman with key employees in the group and the exchange of necessary documents via fax constituted embezzlement. At the time of the shareholders' meeting, group advisory lawyers including myself and personnel of Chairman J were all monitoring the Vice Chairman's attendance.

When I asked Chairman J,

"What if the Vice Chairman doesn't show up?"

due to their past romantic relationship, Chairman J, who knew the Vice Chairman well, replied,

"She won't be the one to miss it."

As expected, the Vice Chairman appeared on time with her own lawyers.

At the shareholder's meeting, the Vice Chairman made tearful pleas, but J, who had already made eye contact with a young woman, coldly ignored the Vice Chairman's pleas and continued with the meeting. Ultimately, the Vice Chairman was dismissed based on the shareholder vote. Afterward, the Vice Chairman initiated a lawsuit to reclaim her rights within the K Group.

The situation was not as simple as it seemed. Here are some reasons why:

1.   The Chairman and Vice Chairman were in a romantic relationship, so they had divided the positions of CEO and director of several subsidiary companies among themselves. They convened the shareholder meetings of these companies simultaneously on the same day and time to swiftly dismiss the Vice Chairman from all her positions, which was allegedly unfair.

2.   When the Chairman and Vice Chairman were still in a relationship, the Chairman had given the Vice Chairman a personal agreement promising to give her 300 billion won.

3.   The Vice Chairman had filed for an injunction to preserve his position, claiming that her dismissal from the position of representative director of K, a holding company within the K Group, was unfair. However, there was a precedent in the legal system indicating that the mere act of establishing a new corporation does not necessarily constitute embezzlement.

4.   The Vice Chairman owned a building in New York, which was acquired using the K Group's funds. The issue of whether the building should be returned was being litigated in a US court.

5.   The Vice Chairman's younger brother, with the Vice Chairman's influence, had been employed as a CEO of a K Group subsidiary and was caught inflating construction costs to embezzle large amounts of money.

6. The prices of supplies from the group's suppliers were unreasonably high due to illegal collusion between the Vice Chairman, his younger brother, and the suppliers.

Not only did I spearhead the entire lawsuit, but I also assumed the responsibility of exposing the illicit actions perpetrated by the Vice Chairman and his sibling, ensuring that they were subjected to criminal prosecution. In pursuit of this objective, I exclusively occupied the Vice Chairman's office within the Group.

I proceeded to summon employees individually, interrogating them regarding their prior interactions with the Vice Chairman. However, I discerned an anomalous pattern. The Chairman's son had assumed a pivotal role as a department head within the Group, and he was surreptitiously impeding my investigative efforts.

Later on, it was discovered that the Chairman's son was siding with his mother, and had been carefully observing his father's behavior towards a young woman. In addition, the Chairman's wife, who was a deaconess at a large church in Gangnam, had hoped to resolve the situation quickly and quietly by paying the promised 30 billion won to the Vice Chairman and settling their relationship.

Nevertheless, it is likely that he was displeased with my appearance and interference and trying to find a way to undermine me, whom the Chairman absolutely trusted. Regrettably, I failed to recognize this reality.

Negotiations with the Metropolitan Investigation Unit

As I worked in the K group, my room was conveniently located right next to the chairman's office, allowing me to frequently have lunch or dinner with Chairman J and engage in stimulating conversations. During these encounters, the Chairman would occasionally reassure me by saying,

"After this case is settled, we plan to appoint Attorney Yoon as our group's overseas business manager or advisor, so there's no need to worry."

The Chairman of K Group appeared to be a mild-mannered individual who had once promised to give 30 billion won to the former Vice Chairman whom he had loved, and had agreed to give 50 billion won to the woman he currently loves. Consequently, I harbored a subtle hope that some leftover crumbs would fall to me after the case was over, but my expectation turned out to be completely misguided.

Looking back, there were several incidents that could have revealed his character, but I failed to notice them due to the mistake of trusting Chairman J too much from a common sense perspective like ours.

When I was investigating K Group to hold the Vice Chairman criminally responsible for what she had done, there were difficulties. If I was to report issues such as embezzlement or misappropriation to the investigative agency, there was a high risk of exposing other parts of K Group, which could cause harm to Chairman J personally. For example, Chairman J had already paid 100 billion won out of 300 billion won to the Vice Chairman for the agreement, and since it was paid with company money, there was a risk of embezzlement or misappropriation for Chairman J.

To resolve the situation, I arranged a meeting with the team leader of the Metropolitan Investigation Unit (MIU) for an informal investigation and we agreed to confine their investigation to the illegal activities of the Vice Chairman only. However, this was an unconventional agreement at the time, and some lawyers associated with K Group expressed their concerns to me. This happened about 10 years ago.

Anyway, the method I used was to conduct a personal investigation within the group and provide the information to the MIU, where they would fact-check and decide whether to conduct an investigation or a search and seizure. It was agreed that we would consult with each other to determine whether there would be any impact on the K Group before proceeding with their investigation.

At that time, I received the news of the death of the team leader's older brother at MIU. So, I inquired Chairman J about it.

"Chairman, I heard that the team leader at MIU, who is in charge of investigating our case, has passed away."

"Is that so? What should we do then?"

"Wouldn't it be appropriate to offer condolences on behalf of the chairman, at least with a token of money?"

"I don't know how much is appropriate these days... Would around 50,000 won (equivalent to $60AUD) suffice?"

At that moment, I was shocked. It was below common sense for the group Chairman to think of giving only 50,000 won as a tip for the funeral offering to the brother of the MIU team leader, who was responsible for investigating the K Group case, in light of the same amount usually given to his own driver when the driver had to wait for us during our lunch.

At that time, Chairman J was one of the wealthiest people in the country, ranking 8th in personal assets. However, when it came to spending money, he had a tendency to gauge his spending based on the status of the recipient.

As someone unfamiliar with the culture of giving money or congratulations in Korea, I turned to P, who was close to Chairman J, for advice. He strongly advised me to spare no expense in this situation, as it was a legal opportunity to give a bribe, and that we should do whatever it takes to influence the MIU team leader, even if it meant spending a lot of money.

As a result, I found myself unexpectedly tasked with delivering a huge sum of cash to the team leader of the MIU. In subsequent investigations involving the Vice Chairman, the team of the MIU was very cooperative with me.

From my experience with the MIU, I realized two things: first, that wealthy people tend to treat others according to their social status, and second, the power of bribery is truly formidable.   While Chairman J had intended to offer an amount of money appropriate to what the average person might give as a token of condolence, the K Group consultant saw this as an opportunity to give a legal bribe. As to which approach is wiser, I leave that for you to judge.

To me, either way is not just!

A Place Like Swamp

Looking back, K Group is remembered as a muddy place. Despite the appearance of everyone being subservient and cooperative towards me on the surface, behind the scenes, they continuously criticized and attempted to prevent Chairman J from trusting me by any means possible.

Mr Choi, who was the brother of the son-in-law of Chairman J and worked for a prominent law firm in Korea, joined K Group naturally due to the controversy involving the vice chairman. During a conversation, he told me that he admired former President Roh Moo-hyun and commented

"I like President Roh Moo-hyun, and you look a lot like him, Lawyer Yoon,"

seemingly trying to be friendly to me.

However, it turned out that Lawyer Choi was working closely with J Chairman's son and they had planned to force me out, reaching some kind of agreement. Unaware of this fact, I temporarily left for Australia to take care of some unfinished business. Right after I left Korea, Lawyer Choi approached his in-law, J Chairman and said,

"Yoon, the lawyer, is a person like a lawyer who cannot stand in court."

"While working in Australia, I received a phone call from Chairman J's mistress, Ms Choi, who asked,

"Lawyer Yoon, are you not qualified to appear in court?"

"What are you talking about? Why do you think I am not qualified to appear in court?"

"At the moment, Lawyer Choi told Chairman J that Lawyer Yoon was not qualified to appear in court, and as a result, Chairman J and I made a bet on it.   If Lawyer Yoon is proven to be unqualified to appear in court, we will remove Lawyer Yoon from all K Group business. If it is proven that Lawyer Yoon is qualified to appear in court, we have agreed to send the people who conspired against Lawyer Yoon, including Lawyer Choi and the head of the department, out of K Group. Therefore, please bring evidence that you are a qualified lawyer when you come to Korea."

The situation was truly perplexing, as those who had previously spoken amiably before me were now seen conspiring against me in front of Chairman J. It left me with a bitter feeling and fostered the impression that K Group was an entity akin to a murky quagmire.

In retrospect, I was reminded of the first words Lawyer Choi spoke to me during our initial meeting.

"How are you planning to cope with this murky and unpleasant environment after living in comfort in Australia?"

It is possible that Attorney Choi may have misconstrued the legal system of barristers in Australia and the UK. These jurisdictions traditionally divide English common law lawyers into two categories: solicitors and barristers. While these titles continue to exist, individuals registered as lawyers in Australia are permitted to utilize both the titles of solicitor and barrister. Consequently, I have elected to make use of both the title of barrister and solicitor.

The matter was expeditiously resolved in my favor through the submission of a translated version of the pertinent provisions of the Legal Practitioners Act of Western Australia to J, the chairman of K Group in Korea. Subsequently, Lawyer Choi and the department head were compelled to depart from K Group. It may be inferred that J, having made a commitment to his girlfriend, was unlikely to have failed to uphold it.

As a cost-saving measure for K Group, I collaborated with a

personally known lawyer as a non-resident counsel. Nonetheless, J's son persuaded the chairman that they needed a Korean lawyer who could work and reside alongside me. Consequently, without my prior awareness, the company hired another Korean attorney to work as my assisting counsel while I was in Australia.

Subsequently, it was revealed that this Korean lawyer, acting on the directives of J's son and the brother of his son-in-law, who was also a lawyer, had been assigned the role of monitoring my actions. Additionally, during my visit to Australia, this lawyer, unbeknownst to me, criticized me as per their instructions. When I returned to Korea and met with J, he abruptly remarked,

"Mr Yoon, let us cease this matter at this point,"

without providing any explanation."

When I asked,

"Why are we stopping now without even concluding the ongoing lawsuits in Korea and the United States?"

Chairman J did not provide any explanation, but simply stated,

"I just want to do everything the Vice Chairman wants and resolve the case as quickly as possible."

I refrained from further inquiries because I felt exhausted by working with someone who was so gullible.

When J, the chairman, was with me, he would speak as if he would do anything I wanted, but he never kept any of his promises. It was all lip service aimed at exploiting me.

A Memorable Flight Turbulence

Once, I thought it was cool to work while traveling abroad. However, while working for K Group, that became a reality. To sustain my work in Australia, I had to travel there for a week every month, and sometimes I had to visit New York for discussions with a US law firm while staying in Korea for three weeks. Since I used a corporate card for expenses, I always traveled business class, and although I sometimes returned on the evening flight after meeting with US lawyers in New York in the morning, I didn't feel particularly tired.

Asiana Airlines Flight

One day, I boarded an Asiana Airlines A380 to the US. In-flight service began when we reached the Pacific airspace. I ordered seaweed soup and bibimbap, but just as I was enjoying my meal, there was a loud noise followed by the plane beginning to shake violently.

The seaweed soup and bibimbap, along with the tray, shot up into the air and the trolley for the in-flight service that the flight attendants were pulling around also flew up into the air, hitting the legs of the flight attendants. The overhead shelf above the head also opened with a creak, and some luggage began to fall as the aircraft began to shake and make a "thud, thud, thud" vibrating noise as it began to descend towards the ground.

As this situation continued for several minutes, the sobs of some female passengers could be heard, and everyone held onto the armrests of their seats, preparing for the impending crash. I also held onto the shaking armrest of his seat and tried to focus on whether the soul would continue to hold his consciousness after death.

Later, upon recounting to my spouse the sensations experienced during the airplane crash, she admonished me, arguing that I ought to have composed a final testament to my family under such conditions.

At that moment, it seemed like my entire life was flashing before his eyes, and he was preparing for the moment of death like a well-trained soldier.

After a few minutes of severe turbulence and deafening noise as though the plane was about to break apart, it suddenly went silent and the safety belt warning light turned off. The flight attendants immediately started tidying up the cabin.

As I regained my composure and looked around, I saw that one flight attendant was receiving emergency treatment for an injury sustained when a trolley fell on her leg. The cabin was also in a state of disarray, with tableware, food, and luggage scattered about. I wondered how they would handle all the trash, but then I saw that they had piled everything up between business and economy class like a wall.

I waited, expecting that they would provide another meal after they finished cleaning up, but they never did. When I asked a flight attendant why we weren't being served another meal, she explained that because of the turbulence, they couldn't serve us and that we would have to wait for the next meal service in about four hours. She suggested that if we were hungry, we could go to the business class lounge and have some snacks like peanuts.

Upon inquiring with the flight attendants subsequent to the incident, they conveyed that it was their inaugural encounter with such an event. Following my arrival in New York, perusing the morning newspaper,

I chanced upon a concise article concerning Asiana Airlines, which had been en route to New York and experienced an accident in the Pacific. Based on my understanding, the flight duration between Korea and the United States is typically around 13 hours. As per standard practice, the pilots would have been resting and relying on the autopilot for most of this time. It is my belief that the aircraft encountered severe turbulence during this period.

I took the flight back to Korea the next day, and the flight attendants were familiar faces. It turned out that they were the same flight attendants who were on the same flight I had taken yesterday. Fortunately, the route back to Korea was relatively smooth and safe, but I fell asleep on the plane and had a nightmare about the plane crashing upside down and catching fire under my legs. The shock of that day made me realize that

"humans are happiest when they have their feet on the ground".

Korean Air Flight

Upon further reflection, it appears that the turbulence experienced by I was not an isolated incident. In September 1999, I embarked on a journey from Australia to Korea in the company of my family. At the time, I had made the decision to forego theological studies and pursue a career in business in Korea. During our flight from Hong Kong to Seoul aboard a Korean Air aircraft, the clear skies that we had enjoyed in Hong Kong gave way to turbulence upon entering Korean airspace, which gradually intensified. Upon our descent for landing at Gimpo Airport, the situation became considerably more severe due to an approaching typhoon, resulting in heavy rain and strong winds that contributed to the aircraft's significant oscillations.

To make a landing with the wind on the runway at Gimpo Airport, the aircraft had to gain an incredible speed. Everyone watched with bated breath, but in the end, the landing was unsuccessful, and the plane had to take off again into the sky. The aircraft then made a large turn over the airspace of Gimpo Airport, where rain and wind continued to pound the plane relentlessly.

The aircraft made another attempt to land, approaching the runway at Gimpo Airport. As the aircraft neared the point of contact with the runway, the sound of gusting wind caused it to become unsteady, ultimately resulting in an unsuccessful landing and prompting the aircraft to ascend back into the sky.

I thought to myself,

'It would be better to land at Kimhae Airport or any other runway in Korea...'

However, I was reminded of a story I heard when I worked at Room No. 100 in Kimhae Airport many years ago.

If an aircraft makes an emergency landing at another airport, it costs the airline a significant amount of money. That's why Korean Air, for example, was nicknamed "KAL[65]" for its sharp and precise landings to avoid extra expenses. Therefore, "KAL" must have been changed to "KE" these days.

Regardless of my wishes, the aircraft was making a large circle in the sky, battling strong winds for the third attempt. The intensity of the wind had increased compared to earlier, causing my family of four to tremble with anxiety, holding each other's hands on both sides.

I had a thought that 'coming to Korea to pursue economic activities instead of pursuing theology might not have been God's will'. At that moment, I felt extremely uneasy, thinking that we might be receiving God's punishment and could all die. Though I have since moved away from these superstitious beliefs, at that time, I tried to interpret everything according to God's will.

---

[65] "KAL" phonetically corresponds to the Korean word for sword.

The sight of other passengers trembling with fear and holding their breaths was pervasive. As the aircraft descended towards the ground for landing, the intense wind caused the plane to shake violently. Despite the sound of the wind roaring and pushing the aircraft back, it managed to overcome the opposing forces by accelerating even more to safely touch down on the runway. The thunderous noise was so intense that it felt like the whole earth was trembling.

When the plane finally landed safely, all the passengers erupted in cheers and applause, a sign of relief that they had survived the ordeal.

Based on my experiences, I have come to the conclusion that frequent travel may not necessarily equate to a good quality of life. As one ages and travels more often, the likelihood of encountering potentially hazardous situations increases. From this realization, it appears that leading a simple life centered around family and rooted in stability may contribute to a greater sense of overall contentment.

Unusual Client

In recent times, there has been a rise in the number of Korean tourists visiting Perth, and as a result, there have been occasional instances where they fail to declare Korean food at the airport and are subsequently prosecuted. Upon entry, they indicate on their arrival card that they are not carrying any food, but during customs inspection, it is discovered that they do have food in their possession.

In most cases, this may be considered an unintentional omission, and the individuals are given a warning, have their undeclared food confiscated, or receive a fine. However, in some cases, tourists have deliberately lied about not having any food during customs inspection, leading to prosecution and a court trial. While in Korea, there may be a more lenient attitude towards lying during customs inspections, Australian society strongly disapproves of dishonesty, and deliberate misrepresentation during customs inspection could result in charges of misrepresentation and corresponding punishment.

Australia is known globally for its strict regulations on food importation due to its unique geographical isolation from other continents. Despite this fact, a recent incident occurred at Perth Airport where an individual was caught and subsequently prosecuted for attempting to bring Korean food into Australia.

A woman arrived at Perth Airport in Australia carrying a significant amount of traditional Korean food, including sundae, tteokguk, and kimchi, which she had packed for her younger sibling studying abroad in the country. Accompanied by her two young children, she had to manage a substantial amount of luggage alone. However, a momentary mistake led to her Australian experience turning into a nightmare.

At around 10 PM, I received an urgent phone call on my mobile phone.

The woman on the other end pleaded with me to help her with a court hearing scheduled for tomorrow at 10 AM. As a fellow Korean living overseas, it was difficult for me to refuse her plea for help. Even though it was a holiday for me, I couldn't help but think that if it were me in her situation, I would want someone to help me too. So, despite the late hour, I agreed to meet her at a nearby McDonald's at 11 PM to discuss the case. With the hearing the following morning, she had no time to waste, and I was happy to offer my assistance.

According to her explanation, she was preoccupied with taking care of her two young children who were feeling unwell and vomiting during the flight, and her limited English proficiency prevented her from fully understanding the contents of the immigration card, causing her to mistakenly declare that she had no food. While I could sympathize with her situation up to this point, I found it difficult to understand why she continued to insist that she had no food when asked by customs officials upon arrival at the airport. When I questioned her about it, she explained that she had misunderstood the question "Do you have any food?" as "Do you have any fruit?", and had therefore answered "No" thinking that they were asking specifically about fruits.

As I was reviewing the investigation process throughout the night to prepare for the trial the following day, I came across the record of the phone interpretation that took place during the customs inspection. Upon examining this interpretation, I realized how crucial accurate interpretation is, as it had been interpreted incorrectly.

The information conveyed through the interpreter was that the individual had brought food, but failed to declare it on their immigration card. However, only the fact that she responded "No" to the customs officer's question regarding the presence of food was conveyed through the interpreter, without any explanation as to why she answered in the negative. This suggests that the interpretation was inadequate in conveying the individual's response accurately.

In any case, the individual in question was prosecuted in Australia for violating sections 67 of the Quarantine Act and 234 of the Customs Act. Section 67 of the Quarantine Act is stated as follows:

A person is guilty of an offence against this subsection if:

> *(a) The person imports, introduces, or brings into any port or other place in Australia, the Cocos Islands or Christmas Island any thing: and*

> *Maximum penalty : Imprisonment for 10 years*

Furthermore, section 234 of the Customs Act, which was also violated, is stated as follows.

A person shall not:

(d) do any of the following:

> *(i) intentionally make or cause to be made a statement to an officer, reckless as to the fact that the statement is false or misleading in a material particular;*

. . .a penalty not exceeding 500 penalty units

After being charged with violating Section 67 of the Quarantine Act and Section 234 of the Customs Act, the female client who visited me the day before the hearing agreed to meet me at the courthouse at 10:10 am. Violating Section 234 of the Customs Act can result in a fine of up to $25,000 (Unit 500), while violating Section 67 of the Quarantine Act can result in imprisonment for up to 10 years without a fine, making it a serious charge.

Imagine visiting Australia with joyful expectations, only to end up facing a maximum sentence of 10 years in prison. It's hard to fathom the emotions one would feel in such a situation. I did my best to help her avoid the maximum sentence of 10 years in prison, considering the emotional toll it would take on her as a mother traveling with her two young children. It must have been disheartening for them to shuttle back and forth between the court and the lawyer's office without any opportunity to rest comfortably at home or enjoy sightseeing.

The next day, I arrived at the courthouse ten minutes before our scheduled meeting time, but the customer arrived at 10:20 with her two children and younger sibling. As the hearing was already running late, I hurriedly urged them to go inside, leading the way towards the courtroom. As we walked, I explained to the customer that she had been charged with violating customs and quarantine laws, and that being charged with section 67 of the Quarantine Act meant a maximum sentence of ten years' imprisonment without a fine. Due to the severity of the charges, I suggested that we seek an adjournment for a week to have more time to prepare her submissions.

However, this client mistakenly sought advice from the Korean interpreter hired by the prosecution, asking if what I had said was true. Despite not being a lawyer, the Korean interpreter claimed to be the court interpreter for my client and boasted about her extensive experience, saying

"I had never seen anyone receive a prison sentence based on my own experience."

She even questioned the validity of my advice to the client by asking,

"Who says that?"

The actions of this court interpreter were unprofessional and could potentially violate her code of conduct as an interpreter. Upon hearing this, the client immediately confronted me in court, asking why I had threatened her with imprisonment when the interpreter had assured her that she would not receive a custodial sentence.

I asked the interpreter,

"Did you advise our client that there would be no imprisonment in the indictment?"

In response, the female interpreter said that she knew so from her own experience and would go to the prosecutor to confirm whether there was imprisonment in the indictment. It was truly beyond common sense for my client to follow the advice of the Korean interpreter engaged by the prosecution, but in the presence of me and my client, the prosecutor confirmed with the client first saying,

"The contents of your lawyer's advice were correct."

However, she only stated,

"The prosecution would not impose imprisonment as the suspect was considered a temporary visitor."

She correctly informed her with the words,

"The judgment would ultimately be made by the judge"

and advised her to consult with her lawyer for further details.

I convinced the client that it would be disadvantageous to go to trial immediately due to the seriousness of violating customs and quarantine laws. Therefore, I suggested adjourning the hearing for three days and reached an agreement with the prosecutor's office to adjourn the hearing.

The night before, a person who had been begging,

"Please help me, lawyer. I will pay the lawyer fee as soon as the trial is over tomorrow."

came to our office after the hearing was adjourned and got angry, claiming that she had not agreed to the adjournment and that I had acted unilaterally. She also demanded that I take responsibility for her loss of time due to the adjournment she didn't agree, and complained that I didn't even acknowledge her children or say hello at the court in the morning. After making various complaints, she finally said,

"I cannot pay you the lawyer fee now, but will pay it at my discretion depending on the outcome of the hearing in three days."

I thought to himself,

"Well, are there really such people in the world?"

I had no chance to greet the client's children because the client arrived late for the hearing and had to hurry to the court, so there was no reason for me to feel guilty about not greeting them. As for the greeting itself, isn't it proper for children to greet adults first? Feeling like she was in a strange country, I spoke without any excuse.

"I apologize for not greeting your children first. You don't have to pay for the lawyer's fee, so please look for another lawyer and leave the office,"

I said, closing the consultation note and preparing to leave the meeting room. However, the client immediately changed her tune and began making excuses, saying something like

"That's not what I meant...blah blah blah."

In the end, the client promised to pay only a portion of the legal fees today and the remaining balance on the day before the hearing. With this promise, I agreed to continue with the case. She asked me to contact her as soon as the written pleadings were ready. Despite being on vacation, I could not entrust this job to another lawyer due to my sympathy for a fellow Korean citizen with two young children facing a hearing in a foreign land. I gave up my vacation and worked hard to prepare the written pleadings before the day of the hearing.

On the eve of the hearing, I informed the client by phone that the written pleadings to be submitted to the court the next day were ready and requested a meeting to discuss them. This was also to ensure that I received my legal fees before the hearing, as it was agreed that the fees would be paid by the client up until the day before the hearing. Given the client's personality, I was worried that the client might refuse to pay the legal fees in some way after the hearing. Furthermore, as a temporary visitor who did not reside in Australia, the client could simply return to Korea immediately after the hearing.

"I'm sorry, but I can't review the written pleadings you've prepared because I don't understand English well. Would it be possible to email them to my husband in Korea?"

I sent the written pleadings to the client's husband via email, and since I was on vacation, it would be inconvenient for me to go to the downtown office. Therefore, I suggested meeting at the McDonald's near my house where we first met to discuss the content of the pleadings together.

"I will check with my husband to see if he has received the written pleadings, and then I will contact you."

Later, a call came through from the client after a long while, but her attitude had significantly changed. After struggling alone with the indictment, on the eve of the hearing, at 10 PM, the client called me on my mobile and urgently requested a meeting.   However, the client demanded compensation for the time lost due to the adjournment of the hearing, claiming that she had not agreed to the adjournment. Although I vaguely sensed how strange this client was for getting angry with me for not greeting her children first, I could not have imagined such behavior.

Probably after confirming that the written pleadings had been received by her husband, the client was verbally abusive to me, saying things like,

"Even if you're on vacation, shouldn't you come to meet the client wherever they want?"

and

"Even if my case carries a maximum sentence of 10 years in prison, you shouldn't tell the client directly but instead reassure them that there's nothing to worry about."

She also accused me of threatening her by being too direct. Due to these reasons, she refused to meet with me and insisted on going to court the next day without a lawyer, telling me to drop the case and refund the retainer fee she had previously paid.

Although I had experience dealing with some irrational Iranians and people from the Middle East, this Korean client seemed to go too far. After that, the frequent phone calls from the husband abruptly stopped, and even emails sent to him received no response. Later, it was discovered from the hearing records that she had used my written pleading to reach a resolution of a minor fine in the hearing.

As a Korean lawyer, I usually represent Korean clients and works for the protection of the human rights of Koreans against Australians. However, due to the significant difference in behavior of some Korean clients who was an angel in borrowing but became a devil in repaying, I sometimes suffer from severe stress.

Difference Between Rich and Poor

The Chairman J of the K Group was the richest person I had ever met in my life. Of course, I had also met K, the Chairman of the H Group, during a venture investment briefing in the past, but those encounters were just brief and passing, while I had personal relationships with J for nearly a year, having meals together. I share my experience with J and his family to help understand the barrier between the rich and the poor.

The Skills of Wealthy People

Not only Chairman J, but also most of the wealthy people I have encountered had exceptional abilities. Regardless of whether those abilities were good or bad, they possessed outstanding talents compared to others, and how they utilized those talents determined whether they became wealthy or poor, in my opinion.

I have also witnessed individuals who became deeply devoted to Christianity at a young age, donating all their assets to the church and living in poverty for the rest of their lives. From my perspective, these individuals could be seen as having fallen under the spell of their beliefs.

When I was young, there was an ice cream treat called "Ice Keki," which would be referred to as a "popsicle" nowadays. I accompanied a friend to the factory to obtain a box of popsicle for sale. As far as I can recall, I could obtain 10 free pieces for every 20 sold, which meant I could enjoy 10 of them for free before attempting to sell the remaining 20. Then, I attempted to sell the remaining 20, but I couldn't sell even a single one. The reason was that I lacked the courage to shout out "Ice Keki" and only wandered around deserted alleys. Eventually, all 20 of them melted, and I had to endure my mother's scolding, and my mother had to pay the factory for the remaining 20.

The Chairman J also disclosed to me that he had sold Ice Keki during his childhood. He initially invited all the local children and offered them free Ice Keki. He then encouraged them to bring in any discarded household items they had at home, promising to exchange them for free popsicles. Eager to obtain the treats, the children brought various household items, such as old utensils and iron pots, without seeking parental approval. J subsequently took these items to a scrap dealer and profited multiple times more than what he had earned from the sales of Ice Keki, according to his narrative.

Chairman J was never swayed by any belief or religion, and as such, did not have any religious affiliations. However, it is known that Chairman J's wife is a member of Somang Church in Gangnam. During the time that I spent with Chairman J, there were several occasions when mayors and politicians expressed interest in meeting him, but Chairman J refused to meet with any political figures.

Emperor's Morality

Chairman J's wife was no ordinary person. Despite everyone knowing about her husband's past affair with the vice-president and the ensuing lawsuit resulting from his current relationship, she appeared unfazed and unbothered by his actions.

Chairman J's wife also operated as the CEO of one of K Group's subsidiaries and owned shares in other subsidiaries, so perhaps she was not financially lacking. Alternatively, maybe as a member of the Somang Church, she had a heart to "love her enemies" and understood the women involved in her husband's extramarital affairs. . .

One day, Chairman J's son got married. Prior to the marriage, I was asked about a prenuptial agreement. I then recommended a divorce lawyer he knew to the son and advised him to go there to seek advice on the prenuptial agreement and to prepare necessary documents.

A week after the wedding, Chairman J arranged a dinner party with me and key executives of the K Group, following the son's honeymoon. After the meal, they rented out a section of a karaoke room in Gangnam and had a drinking party together. Several hostesses joined them at this place, with Madame sitting next to Chairman J and the other hostesses sitting next to me and Chairman J's son.

As I couldn't drink, I requested the hostesses to attend to the drinking executives sitting next to me, and they ended up serving on both sides of Chairman J's son. I witnessed Chairman J's son engaging in inappropriate behavior such as kissing the hostesses without any care that he was being watched, and I clicked my tongue in my heart.

'How could he behave like this just a week after his honeymoon? And in a place where his father and other high-ranking executives of the K Group were present...'

It was beyond comprehension.

Chairman J didn't seem to care at all about his son's behavior. A few days later, while taking an evening walk with the Chairman, I casually asked,

"Chairman, is your son enjoying his honeymoon?"

"Well, our daughter-in-law told us that they had a big fight and haven't been talking since they got home late after a drinking party," he replied.

"Oh, what will you do?" I asked.

"I'm worried that my daughter-in-law is too picky, and my son won't be able to freely cheat on her," he said.

I was speechless. I couldn't understand how someone could be so confident in expressing such unethical thoughts. Perhaps the wealthy have a different set of ethics than the rest of us, otherwise they couldn't think like that.

Nietzsche distinguishes moral concepts into master morality and slave morality. He believes that 'goodness' is power and 'evil' is weakness. 'Badness' arises from weakness and 'happiness' is the growth of power that overcomes resistance.

I believe that some wealthy people are living by an emperor's moral code. The emperor's morality is one who sets their own values and determines what is good and evil for themselves. In contrast, people with a slave morality try to follow the opinions of powerful people and accept them. This is because they cannot determine their own values.

In Korean society, the reality is that descendants of pro-Japanese collaborators, who have an emperor's moral code, have seized the top of society. Meanwhile, the general public and poor descendants of independence fighters who are trapped in a slave morality structure have no choice but to sympathize with them. It is a sad reality.

Death of My Parents

When I was young, my mother was very often ill. So whenever she thought that living with severe pain would make it difficult for her to live long, she would leave me with the advice to take good care of my siblings and live well. As a result, I have lived my life preparing for death.

My groaning mother, fortunately or unfortunately, passed away on 17 July 2022, living about three years longer than my father. However, those three years were a period of pain not only for my mother but also for all of us siblings.

Resentment of My Father

During my father's funeral in September 2019, my mother collapsed and was rushed to the emergency room. After the funeral, she underwent a thorough examination, and the results showed that she had:

- Advanced stage endometrial cancer

- Three aortic aneurysms

- 15% kidney function

- Early stage dementia

- A combination of problems including high blood pressure, high cholesterol, and diabetes.

Because my father hated going to a hospital so much while he was alive, she had been relieving her symptoms with medication without going to the hospital. But in the end, it had developed into a serious illness as she got older.

Even though my father had already passed away, I don't know how much I resented him when I heard my mother's medical diagnosis.

One of the resentments towards my father was because of something he used to say as a habit, as if it were a joke, while the two of them were still alive.

"Honey, if I die first, I'll come pick you up within a few years."

Surprisingly, it seemed like that habit had become a reality. I stopped believing in the afterlife at some point, and my energy for preparing for the afterlife changed to a mindset of using it for myself, my family, and my friends while I am alive.

However, I couldn't help but resent my father when my seemingly healthy mother was diagnosed with these illnesses after my father's funeral and couldn't even move freely.

The Surgical Decision Dilemma

I decided to bring my mother to Australia when she had some consciousness and strength to move. In late November 2019, I brought her to Australia in business class, paying for her to lie down during flight since it was difficult for her to sit for long periods of time.

As I stayed with my mother in Australia, I wanted to take care of her with all my heart, but she began to have difficulty breathing at night, which made things very tough. After only three weeks, I had to urgently send her back to Korea. My heart felt like it was being torn apart at that time. I knew deep down that this was the last time I could spend with my mother in Australia.

Through my youngest sibling, we decided to take my mother to Busan University Hospital and look for the best treatment.

The doctors answered that they could perform surgery in obstetrics and gynecology, internal medicine, and cardiology, but they avoided giving a definite answer when asked if my mother could survive the surgery. They said they could perform the surgery, but they could not take responsibility for the results. This caused us a lot of deliberation.

Apparently the Korean doctors seemed eager to perform the surgery and influenced my mother to feel she wanted to undergo the surgery. Consequently, my mother requested that I permit her to undergo the surgery, stating that she could wake up once the procedure was completed.

However, because she had three aortic aneurysms, they could not perform all surgeries at once and had to prioritize the most urgent one and observe the results before proceeding with the others. We were worried that if she underwent the surgery, the rest of her life would be wasted as an experimental subject in the hospital.

At that time, a female doctor at Daedong Hospital in Busan told us that her mother had experienced a similar situation to ours and advised us that it would be better for my mother to live comfortably without undergoing the surgery and pass away peacefully instead of suffering from the pain after the surgery.

Furthermore, Dr. Choi, whom I had a personal connection with, also gave me the same advice, so I refused the surgery with peace of mind. However, my youngest sibling became upset, questioning how I could refuse the surgery when the doctor said it was necessary. The criticism even included the accusation that I was trying to save money on my mother's surgery costs.

But at that moment, my decision was based on my concern for my mother's quality of life during her remaining time, rather than how long she would live.   Now, all of us believe that my decision at that time was correct.

<u>Tyranny of Nursing Hospital</u>

While medical technology in Korea has advanced to a surprising extent, regulations and accountability for doctors and hospitals are surprisingly lax compared to other countries. In Australia, it is unthinkable for a doctor to sexually assault a young female patient in a surgical room, but such news has become all too common in Korea. Reports of excessive anesthesia or patients dying due to negligence in the surgical room are not surprising news.

A noteworthy fact is that despite their transgressions, these medical practitioners are able to continue performing medical procedures

"I want to touch more" Operating Room Anesthesia Patient Molestation Doctor Sentenced to 3 Years in Prison

Jang Jimin Guest Reporter ☆

Input2021.11.26 02:57 Modified2021.11.26 02: 57

Korea Economic Daily Report on 26/11/2021

without having their licenses suspended or revoked. There have been loud calls for institutional reforms to address this issue, and if the legislative branch were to pass a reform bill that reflects the public's demands, the medical association *en masse* refused to treat patients, making the healthcare system in South Korea ineffective.

My mother spent some happy times attending an elderly school and making new friends while living with my younger sister. Unfortunately, one night my mother tripped and fractured her hip on her way to the restroom. She was hospitalized and couldn't return home, eventually passing away.

At that time, the world was in a state of panic due to the COVID-19 outbreak. The nursing hospital where my mother was staying prohibited all family visits during a period when the fear of infection was high. As a result, she was left almost neglected, but we were unaware of this at the time.

The happy times at the elderly school

(mother on the far right)

During my mother's staying at the nursing hospital, she demanded for various food from us.   From time to time, my younger sister bought plenty of food and had them delivered to my mother in order for her to share the food among patients in the same room.   However, the food would quickly disappear within a day or two.   We were pleased that my mother could consume so large food because it meant to us that she was so healthy.

One day, my mother expressed a desire to eat "chonggak kimchi" (a type of Korean kimchi). So, my younger sister personally made and sent her some "chonggak kimchi" to the nursing hospital. The next day, a nurse from the nursing hospital called our younger sister and asked if it would be possible for my sister to sell some of the "chonggak kimchi" because it was so delicious. This call finally revealed to us the reason why all the food my younger sister sent seemed to disappear so quickly.

When my mother was conscious and able to eat, she would order tasty food to share with the nurses and staff at the hospital, and consequently, she became quite popular and was well treated by them. However, as she became less mobile and her consciousness became less stable, she was left almost neglected.

As soon as the border opened, I visited Korea to see my mother in a nursing hospital. However, I was told that I had to pay a visitation fee of 50,000 won (equivalent to $60AUD) and that the visitation time was limited to one hour, all due to COVID policies. Instead of that, I suggested temporarily discharging my mother and spending time with her at my sister's house.

While staying with my mother and sister, I took care of my mother by massaging her legs or adjusting her position when she complained of pain at night. After spending a happy week with her, I had to send her back to the nursing hospital. However, when I tried to re-admit her, I was told that I needed to pay a readmission fee of 220,000 won (equivalent to $280AUD), which I thought was unfair, but I had no other option.

My sister called me shortly after I readmitted my mother to the nursing home and returned to Australia. While my mother was staying with me, I spent the entire night adjusting her position to relieve her pain. When my mother was readmitted to the nursing home, on several occasions she asked the caregiver to help her change her position instead of asking me. In response, the caregiver threw a pillow at my mother and yelled at her,

"If you're going to act like this, why did you come back to the hospital instead of staying at home?"

My sister told me that she demanded corrective action from the hospital over the phone, but hearing such news from Korea made my blood boil, and what frustrated me even more was the fact that there was nothing I could do from Australia for my mother who was in Korea.

Due to the slight easing of the COVID-19 pandemic, the cost of visiting my mother has been reduced from 50,000 won (equivalent to $60AUD) per person to 5,000 won (equivalent to $6AUD), which is said to cover the cost of COVID-19 testing. One day, when I visited my mother, she burst into tears as soon as she saw me. When I asked what was wrong, she said she was in excruciating pain in her back. I immediately called the person in charge of the nursing hospital, and they promised to provide painkillers to my mother. The nursing hospital's tyranny, which showed such irresponsibility towards their patients, seems to have no bounds.

Before returning to Australia, I visited my mother for the last time, and she weakly said something to me in the Korean language. I bent down and put my ear close to her mouth, asking her to repeat it.

"You are a good son," she said.

I lived my whole life as my mother's son, with the willingness to do anything for her, but eventually, the day after I returned to Australia, my mother passed away.

Despite the expensive airfare, I wanted to be there for my mother during her final moments. In 2022, the year she passed away, I traveled to Korea three times. I think my mother sent me to Australia with a compliment of "you're a good son" while worrying about me, and then passed away.

I too will inevitably depart from this world after my parents one day, and it appears that the moment has arrived for me to reflect on what constitutes a death that is considered blessed.

With my parents in 2018

Chapter 10 Happiness and Sadness

At Kings Park in Perth

Memories of Tongyeong

On every occasion of my visits to Korea, there is a particular destination that I unfailingly attend, namely Tongyeong, dubbed the Naples of the East. Whether I venture there on my own, accompanied by my wife, or in the company of friends who have joined me from Australia, this place holds an unshakeable appeal.

It is the residence of the esteemed accountant, the late Kim Yong-ryul and his wife Yoon Deok-ja, whom I hold in high regard and deeply esteem. The mere thought of them stirs up profound emotions within me.

To my wife, they represent a sort of parental figure, while to me, they are akin to close family members. Despite my unannounced visits and extended stays, Kim Yong-ryul and Yoon Deok-ja have never once betrayed any signs of discomfort, a testament to their unshakeable hospitality.

With a notable sense of audacity, I have on numerous occasions brought along my Australian acquaintances to their abode, yet they have consistently welcomed us with unbridled warmth and cordiality, never failing to extend their generosity to us.

One day, when I expressed my gratitude to Yoon Deok-Ja by saying, "I will definitely find a way to repay the favor you have shown me," she replied:

"Mr Yoon, we give with a joyful heart because we have become financially capable. If you have goodwill towards us, please pay it forward to others."

In most cases, when something good happens to our friends, we expect our friends to treat us with comments like, "You owe me one." However, Kim Yong-ryeol had a different approach. Whenever something pleasant happened to me, he refused to be treated and said,

"We are the one who should buy celebratory wine to share your joy."

Once, Kim Yong-ryeol expressed his interest in experiencing life in Australia, saying that he would not have such an opportunity in a Korean household,   I introduced him to my Australian friend's house so that he could do a homestay to learn English and culture.

He would visit my home on weekends, and we would have meals together and engage in social activities. At the time, I was studying theology and was in a financially challenging situation, so despite being unable to provide lavish hospitality, I was humbled by his expressions of gratitude and appreciation every time I visited them in Tongyeong, as if I had done him a great favor while I was the one receiving their generosity.

During the period when my father passed away, he was battling stomach cancer. Unaware of this fact, I had already sent my mother and father off before contacting Yoon Deok-ja about the situation. Yoon Deok-ja informed me that Kim Yong-ryul, her husband, had already passed away due to stomach cancer.

Currently, Yoon Deok-ja remains alone in Tongyeong. Last year, in late 2022, when I visited Korea for the purpose of handling my mother's remains, I also visited Tongyeong with my Australian friends. Once again, I was grateful to witness that Yoon Deok-ja remained as optimistic and positive in life as ever, living a life that reflects the character of both her husband, the late Kim Yong-ryul, and herself.

The opportunity to become acquainted with the couple, the late Kim Yong-ryul and Yoon Deok-ja, was a great fortune and honor for me. I sincerely hope that Yoon Deok-ja will continue to live a life full of happiness and positivity for the remainder of her days.

Reversed Relationship

One day in 2007, I was invited by the Korean community leader at the time to his house with my spouse. Although we didn't know the reason behind, we went to his house and met S and his family. He greeted us with a smile and told us that he had also come to study in 1987 and had known me during that time. I couldn't remember him at all, but I felt it would be impolite not to recognize him, so I greeted him as if we had met after a long time.

S had three daughters, including one who was the same age as my daughter. He came to Australia with his wife and daughters to start a new life in his middle age, which caught my attention. As a result, our families became very close.

Then one day, another couple, L, came to see me. They were people whom I had never met personally, but they came to me because they wanted to talk to me about something. I thought it might be related to personal religious counseling, as I had a lot of experience counseling some of the Perth expatriates on their individual faith journeys during my theological studies.

However, as I listened to them, I found out that it was about S, who had been very close to our family at the time.

To summarize, Mr S approached Mr L in a similar way as he did to me and maintained a close relationship. Later, Mr S asked Mr L for a loan of several hundred thousand dollars for his business, but now he is avoiding to pay it back.

Upon reflection, I remembered that Mr S's behavior was not normal. Therefore, I warned my wife to never have any financial dealings with Mr S's family. In fact, Mr S's wife had previously requested a loan from my wife on several occasions, but she had politely declined due to my warnings.

After hearing the details from Mr L, it became clear that this was not a simple financial transaction between the two parties, but rather a shameless criminal act committed by Mr S.

Upon finding themselves in a difficult situation, Mr and Mrs L reached out to me, as I was close to Mr S, to mediate and help them receive the money they were owed from him. I promptly called Mr S and tried to persuade him to fulfill his obligation.

However, it was surprising that Mr S had a different understanding of common sense compared to ours. To be more specific, Mr S was willing to return the money to Mr L only if he acted according to Mr S's preferences. He accused Mr L of not being prepared to receive the money from him. It was like the saying "an angel in borrowing and a devil in repaying" applied to this person.

After becoming a lawyer, the dispute between Mr L and Mr S continued. Despite our close relationship, I realized that I couldn't associate with someone who held such irrational beliefs, and thus decided to sever ties with Mr S.

Instead, a new relationship began with Mr and Mrs L, who I had frequently met due to Mr S's problems. We started meeting once or twice a week to eat out together. During our time together, I noticed how considerate Mr and Mrs L were towards their neighbors, which made me appreciate them even more. As a result, I developed a long-term relationship with this couple.

Mr L expressed his gratitude for having gained a relationship with our couple instead, despite losing hundreds of thousands of dollars through his association with Mr S. I, too, highly value my relationship with the L couple.

My wife and I are both the eldest child in our respective families, and we are not accustomed to addressing others as "big brother" or "big sister." Despite this, Mr L and his wife have shown us more kindness and care than our own siblings. While I cannot use the titles of "big brother" or "big sister," I hope that they understand that we hold them in high regard and treat them as if they were my own family.

The Daughter of My Father's Friend

Kim Sun-hee is the daughter of my father's friend. I've heard that when my father was young, he used to drink a lot and wasn't very responsible. However, when Sun-hee's father introduced him to the church, he underwent a complete transformation.

As they continued to rub elbows with each other, their passion for their faith became a competitive drive, spurring them to complete their theological studies and become pastors.

The impression I have of Sun-hee's father is that he had a strained and hoarse voice, likely due to his frequent praying and sermon. During his visits to our home, he often spoke about his daughter, who was several years younger than me. One memorable phrase he uttered was,

"My daughter, Hee-ya, is fussy about food, so her mom must feed her with rice mixed with egg yolks."

The adult acquaintances of Kim Sun-hee referred to her with the affectionate nickname 'Hee-ya'. During a period when eggs were considered a rare commodity, her father boasted about her habit of mixing rice with egg yolks, as a sign of her family's social status. Consequently, it is reasonable to assume that Kim Sun-hee grew up in a privileged and affluent environment.

Although the exact date of his passing is unknown to me, Sun-hee's father had passed away prior to my knowledge. I presumed that Sun-hee was leading a content life with her mother. As an adult and during my tenure at the Changseon police substation in Busan, I received news of Kim Sun-hee's mother's hospitalization and paid a visit to her at the medical facility.

As Sun-hee left for a brief moment, her mother turned to me and spoke with a somber tone, almost as if leaving her final wishes.

"Soo Yong," she said,

"If I pass away, please take good care of my dear Hee-ya who will be all alone."

As I stood by Sun-hee's mother's hospital bed, I spoke with a reassuring tone.

"Please don't worry, I'll do everything in my power to be her pillar of strength and support."

Afterwards, we met again at the funeral after Sun-hee's mother had passed away. Sun-hee seemed to be a deeply religious person, perhaps influenced by her father. The pastor of the church Sun-hee attended requested to have a quiet conversation with my parents after the funeral.

"I heard that you were close friends with Kim Sun-hee's father," the pastor said.

"Yes, that's right," my father replied.

"Sun-hee is an adult now, but she'll need to start a family and live on her own. I believe you'll take care of her well, just like her parents did."

"Yes, we also consider Hee-ya as our own daughter," my father said with a nod.

"I know that you have a son of the same age as Sun-hee?" he asked.

"Yes, you mean Soo Yong,"

"Well, what do you think about the two of them getting married?"

Kim Sun-hee on a trip to Jeju Island

"Hee-ya and Soo Yong are both adults now, and they should be the ones to decide if they want to get married or not. How can parents force their children to marry someone?" **my father replied.**

"Of course, I understand. I'll make sure to take care of Sun-hee until she gets married, so hopefully, they can get to know each other better,"

"Okay, I understand."

Later, my parents called me and asked for my opinion. During the funeral, I noticed that Kim Sun-hee seemed to be strongly attached to a young pastor she knew, so I replied,

"Perhaps, Hee-ya has someone she's currently dating with"

I didn't think that Kim Sun-hee, who grew up in a wealthy family, would marry into our poor household. Rather, I hoped that she would end up with that young preacher whom I saw at the funeral.

Later on, when my parents invited this pastor to my wedding, he expressed his discomfort saying,

"How can you allow your son to marry a woman other than Sun-hee despite our agreement?"

My father added,

"How could parents reject the bride when their son has brought to marry?"

Afterwards, I lost contact with Kim Sun-hee as I got married to my current wife and came to Australia for further studies. Looking back, I realize how fleeting human relationships can be.

During the time when I claimed to be running a venture business and staying in Seoul around 2000, I received news from my parents that Kim Sun-hee had gotten married and was living in Ilsan, Gyeonggi Province. Ilsan was not too far from where I was living at the time, so I got her phone number from my parents and contacted her. Kim Sun-hee had married and was raising a son who was similar in age to my own son. Although we were each living in our own households, Kim Sun-hee felt like a close relative.

Kim Sun-hee and her husband, Kang Sung-gu

Her husband, Mr. Kang Sung-gu, has been working as a software programmer with a similar career as mine. Unlike myself, he has read numerous books, and when we meet and have conversations, my wife and I find it enjoyable to hear about his profound knowledge and philosophy.

Hence, it is imperative that my spouse and I include Mr. and Mrs. Kim Sun-hee on our list of essential contacts to meet during our visits to Korea. I hope that she spends a happy retirement with her excellent husband and well-raised son.

Little Happiness

As I age, maintaining good health has become a challenge for me. I have never been a fan of exercise and waking up early in the morning, but a few years ago, I was diagnosed with a lump in my liver, which was a wake-up call for me to start taking care of my health seriously.

Since then, I have joined the health center as an annual member and have started exercising every morning. I am also careful about my diet and try to eat healthy foods. I realized the importance of taking care of my body, and now I make it a priority to stay healthy.

On the other hand, my wife and I, along with three other couples, have been meeting every two weeks to explore various trekking courses in Perth for several years now. Considering my aversion to early mornings, we schedule our meeting at 9:00 am. We walk for about two hours, have lunch together, and then part ways.

It may seem like an insignificant gathering, but it brings us immense happiness. Despite having different political views, it's a pleasure to walk and discuss a wide range of topics, including politics, society, culture, religion, and economy, dealing with all areas of the world.

I wish for everyone's continued good health and for this gathering to continue until the end of our days. I and on behalf of all the couples participating in this meeting, would like to extend my heartfelt gratitude to Mr and Mrs Kang, who lead the meeting with great care, taking into consideration the physical limitations of some members and discovering and introducing good trekking courses.

Taiwanese friend Max Ma

My wife and I frequently meet and socialize with different groups of people, whether it's weekly, biweekly, or monthly. Being someone who usually prefers working independently, I'm not entirely sure how I became so involved in these regular social gatherings. However, through these experiences, I've come to realize that humans are not meant to live in isolation.

Among them, one of the relationships that I treasure the most is with my Taiwanese friend, Max Ma. It all started when Max's wife, Mrs Lee, a Korean woman who was initially a friend of my wife, visited Taiwan several years ago and was admitted to a hospital there due to indigestion. However, the exact name of her disease was unknown, so she was transferred to Samsung Hospital in Korea. It was later discovered that she had cancer, and the couple had to endure a lot of hardship. While staying in Korea to take care of his wife, Max lost a lot of weight.

Mrs Lee, being an Australian citizen, was not covered by Korean medical insurance, and as a result, she was spending over 50 million won per month at Samsung Hospital in Korea. During this time, she was advised that she had a chance for treatment in the United States. However, Mrs Lee did not want to waste the billions of dollars in surgery costs for her cancer surgery with no guaranteed outcome, and made the decision to receive treatment in Australia and asked me for assistance.

Admitting Australian citizens directly from Korean hospitals to Australian hospitals was not an easy task. Prior to Mrs Lee's arrival, the Australian doctor had to review the voluminous medical reports containing all of her hospital records and current condition at the Korean hospital. Furthermore, Mrs Lee had to be admitted to an

Australian hospital immediately upon her arrival and treated, but unfortunately, such a system did not exist in Australia.

In Australia, when someone needs to be hospitalized, the usual process is to send a referral to the hospital through a home doctor and then wait for the hospital to contact you, which often takes more than a month. The only way to be admitted quickly is to go directly to the emergency room, but even then, there's no guarantee of immediate treatment upon arrival. This was a big concern for Mrs Lee, who arrived in Australia with a stomach tube and respirator and required continuous medical attention right away.

However, Mrs Lee's decision to receive treatment in Australia was driven by her desire to avoid being treated as a mere guinea pig for medical trainees every morning and evening while paying more than 50 million won per month at Samsung Hospital in Korea. In Korean hospitals, patients are often subjected to numerous blood tests and medical procedures without sufficient explanation, and Mrs Lee wished to avoid these sufferings.

Mrs Lee had a comprehensive private insurance policy in Australia, but unfortunately, the private hospital was unable to accommodate her. As a result, it was agreed that Mrs Lee would be admitted to the emergency room at Royal Perth Hospital, a public hospital, as soon as she arrived in Australia.

However, unfortunately, Mrs Lee passed away just three days after her arrival at the Australian hospital. Her death highlighted the limitations of Australian hospitals in providing life-sustaining medical care. In situations where there is no possibility of resuscitation, Australian hospitals tend not to invest resources in medically sustaining treatment.

Despite the tragedy, Max and his son Mac found solace in forming a close bond with my family, and we now regularly meet and spend time together as if we are one family.

Max and his son Mac

Thai Friend Nahtaw

While studying theology, I attended the Australian Baptist Church in Kelmscott, where the majority of the churchgoers were white. During one service, a Thai woman and an Australian man shared their experience of doing missionary work in Africa.

It was there that we met Nahtaw, a Thai woman and her white husband, Harvey. My initial impression of Nahtaw was that she was slender, unlike most Thai women, which made me mistake her for a Japanese woman. Nahtaw had beautiful two daughters, one of whom was about the same age as my son. Both daughters are now married and live independently. The memories of the relationship I shared with them are unforgettable.

While I was studying theology, my wife had to go to Korea with our second child for her family matter, leaving me and my son to stay in Australia. Due to my reluctance to cook, my son and I resorted to consuming pizza and hamburgers as our primary source of sustenance.

Nahtaw and Harvey and their two daughters

I assumed that he enjoyed these meals until one day he spotted Nahtaw and asked her,

"Ma'am, can you cook rice?"

This inquiry served as a wake-up call and reminded me that my child may have been craving a home-cooked meal all along.

Another day, my son and Nahtaw's second daughter, Malissa, fought so hard that Nahtaw said to my son and Melissa,

"If you keep fighting, I will make you two get married later."

Then they stopped fighting. Even now, when I meet Nahtaw and Harvey, Nahtaw sometimes reminisces about these stories.

The lives of Harvey and his wife, Nahtaw, have been a source of inspiration to us, as they always maintain a positive outlook and never lose their sense of humor or composure. They were dispatched as Christian missionaries to Zimbabwe, Africa, where they selflessly volunteered for several years before returning to Australia to serve as civil servants in the Department of Agriculture WA. However, when an opportunity to serve as missionaries arose in Kazakhstan a few years later, they made the difficult decision to resign from their government jobs and relocate with their entire family to Kazakhstan.

While they were engaged in missionary work in Kazakhstan, I shifted gears from running a software venture business in Korea to pursuing a biotechnology venture in Daejeon. Despite this change, I still felt compelled to invite Nahtaw's family members to visit during my time in Korea and bring some joy into their lives, while also supporting the missionaries in their work.

While Nahtaw and her husband, along with their two daughters, were staying in Korea, we traveled throughout the country, visiting cities such as Seoul, Busan, Daejeon, Tongyeong, and Chuncheon, and enjoyed many happy times together. Nahtaw, in particular, loved everything about Korea, so it was a pleasure to introduce her to different aspects of the country.

During their stay in Korea, concerned about Nahtaw's daughter, Amy's acne-prone skin and its potential impact on her well-being, I accompanied her to a nearby dermatologist. After examining her, the dermatologist was impressed by her beauty and generously offered to provide free acne treatment during their stay in Korea. Subsequently, Amy underwent acne treatment during their time in Korea.

Additionally, Harvey received dental care for cavities at a clinic where my younger sister was employed.

When they left for Kazakhstan, I gave them my digital camera as a gift. I tried my best to ensure that all of these families had a sense of happiness.

Nahtaw and Harvey, who returned to Australia after completing a mission in Kazakhstan, lived in Esperance and recently moved closer to my house to live close to their two daughters living in Perth.

I hope that the lives of Nahtaw and Harvey, who have lived their lives with a heart of practicing faith toward God, will be filled with God's blessings.

Friend's Daughter

As a detective for foreign affairs stationed at Room No. 100 in Gimhae Airport, I had the pleasure of working with Detective Lee, who stood out among my colleagues for his exceptional competence, towering stature, and handsome appearance. Despite my no-nonsense approach and lack of connections, Detective Lee treated me with a level of respect and kindness that I greatly appreciated.

With the late detective Lee

However, I couldn't help but notice Detective Lee's extravagant spending habits, particularly when it came to drinking. While my monthly salary barely exceeded 200,000 won, Detective Lee would effortlessly spend more than that amount on a single night out. I found myself intrigued by his seemingly unlimited financial resources and often wondered how he could afford such a lavish lifestyle.

Detective Lee's transfer to Room 100 at Gimhae Airport was a privileged appointment that he received while serving in the secretary's office for the head of the

Busan Police Department. We called it a parachute appointment[66]. There are speculations that the seemingly endless financial resources of Detective Lee may have been attributed to pocket money or gifts from wealthy businessmen in his network.

Detective Lee provided me with an opportunity to experience lavish room salons and karaoke that were beyond the means of ordinary people when I was young. Despite being unable to drink, I enjoyed the delicious snacks and unique atmosphere. Whenever Detective Lee invited me to join him, I would eagerly accept without hesitation.

After spending the entire night at a bar, Detective Lee mentioned he needed to change his clothes for work the next day and invited me to his home. When we arrived, I saw Detective Lee's wife holding their newborn child, and little did I know that my relationship with the child would continue.

While pursuing theology studies after immigrating to Australia, I received a phone call from Detective Lee, asking for my assistance with his daughter's education. He expressed interest in having her live with us in Australia to learn English and immerse herself in the local culture.

Without any hesitation, I accepted Detective Lee's request. Despite being three to four years older than me, I never referred to him as an elder brother. In Korea's hierarchical culture, this could have been viewed as arrogance, but Detective Lee always showed understanding and consideration towards me. I was grateful for his kindness.

I couldn't believe how quickly time had flown by when Detective Lee's child, who I once saw in swaddling clothes, came to visit me in Australia as an elementary school student. As I write this

---

[66] A "parachute appointment" is when a person is appointed through their connections, often based on nepotism, regardless of the existing organizational system.

autobiography, Jisoo has already turned 30 years old.

Several years ago, Detective Lee passed away from lung cancer, despite his enjoyment of drinking and smoking. After his death, Jisoo told me that she wished that I were her father. I made a commitment to treat Jisoo as my own daughter. However, I realize that this is only my

With Jisoo in 2018

personal desire, and I still feel a sense of remorse towards Jisoo.

Whenever I visited Korea, I could always get in touch with Jisoo, but often I had to leave without meeting her. It's regretful that I haven't been able to create many memories with Jisoo, who affectionately calls us "little dad and little mom".

The reason why I hold Jisoo in such high regard is likely due to her spending some of her formative years with us. However, above all, it is because she is the daughter of a person who once took care of and guided me like a brother. My daughter, who is unaware of these circumstances, can sometimes become envious.

Jisoo on her recent birthday

Perhaps when she gets older and if one of her friends passes away before her, leaving children behind, she may come to understand my sentiments as she looks at the remaining children of her deceased friend because that is my mind towards Jisoo.

Regardless, it is my wish to witness Jisoo promptly encountering a suitable partner, and establishing a blissful household.

Passing Fate

Throughout my life, I have encountered numerous relationships that could have easily been fleeting, yet many of them have persisted and developed into meaningful relationships. Among these relationships, I would like to highlight the two most significant ones that have left a lasting impression on me.

Good Neighbor

During my time working in venture business in Korea, my place of residence was a Goyang apartment in Gyeonggi-do. Because my office was set up in Mapo-gu, it was easy to commute from Goyang through Jayu-ro.

Our next-door neighbor was Hyeyoon, who shared the same age as our daughter. Hyeyoon's family temporarily stayed in Goyang while their Sangdo-dong apartment underwent reconstruction. Hyeyoon frequented our home for playtime, and my wife, who enjoys being around kids, treated Hyeyoon as if she were her own daughter.

When the cheerful Hyeyoon was playing at our house, her older sister Hyeri would come over and take her home, saying their mom had called for her. Through this, Hyeyoon's mom and my wife became close neighbors, and as a result, the husbands joined in and the two families started to socialize over meals together. Although it was natural to have this kind of interaction as neighbors living in adjacent apartments, we became close enough that we even traveled together to Jeju Island at one point.

Current Appearance of Hyeyoon

After leaving my venture business and relocating to Daejeon to establish a biotechnology business, Hyeyoon's family once visited us in Daejeon.

During our time living in Australia, Hyeyoon's parents requested our assistance in enrolling their elementary school-aged daughter in an Australian school to provide her with the experience of living and studying abroad.

Without hesitation, we welcomed Hyeyoon and enrolled her in a private school in Australia. During her studies, she lived with us for a few months. Perhaps because of this relationship, when I look at Hyeyoon, my daughter's friend, unlike other children, I feel like I'm meeting my daughter.

However, Hyeyoon's parents eventually divorced after a long separation, and both Hyeyoon and her sister now live with their mother. Hyeyoon's mother is a smart, capable, and determined woman. It is not easy for a single mother in Korean society to raise two daughters, but she managed to send both of them to university and get them jobs at major corporations, taking great pride in her daughters' success.

During my visit to Korea in 2022, Hyeyoon's mother offered us to use her own Gangnam studio apartment while we stayed in Korea. While we once lived in adjacent apartments and our relationship may have been fleeting, the connection between Hyeyoon's family and mine has developed into something distinct and meaningful, and we have continued to maintain this bond to date.

Relationship in Chuncheon

I had only heard of Chuncheon as a lakeside city, which had nothing to do with me. Therefore, I never even traveled there once. However, by chance, I got to know the Lee family in Chuncheon, and ended up going there often as if it were my own hometown.

While I was doing venture business in Korea, I missed Australia a lot. So, our family decided to take a trip to Australia. The feeling of arriving in Perth, Australia as a student, arriving to settle down with an immigrant visa, and arriving as a tourist from Korea were all different.

Upon the arrival of my family in Perth, they initially stayed with Jennifer while also visiting Nahtaw in Esperance. Subsequently, I flew to Perth independently to reunite with my family. Upon my arrival, we moved to stay with our esteemed acquaintances, Mr and Mrs Oh.

After enjoying our time in Perth, we headed to the airport to begin our journey back to Korea. As we said goodbye to our friends and went through the departure process, we received the unfortunate news that our Cathay Pacific Airlines flight had been cancelled due to a technical issue.

We had planned to spend two nights in Hong Kong before heading back to Seoul the following day. However, due to the flight cancellation, our plans were completely disrupted. The airline staff offered to arrange for our departure on the following day, and we were provided with accommodation at the Novotel in Perth city center for that night. As we were leaving the airport to take a taxi with our round-trip voucher, Mrs Lee, the wife of Mr Lee who was scheduled to leave on the same flight as us, asked me what was going on. They did not even know that the flight had been cancelled, as their English proficiency was limited. Therefore, I approached the airline staff and arranged for them to receive accommodation and a taxi voucher as well..

Traveling in Hong Kong with

Mr Lee's family in 2001

Mr Lee Sang-woo and his family were on their way back to Korea after coming together to Perth to send their son for studying. During their conversation at that time, my family mentioned that they would stay in Hong Kong for a few days before returning to Korea. Mr Lee's family also wanted to go sightseeing but couldn't due to their limited English proficiency. I then helped them change their flight schedule and they decided to go sightseeing together in Hong Kong.

Due to these events, I and Mr Lee have stayed in touch and maintained their relationship. Their son successfully completed his studies in Australia and obtained an accounting qualification, as well as permanent residency. However, he decided to return to Korea to continue his father's business, giving up his permanent residency in Australia and immigrating back to Korea where he was required to complete his military service in Korea,

It is possible that Mr Lee Sang-woo has accumulated substantial wealth, as evidenced by his son's decision to renounce his Australian permanent residency and complete mandatory military service in Korea. However, the source of his wealth remains unclear. Nevertheless, it is undeniable that he is a well-off individual in Chuncheon.

Despite being older than me, the Lee couple is humble and both appear to have good health with a healthy complexion. I have not been able to meet them since the outbreak of COVID-19, but recently received a wedding invitation for their son, which made me reflect on how much time has passed.

Precious Relationships

While it's impossible to list them all, I have many precious relationships. Some of them are like benefactors, but most of them have a feeling of family. Therefore, even if they don't meet often, they always occupy a place in my heart as family members. Since mentioning their real names could be problematic, I won't disclose them. However, there are the Ohs and the Lees, married couples who came to Australia as international students around the same time as me.

The Oh couple were close friends of mine, and they discussed various topics with them, including matters of faith in their younger years, and had a significant influence on each other. While I have transitioned from the computer industry to becoming a businessman and a lawyer, Mr Oh has remained consistent in his career in software development. I admire Mr Oh's dedication to one industry, likening it to that of a steadfast old woman serving only one husband throughout her life.

Despite infrequent meetings, the Oh couple always maintain a comforting presence in my life with their unwavering character. Oh and his wife prioritize their health with strict diets and exercise routines, resulting in a youthful and energetic appearance. As a result, I

With Mr Oh in 1987

believe that Mr and Mrs Oh will likely outlive myself and my spouse, and have even considered entrusting future matters to the Oh couple.

One of the most valuable relationships among them is the one that was rekindled after a separation. Mr and Mrs Lee are close friends whom I met while studying in Australia in 1987. Although they had a brief encounter with myself and my

With Mr Oh in 2007

spouse in Perth, they parted ways on their journey to Sydney. An incident that still resonates with me is when Lee and his wife bought a box of shrimp crackers in Sydney and sent it to me after learning of my love for them. Following that, I lost touch with the couple, but in 2007, while preparing for judicial training in Canberra, I was fortunate to reconnect with them.

Mr and Mrs Lee later moved to Perth, where I live, and at that time, I and my wife were so happy to feel like their close family was coming to Perth. I even encouraged them to buy a house in the neighborhood where he lives, but for some reason, they bought a house in a distant place that is about an hour away by car, which left me feeling somewhat disappointed. When I first immigrated to Australia and bought a house in Kelmscott, it was because my Australian friend, Neville, lived in H untingdale at the time. However, Mr Lee and his wife bought a house in a faraway place, making me think that I couldn't control my relationships with people as easily as I thought. Nevertheless, I continue to meet with this couple regularly at least once a month and maintain their friendship. They are a couple who hold a dear place in my heart.

There are also people whom I personally admire. There are many couples such as Mr and Mrs Ji, Mr and Mrs Yoo, Mr and Mrs Han, but I refrain from mentioning their real names in case of possible privacy concerns.

The Ji couple is someone whom I personally admire. They shared many conversations about faith during their youth, and had a deep emotional connection. While most churchgoers tend to focus on others only if the goal is evangelism, the Jis never forgot to care for my family, even while being busy as elders in their own church. I am extremely grateful for their kindness, which is always remembered. During the years of my study in Australia, when our first child was born, the Jis provided basic necessities such as a crib and a stroller. As our children grew up, the Jis always kept my freezer filled with ice cream, which not only made the children happy, but also me loving snacks. Although they have moved to the eastern part of the country to enjoy their retirement, I hope they remain healthy and happy.

One of the most compassionate and capable parents in Australia that comes to mind is the Yoo family. The Yoo couple, who currently run a restaurant in Perth, have raised their two sons and one daughter remarkably well, and there is much to learn from their way of life.

Our couple has a tendency for the wife to vent her dissatisfaction with me to our children during conversations. However, in the case of the Yu couple, when the father scolded the children, the mother comforted them while also saying "But apologize to your father for what you did wrong!" and ultimately taught the children to accept their father's discipline. As a result, even as adults, their three children still obey and honor their father. While we may not be able to apply the parenting methods of the Yu couple to our own adult children, I am writing this to emphasize the importance of a united front between parents in raising children. The obedient behavior of their three children has been passed down to their own children, and the Yu couple, who never tire of boasting about their grandchildren every time I see them, are enviable.

I also cannot forget the connection with Mr and Mrs Han, who are much older than me. It was during my study in Australia when I was living in a small apartment in Wembley. Mr Han had arrived in Australia as an investment immigrant at a young age and visited to prepare for settlement, such as purchasing a house, before his family arrived. We first met at a Korean church. I had a thought that he might feel lonely coming alone to Perth, so I invited him to my small apartment for dinner.

The dinner that the poor student couple prepared may not have been very delicious, but later, after the Han family settled in Perth, they invited my family to their home for a meal as a thank-you gesture. This relationship has continued until now. We meet almost once a month, share our opinions on politics, religion, social issues, and learn a lot from each other's vast knowledge. It seems that they have a

With Mr. Han and his wife in 2022

principle of living independently without depending on others, and even when I offer to drive them home or pay for the meal instead of them, they politely decline. The always dignified and polite appearance of the Han couple now seems to be aging and it breaks my heart.

In addition, there are many valuable relationships that I cherish and have maintained over time. However, I am unable to introduce them all due to my wife's opposition, which is regrettable. To borrow her words, it feels like we would be exposing all of our privacy. I hope that those acquaintances who were not mentioned here do not feel disappointed.

Epilogue

I believe it was a wise decision to update my autobiography and have it translated into English. As I am approaching my mid-sixties, I realized while writing this autobiography that my motivation and actions are not the same as they were before. In other words, writing a book may not be easy as I get older.

Fortunately, based on the autobiographical essay I wrote earlier titled "My Experiences in Korea and Australia," I was able to recall many memories and supplement many parts of my life while summoning my memories of my life, which has led me to think deeply again.

Looking back, there have been so many events in my life that it was regrettable that I could not include them all in this one book. However, I selected the ones that occupy the most space in my memory.

It's my story, and there is nothing to be proud or ashamed of.

While writing, I sometimes felt melancholy, wondering who would be interested in the life story of a non-celebrity like me. Nonetheless, I continued to write without any hesitation because this book is not written with the intention of seeking attention for myself, but rather as a personal desire to leave a record for my children and friends.

For those who have the opportunity to read this book, I hope that my life story has at least one valuable lesson to learn from.

My Family in 2008

- Australian Lawyer
- Advisory Lawyer for Korean Association of Western Australia
- Advisory Lawyer for Korean Overseas Traders Association
- Former Managing Director of Asotech Co., Ltd.
- Former Director of Avnet Korea Co., Ltd.

INDEX

'Children of the Dark, 114

1 John 4

    18, 41

a collapsed sewer, 25

a descendant of the Yoon's head family, 54

a drawing contest, 20

a hedge of the flowerbed, 12

a loner, 37

a senior deaconess, 46

administrative litigation, 257

an act of desertion, 68

ASoTech, 479, 502

ASoTech Co., Ltd.,, 457

Australian Baptist Church, 616

Australian Baptist Union, 381

average balance rate, 475

Bansong Elementary School, 19

barrister and solicitor, 553

barristers, 553

Bechtel Corporation, 112

Beolteog-Injection, 412

biblical teachings, 38

black pork, 86

blessing, 46

briquette fire, 31

Brother Welfare Center, 125

Bugok Middle School, 35

Bupyeong Police Academy, 113

bus stop, 37

Busan District Prosecutor's Office, 283

Busan University, 307

Business Activity Statements, 463

car painting factory, 36

Casuarina Prison, 334

Central Intelligence Agency, 92

Chairman J, 577

Cheolhakgwan, 138

Cheongdeok Church, 39

Choedaepo restaurant, 502

Choheung Securities, 486

Choi Jae-ho, 494

chonggak kimchi, 589

Christian Review, 342

clinical trials, 126

collective training, 64

Combat Police Force, 58, 63

Combat Police Forces, 83

compatibility, 539

Computer-Aided Software Engineering (CASE) tool, 275

contribution, 49

Copyright Association, 288

cousin brother, 51

Crocodile Dundee, 217

Daedong Hospital, 586

Department of Family Medicine, 466

Department of Health, 408

Devil's Island, 75

Donggwang Police Box, 113

drunken master, 495

EBED, 456, 485

economic power, 19

economic support, 50

embezzlement, 541

emergency measures, 132

English basics, 54

False Accusation, 308

financial dealings, 600

first cousin once removed, 92

foreign pen pals, 44

Forner, 456, 494

full seats., 499

Gangwon-do, 418

garage sales, 384

Gimhae Airport, 185

glabella, 13

Gohwa Church, 368

Gonyok, 46

Goods and Services Tax, 463

GoStop, 167

greater distress, 68

GST, 463

guinea pig, 614

handicapped, 418

Hippocrates, 417

Human Resources Development Service of Korea, 62

IMF foreign exchange crisis, 341

Incheon International Airport, 418

individual tutorial sessions, 526

Iranian embassy, 512

Jeju Airport Security Unit, 83

Jessica, 44

Jindotgae One alarm, 80

John 4

18, 41

Judicial Research and Training Institute, 537

Jung Won-seop, 322

Jungbu Police Station, 114

K Group, 541

KAL, 561

Kangjeong Coastal Guard Post, 76

killing two birds with one stone, 26

Kim Soo-chang, 321

Kimhae Airport, 561

Korea and Australia I Experienced, 1

Korea Computerware Co., Ltd, 311

Korea Technology Finance Corporation, 315, 452

Korean embassy, 516

Korean National Police Agency, 118

Korean Red Cross logo, 262

Korean version of Auschwitz., 125

KOSDAQ, 486

lawless behavior, 68

loom operator, 329

lump on my buttocks, 98

lynx, 38

mandarin fields, 84

master morality, 581

medical technology, 105

mere sympathy, 8

merger agreement, 490

Mild Coffee, 174

Military Manpower Administration, 255

Moon Kyung-soon, 28

multiple demonstrations, 92

Murdoch University, 338

my aunt-in-law, 51

my toys, 5

my youngest maternal uncle, 50

Myeongdo, 139

National Bank, 479

NewsTapa's special project, 132

Nicene Creed, 344

Nietzsche, 581

No Parking on verge, 398

no suspicion, 283

Nonsan Training Center, 63, 66

North Korean flag, 508

Notification of Change of Ownership, 428

Nurturing Membership Fee, 17

obstetric, 243

parenting methods, 5

Park Geun-hye, 299

Participantism, 479

password input keypad, 478

Philosophy Hall, 139

physiognomy, 539

place of misfortune, 12

pleurisy, 96

Police Headquarters, 63

President Park Jung-hee, 82

Prosecution Republic, 273

quality control, 498

referral, 613

register my transfer, 83

repertoire, 4

res judicata, 303

righteous policy, 85

Road Traffic Act, 392

Saemaul Movement, 24

School Membership Fee, 389

searchlights, 79

section 234 of the Customs Act, 567

sections 67 of the Quarantine Act, 567

senior deaconess, 45

shameless criminal act, 600

Sheol, 373

skilled general, 5

slave morality, 581

Snow White and the Witch, 21

solicitors, 553

student classes, 37

Suni, 8

Tak Myung-hwan, 343

talk dirty, 36

tax audit, 439

the abuse of power, 273

the early morning prayer, 47

the girl with polio, 8

the military government, 93

the most compassionate and capable parents, 635

the offering box, 49

the operator, 39

The parable of the talents, 377

Truth and Reconciliation Commission, 325

UDT, 73

unfairness, 286

Unicle, 274

value-added tax, 460

VAT, 460

violation of the program copyright law, 284

Wang Gocham, 79

written pleadings, 573